PEOPLING THE PLAINS

PEOPLING

UNIVERSITY PRESS OF KANSAS

THE PLAINS

Who Settled Where in Frontier Kansas   James R. Shortridge

Published by the
University Press of
Kansas (Lawrence,
Kansas 66049),
which was organized
by the Kansas Board of
Regents and is operated
and funded by Emporia
State University,
Fort Hays State University,
Kansas State University,
Pittsburg State University,
the University of Kansas,
and Wichita State
University

© 1995 by the University Press of Kansas

Library of Congress Cataloging-in-Publication Data
Shortridge, James R., 1944–
Peopling the plains : who settled where in frontier Kansas / James
R. Shortridge.
      p.   cm.
Includes bibliographical references and index.
ISBN 0-7006-0697-1 (cloth)
1. Kansas—History.   2. Kansas—Geography.   3. Land settlement
patterns—Kansas—History.   4. Kansas—Population—History.
I. Title.
F681.S55   1995
304.8′781′009034—dc20   94-45603

British Library Cataloguing in Publication Data is available.

Printed in the United States of America

10   9   8   7   6   5   4   3   2   1

The paper used in this publication meets the minimum requirements of the
American National Standard for Permanence of Paper for Printed Library
Materials z39.48–1984.

FOR GEORGE F. JENKS

who talked about frog hairs

and number eight pickles,

and epitomized all that

a professor should be.

Contents

Preface

This book was conceived rather indirectly out of a personal, long-term curiosity about the political and social geography of Kansas. My initial questions were sporadic and seemed quite unconnected one to another. Why, for example, have people in some sections of the state consistently voted Democratic; are the mindsets of eastern and western Kansans as different from one another as sometimes asserted; how did Methodism come to be the religion of choice over most of the state? As I sought answers, I gradually began to realize that these puzzles were not as unrelated as I had thought. The themes of nativity and migration arose repeatedly. Whether or not the cultural heritage of the frontier population could fully explain the question at hand, it was always involved. In time, I came to see population origins as basic for cultural studies in the way that bedrock geology is for earth science, a foundation upon which varied superstructures have been constructed. In this study I seek to assemble that influential social foundation for Kansas.

Population origins are so obscure in most countries that students must resort to indirect measures or even guesses for their information; the same is true for Native Americans. In contrast, detailed inquiries into the Euro-American heritage of the United States are possible. Good records exist, and the history is relatively short.[1] Still, the task is not easy. Research at the county or township level must be based largely on assiduous counts made from unpublished census records. Although I can attest that the tedium of such work can sometimes make a person question his or her sanity, prolonged contact with the handwritten names and birthplaces of actual settlers also helps to establish an empathy both for the immense scale and for the personal nature of the westering process. Eight states have been studied at scales comparable to this Kansas effort. Though much remains to be done if we are to grapple competently with the complex cultural geography of the nation, the work is satisfying. I hope others will expand the inquiry to additional places.[2]

The volume before you is difficult to classify. It is an atlas, in part, a series of township-level maps for each county in the state at their times of immediate postfrontier development, but I have written more text than is typical of atlases. My goal was to document and map the selective migration to Kansas of people from different places of birth, to account for the resultant patterns, and to speculate on the effects of this pattern on the emerging cultural geography of the state. To the extent that the study can also serve as a foundation for additional work on migration and population geography, so much the better. Migration is a central concern in this study, but I did not intend for the book to be a comprehensive population geography. Among many limitations in this regard, it focuses on group rather than on individual behavior, it addresses the important question of population turnover only indirectly, and it makes no effort to deal with intermediate stops of settlers between their birthplaces and their moves to Kansas. Most important, this work treats most locales at only a single point in time.[3]

The University of Kansas supported this research in several significant ways. A sabbatical leave in 1986 provided time for me to immerse myself in materials and ideas about nineteenth-century Kansas; another in 1994 allowed the completion of the manuscript. A grant from its General Research Fund aided the compilation of the manuscript census data, and Barbara Shortridge, Phil Reed, and others at the Cartographic Service laboratory designed and drafted the numerous maps and charts with skill and patience. Beverly Roberts, in the Department of Geography, typed the entire manuscript and endured its many drafts with good humor. For insights on the study of population origins I am grateful for the work of William Bowen, Russel Gerlach, John Hudson, Terry Jordan, Douglas Meyer, Michael Roark, Gregory Rose, William Sherman, and Hubert Wilhelm. Admirable studies of Kansas settlement by J. Neale Carman, Paul Gates, Robert Haywood, James Malin, and Craig Miner have also made my task easier. Finally, I owe particular gratitude to Donna Goltry, an exceptionally able and reliable research assistant, and to Barbara Shortridge, a skilled copyeditor. An earlier version of some materials in chapters 1 and 2 appeared in the Autumn 1991 issue of *Kansas History: A Journal of the Central Plains*.

Graphs and Tables

Maps

1

An Ambiguous Cultural Heritage

In 1854 Kansas Territory was opened to a massive influx of people from the eastern United States and abroad. Just as thirty years before the Kansa, Pawnee, and other native plains peoples had been largely dispossessed in order to make the region a "permanent" refuge for eastern Indians, these eastern tribes were now evicted. The promise of economic opportunity for white Euro-Americans, whether farmers, railroad builders, urban entrepreneurs, or other speculators, had created pressures too strong for the federal government to ignore. Some one hundred thousand people rushed across the Missouri border into Kansas between 1854 and 1860 and, after a lull caused by the Civil War, the migration continued at an even more rapid pace throughout the 1870s and 1880s. The story of this frontier Kansas has been told from many perspectives, including political maneuvering, land policy, adaptation to local environmental and economic conditions, and, more recently, the views of minorities and women. The origins and cultural heritage of settlers, my focus here, is another important aspect of the chronicle.

Why should anyone care about settler origins, especially nearly a century and a half after the fact? The answer lies in the social, political, and economic attitudes that are associated with nativity. All places have social stereotypes associated with them and, typically, these stereotypes have at least

MAP I.I

Traditional rural culture areas of the eastern United States. Modified from maps in Terry G. Jordan and Lester Rowntree, The Human Mosaic, *4th ed. (New York: Harper and Row, 1986), p. 10, and in John C. Hudson, "North American Origins of Middlewestern Frontier Populations,"* Annals of the Association of American Geographers *78 (1988): 411.*

some bases in fact. Such inferences explain why, when strangers meet, the first question asked often is, "Where are you from?" Linkages between place and culture were especially strong before twentieth-century revolutions in transportation and communication, and many of these patterns linger to the present. From a geographer's perspective, knowledge of the population origins of early settlers is essential for understanding the personality of a place, its people's collective pattern of behavior. Pioneers usually establish the cultural tone, and later settlers, even if from quite different locales, typically adopt many of the earlier values and practices.

As an initial step toward understanding the cultural patterns of Kansas, this study explores the population origins of early-day residents. With its central location, Kansas was in a position to receive settlers from the four major regional subcultures that have been identified in the eastern United States (see Map I.I). The stereotypical denizens of these places—Yankee trader (Northern culture), Southern planter (Lower Southern), Pennsylvania yeoman farmer (North Midland), and Kentucky backwoodsman (South Midland or Upper Southern)—could, in theory, intermingle on the plains and also mix with a variety of foreign-born immigrants who had begun to move westward in large numbers at midcentury.[1]

Did a vivid cultural mosaic emerge in Kansas? Statewide population data from later in the century would seem to deny it. They reveal that people born in Ohio, Indiana, and Illinois eventually dominated migration to the state and, consequently, modern scholars usually have classified Kansas as North Midland in temperament.[2] The situation may not be so simple. Yankees, Southerners, Germans, and other distinctive peoples have been important contributors to the state population from the beginning and even have dominated settlement in certain regions. Missourians and other Upper Southern peoples constituted 45 percent of the immigrant population in 1865, for example, and undoubtedly brought with them aspects of the roughshod but egalitarian backwoods culture that had enabled them to colonize the trans-Appalachian frontier with speed and ease.[3] Was this early dominance strong and enduring enough to have left a cultural mark on the state? Similar immigration streams from both the North and South into Ohio, Indiana, and Illinois produced a distinctive series of banded regional cultures within these states. Is this the Kansas reality too? At the other extreme, it is possible that the mixing of these different peoples in Kansas was sufficient to have created a new overall personality for the state, a hybrid that cannot be described adequately with the old Eastern labels.[4]

One might expect that nearly a century and a half of historical inquiry would have revealed the true nature of Kansas society, but the cultural beginnings of the state have long been shrouded by propaganda. As a national focus for the slavery and general states' rights issues in the 1850s, Kansas was rarely discussed in rational terms. Credit for the free-state cause was popularly attributed to the influence of the New England Emigrant Aid Company, and later writers continued to emphasize this Yankee theme. Kansas was the "child of Plymouth Rock," a shining example of the triumph of Puritan virtue over base Southern influences from Missouri and elsewhere.[5] Missouri and Arkansas settlers, one assumes from this rhetoric, returned across the border once the free-state forces were ascendant. Foreign and North-Midland settlers were rarely mentioned. The symbolism of New England heritage and Puritan ideals was used repeatedly by William Allen White in his influential interpretations of Kansas culture, and the idea has continued to the present; a recent history calls it the state's "longest-standing" image. James C. Malin began a probe into the realities behind this perception in 1961; it is time to extend his work with a detailed geographic look at the basic population data.[6]

This book is based on the birthplace information recorded as part of the Kansas state census for the years 1865, 1885, 1905, and 1925. Every federal census since 1850 contains a similar question on state or country of birth, and many Kansas studies have used the easily available statewide figures for 1860. This 1860 survey is suspect as a cultural base, however. The population of the territory was still in great flux at the time as raiders despoiled the Missouri border region, new settlers and adventurers arrived in large numbers, and a major drought was under way that would cause thousands to abandon their claims. Although forces favoring a free-state constitution were dominant in 1860, believers in a Southern-style government had not completely lost hope. For the purpose of assessing the continuing cultural heritage of Kansas, 1865 is a better date for study. By then the free-state/proslavery issue had been settled, and the wartime, opportunistic transients had left the region. The 1865 census should best enumerate the "first effective" settlers, the ones most likely to have permanently molded the raw Kansas landscape.[7]

The philosophy of first effective settlement has guided the choice of dates for detailed examination of each Kansas county. My object was to survey individual townships after they were well settled but before native Kansans constituted a large portion of the total population. For consistency and practicality I decided to stay with state census records and to restrict the detailed township survey to a limited number of time periods. This process captures immediate postfrontier Kansas in four unequally sized chunks that form the basis for the following chapters.

THE PATTERNS IN OUTLINE

Twenty-eight counties in northeastern Kansas each contained a thousand or more people in 1865; their settlement is the focus of chapter 2. Migrants from Illinois, Indiana, Ohio, and other North-Midland states could be found throughout the new territory, but other groups had more specific motivations that produced distinct clusterings. Missourians and other Upper Southerners, who were adjacent to and familiar with Kansas, secured choice townsites and other land near the Missouri and lower Kansas rivers and along portions of the Santa Fe and Oregon trails. Yankees, generally the best financed of the immigrant groups, also concentrated on sites with good potential for commerce. Because of their slightly later arrival, though, they were relegated to sites upstream on the Kansas River. Immigrants from Europe tended to select either urban locations or isolated rural tracts, choices that allowed these groups to maintain cultural cohesion while they adjusted to a new social and economic milieu.

Fifty-three new counties to the west and south of the older core were settled during the economic booms of the early and late 1870s and had achieved a population of a thousand or more by 1885. Chapter 3 focuses on eight of these counties, the initial postwar frontier of the state in southeastern Kansas. A favorable location there on a direct route from Kansas City to the Indian Nations and Texas, plus rich mineral resources and good agricultural conditions, led to rapid railroad development, rampant land speculation, and, not surprisingly, a mix of settlers dominated by veterans of the Union army. The 1885 data portray the region after railroad development but before large-scale mining activity. Black immigrants in several border townships formed the most distinctive clustering in the region; many of them were Texans and part of the post-Reconstruction exodus from the South.

By the time the droughty years from 1879 through 1882 ended a sustained period of postwar settlement, all of central and much of western Kansas was newly occupied; chapter 4 focuses on this vast and quickly settled realm. I argue that railroad policies and variations in the cost of land were key to the settlement pattern that emerged. Upper Southerners, whose culture included a history of cattle trailing and who could see the market potential offered by the new Santa Fe Railroad, were pioneers on the potential rangelands of the Flint and Gypsum hills south of the Santa Fe grant. Europeans, who frequently sought large acreages of land for colonies and who often were unfamiliar with local land policies, tended toward the relatively expensive but otherwise easily secured tracts within the railroad land grants in a wide belt across central Kansas. Iowans and other North-Midland peoples were especially dominant on the cheap, nonrailroad lands near the Nebraska border.

The westernmost twenty-four counties in the state, the High Plains, are examined in chapter 5. Much of this region, in some ways an ongoing frontier in Kansas, is surveyed three times: in 1885, 1905, and 1925. This repetition seems prudent given the local history of boom years in the mid-1880s followed by widespread abandonment in the decade after 1888. Drought and economic depression spawned high rates of population turnover, but the source areas for immigration remained fairly constant over the entire period. Better transportation and improved place knowledge led to less group colonization on this twentieth-century frontier than elsewhere in Kansas, but some banding of cultures is still evident. A presence of Upper Southerners engaged in cattle and freighting businesses is especially clear south of Dodge City.

In an attempt to place the legacy of nativity in perspective, I turn in chapter 6 from an interpretation of settlement patterns to some of the implications and limitations of the process. Composite maps of pioneer nativity regions for the state form a point of departure. Comparison of these regions with some limited, county-level data available for adjacent states suggests that the Kansas border did not serve as a sharp barrier to early cultural diffusion. Within Kansas, though, the traditional zones of South-Midland, Yankee, and European influence can be seen in a wide variety of political, religious, agricultural, and business behavior. The legacy of pioneer nativity endures, but has necessarily faded over the years. New immigrant groups have overwhelmed earlier peoples in extreme southeastern Kansas, in several urban areas, and elsewhere in the state. Hybridization in a cultural sense clearly has occurred on a large scale, and new regional culture values also seem to have formed as part of an adaptation to local conditions and circumstances.[8] I evaluate the scope of these changes and conclude the study with a comparison between the nativity regions and some modern geographies of the state and of the larger Great Plains realm.

SOME THEORETICAL CONSIDERATIONS

Given the veil of uncertainty that surrounds the peopling of Kansas after 1854, it seems wise to begin any new survey with a theoretical perspective. The standard wisdom in migration studies holds that most mass movements can be attributed to economic and cultural motivations.[9] These categories would seem to be encompassing, but it is easy for analysts to treat them in mechanical fashion and thus to create the impression of an economic or cultural determinism that denigrates the central role of individual decisions in the settlement process. Several excellent studies have demonstrated the feasibility of incorporating individual actions into the broader social milieu of the plains frontier. With the exception of work in North Dakota based on a unique statewide set of life histories, however, the scale has been small and the communities studied relatively homogeneous. To execute such research at the state or even at the county level would be an overwhelming project.[10]

The most promising approach for a statewide study such as I undertake here would seem to be a leavening of the standard assumptions about group motivation with an increased sensitivity to the role of individual action. Incorporation of existing local studies is one logical approach. Another is to consider power relationships among institutions and individuals.[11] Power, defined simply as the means of getting things done, operates at scales ranging from the individual, through family and community, to state and country. It integrates economic, social, and cultural behavior. Power includes access to money, of course, but also such varied traits as knowledge of local environmental and business conditions, and position in society. The presence of cultural traits useful in an adaptation to a new environment (the concept of preadaptation) can be seen as another example of power relationships.[12] Ultimately, though, perhaps the most valuable contribution that a statewide study can make is to identify not only the localities where the standard economic and cultural generalizations seem to apply, but also the places where they do not. These latter sites, anomalies on the map, are promising locales to study facets of independent individual action.

A theory to predict the immigration process in Kansas can be divided logically into two components: one to predict the overall number of migrants from various points of origin and another to account for the geographic locations of these groups within the state. The first issue can be approached with a simple question: How many settlers would each state contribute to the total migration flow into Kansas (excluding for the moment those born in foreign countries) if the only criteria were simply the respective populations of the states and their distances from Kansas? The assumptions in this wording are clearly economic, and they ignore the individual, but the question can generate an effective model for addressing the complexities of migration. It filters out the obviously important roles of distance and population numbers and thus allows inspection of other, more localized factors. Any deviation from the model's predictions, a proportionately large or small number of New Englanders, for example, would be a measure of special motivations or inhibitions on their part.

I decided to generate three versions of the prediction model, using population figures from the source states for 1850, 1860, and 1870. The procedure, for each year, was to calculate the ratios of population to distance-from-Kansas for each state, to sum the results, and then to divide each individual state ratio by this sum total.[13] The process yields a predicted percentage of the migrant stream that can be graphed against the actual percentage of the Kansas population contributed by each state (see Graphs 1.1, 1.2, and 1.3).

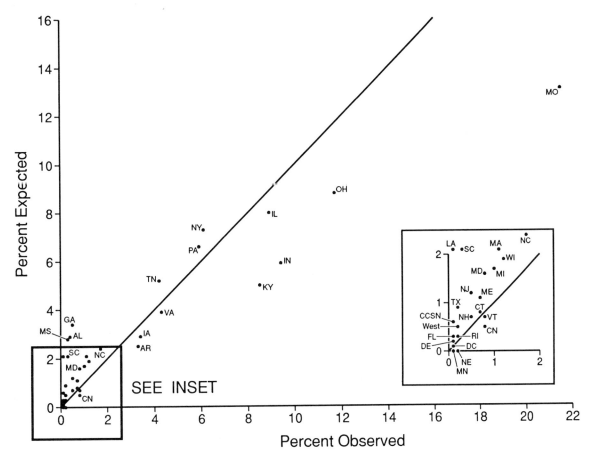

GRAPH I.I
Expected and observed populations in frontier Kansas (1850 population base). Observed data from 1865 Kansas state census; expected data from 1850 U.S. census and Standard Highway Mileage Guide *(Chicago: Rand McNally and Company, 1982). CN denotes the Cherokee Nation, CCSN the combined Choctaw, Creek, and Seminole Nations, and West the states and territories west of Kansas.*

The results of the prediction models for 1850 and 1860 (both compared with Kansas data from 1865) are similar except for Illinois, Iowa, and a few other places that were little more than frontiers themselves at this time and whose populations had risen dramatically between the two census years. Using Illinois as an example, the state sent more people to Kansas than one would project based on its small 1850 population of 851,470 but fewer than one would project using its 1860 population of 1,711,951. A more realistic expectation would employ a population base somewhere between these two extremes and would yield a figure close to the number of Illini who actually migrated to Kansas. Settler numbers from Arkansas, Iowa, and Minnesota are also about as expected based on this logic. Two other states in this growth category, Wisconsin and Texas, sent fewer people to Kansas than expected on both graphs.

Popular mythology predicts that the states of the Lower South would be underrepresented in Kansas because of its free-state status, and the graphs bear out this stereotype. Missourians made several appeals in the late 1850s for the people of South Carolina, Georgia, Alabama, and other states to aid them in the quest for Kansas.[14] Clearly the Southerners either did not respond in the

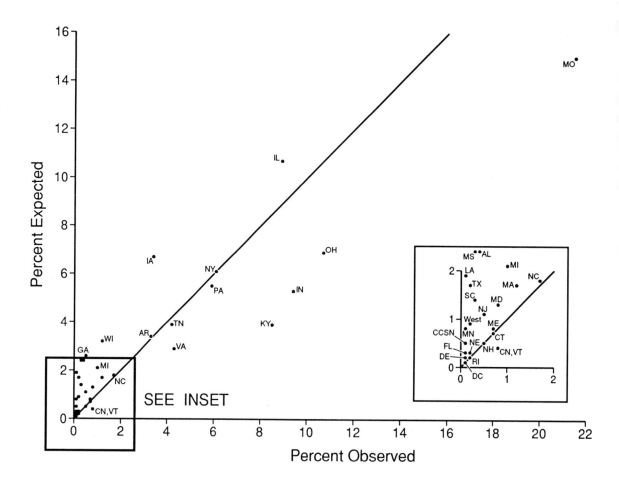

GRAPH I.2

Expected and observed populations in frontier Kansas (1860 population base). Observed data from 1865 Kansas state census; expected data from 1860 U.S. census and Standard Highway Mileage Guide *(Chicago: Rand McNally and Company, 1982). CN denotes the Cherokee Nation, CCSN the combined Choctaw, Creek, and Seminole Nations, and West the states and territories west of Kansas.*

numbers their populations and distances would predict or they retreated quickly from the state once the slavery issue had been resolved locally and the Civil War was a reality. Only 2,035 natives of the Lower South were in 1865 Kansas, too few to be a factor in the emerging state culture (see Table 1.1).

The second category of states somewhat underrepresented in early Kansas challenges stereotypes instead of supporting them. Nearly twelve thousand people from New England, New York, and other Northern states came to Kansas, six times the total from the Lower South but still modestly less than predicted by the model. Only Vermont and Connecticut sent settlers at or above the expected levels. Although the failure of Yankees to dominate Kansas numerically is well known to scholars, an assumption that these people were zealous in colonization activity considering the distance of the migration has been implied in many studies. The discrepancy between image and reality can be lessened a little if one works with 1860 census figures instead of the numbers from 1865. The Northern-culture states contributed 12.3 percent of the Kansas population for that earlier date compared with 8.8 percent in 1865. The overrepresentation of New Englanders as government

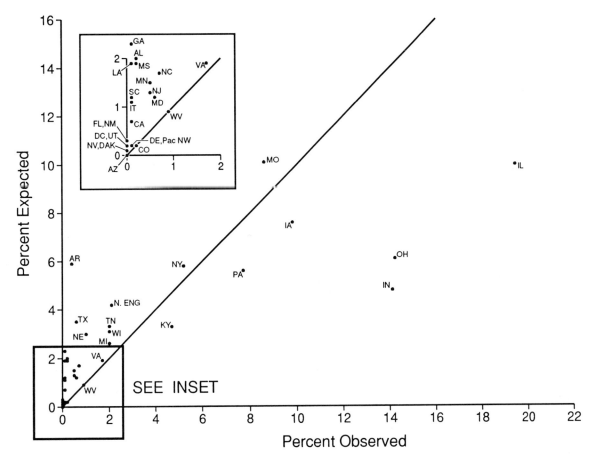

GRAPH 1.3

Expected and observed populations in frontier Kansas (1870 population base). Observed data from 1885 Kansas state census; expected data from 1870 U.S. census and Standard Highway Mileage Guide *(Chicago: Rand McNally and Company, 1982). DAK denotes Dakota Territory, IT Indian Territory, N ENG the six New England states, and Pac NW the state of Oregon plus the territories of Idaho, Montana, Washington, and Wyoming.*

officials, newspaper editors, and similar people of influence in the young state is a more important factor; New Englanders indeed wrote many of the early Kansas histories.[15] This situation deserves closer study, including geographic inquiry. A concentration of New Englanders in urban areas, for example, would help to increase their visibility and influence; a dispersed pattern would suggest a lesser role than is commonly believed.

One of the "laws" articulated by the pioneer demographer E. G. Ravenstein states that "the great body of our migrants only proceed a short distance."[16] The role of Missourians in early Kansas settlement bears out this principle. The 20,817 migrants from there exceeded the total for the next two largest contributing states combined, and Missouri settlers came at a rate far higher than predicted by the distance model. Missouri's population in the 1850s derived largely from Kentucky, Tennessee, and Virginia, the core of South-Midland culture.[17] When the immigrants to Kansas from this entire group of states are summed, the Upper South emerges as the single largest culture represented in the new state. These people probably were concerned less with slavery, rhetoric, and political concerns than is commonly assumed. New farms and businesses beckoned, and they were

Table 1.1. *Place of Birth of Kansans, 1865*

Collection Unit/Culture Area	No.	(%)	Excluding (by %) Kans.-born	Excluding (by %) Kans. & Foreign-born
New England (Northern)				
Connecticut	663	(0.5)	0.6	0.7
Dakota	4			
Maine	645	(0.5)	0.6	0.7
Massachusetts	1,171	(0.9)	1.1	1.2
Michigan	933	(0.7)	0.8	1.0
Minnesota	90	(0.1)	0.1	0.1
New Hampshire	438	(0.3)	0.4	0.5
New York	5,888	(4.3)	5.3	6.1
Rhode Island	169	(0.1)	0.2	0.2
Vermont	791	(0.6)	0.7	0.8
Wisconsin	1,177	(0.9)	1.1	1.2
Subtotal	11,969	(8.8)	10.8	12.4
North Midland				
Delaware	79	(0.1)	0.1	0.1
Illinois	8,554	(6.3)	7.7	8.9
Indiana	9,041	(6.7)	8.1	9.4
Iowa	3,473	(2.6)	3.1	3.6
Nebraska	147	(0.1)	0.1	0.2
New Jersey	437	(0.3)	0.4	0.5
Ohio	11,217	(8.3)	10.1	11.6
Pennsylvania	5,745	(4.2)	5.2	6.0
Subtotal	38,693	(28.5)	34.9	40.1
Upper South (South Midland)				
Arkansas	3,186	(2.3)	2.9	3.3
Cherokee Nation	798	(0.6)	0.7	0.8
Dist. of Columbia	72	(0.1)	0.1	0.1
Kentucky	8,125	(6.0)	7.3	8.4
Maryland	749	(0.6)	0.7	0.8
Missouri	20,817	(15.3)	18.8	21.6
North Carolina	1,673	(1.2)	1.5	1.7
Tennessee	4,094	(3.0)	3.7	4.2

Table 1.1. *Continued*

Collection Unit/Culture Area	No.	(%)	Excluding (by %)	
			Kans.-born	Kans. & Foreign-born
Virginia	4,071	(3.0)	3.7	4.2
West Virginia	57		0.1	0.1
Subtotal	43,642	(32.1)	39.3	43.2
Lower South				
Alabama	423	(0.3)	0.4	0.4
Choctaw, Creek, & Seminole Nations	134	(0.1)	0.1	0.1
Florida	50			0.1
Georgia	452	(0.3)	0.4	0.5
Louisiana	119	(0.1)	0.1	0.1
Mississippi	295	(0.2)	0.3	0.3
South Carolina	309	(0.2)	0.3	0.3
Texas	253	(0.2)	0.2	0.3
Subtotal	2,035	(1.5)	1.8	2.1
The West				
California	21			
Colorado	50			0.1
Idaho	1			
Nevada	1			
New Mexico	51			0.1
Oregon	5			
Utah	42			
Subtotal	171	(0.1)	0.2	0.2
Kansas	24,828	(18.3)		
Foreign Countries				
Austria	42			
Belgium	52			
British America	1,034	(0.8)	0.9	
Denmark	79	(0.1)	0.1	
England	1,623	(1.2)	1.5	
France	465	(0.3)	0.4	
German States	5,142	(3.8)	4.6	

Table 1.1. *Continued*

Collection Unit/Culture Area	No.	(%)	Excluding (by %) Kans.-born	Excluding (by %) Kans. & Foreign-born
Ireland	4,408	(3.2)	4.0	
Italy	20			
Mexico	12			
Moravia	40			
Netherlands	96	(0.1)	0.1	
Norway	162	(0.1)	0.1	
Poland	63		0.1	
Scotland	416	(0.3)	0.4	
Sweden	186	(0.1)	0.2	
Switzerland	441	(0.3)	0.4	
Wales	148	(0.1)	0.1	
Other Countries	25			
Subtotal	14,454	(10.6)	13.0	
Total	135,792[a]	(100.0)	100.0	100.0

Source: Manuscript Kansas state census, 1865.

[a]This total does not include 6,664 residents for whom no place of birth was recorded. Percentages may not total exactly because of rounding.

in the best position to see and to take advantage of the possibilities. Sheer numbers suggest a tremendous potential for cultural impact, an impact heretofore unexplored since Kansas imagery has never acknowledged a Southern presence after the late 1850s.

Ohio and Indiana complete the list of states sending more people than expected to Kansas. Both of these states border the Ohio River, the major east-west transportation artery of the time. Movement by this route to St. Louis and Kansas City was probably easy enough to have encouraged more people to migrate than the numbers predicted by the simple distance measure used in the model.

Most of the generalizations seen for the 1850 and 1860 models hold as well for the 1870 one when it is compared with Kansas data from 1885 (see Graph 1.3). Obvious ramifications from the Civil War explain most of the aberrations: the South remains underrepresented, and residents from the now quite populous states of Ohio, Indiana, and Illinois have moved directly west in extremely large numbers. The percentage of Missouri and Arkansas natives has fallen sharply from the earlier calculations, a result of the surge of migrants from these states in the 1850s not being augmented by large numbers of later movers. The overrepresentation of Pennsylvanians is the most intriguing anomaly on the graph. Relatively few residents of the other industrializing Atlantic seaboard states opted to come to rural Kansas.

When adjustments are made for the strife in the South and the ease of migration directly westward in the 1870s along the latitudinal bands favored by the railroad routes, it is remarkable how well the prediction models explain the gross components of Kansas settlement. The rhetoric of the 1850s and the long-standing beliefs derived from this age about Yankee dominance and Southern absence have made people assume that the migration to the state was more political and complex than it was.

THE CASE FOR CLUSTERED SETTLEMENT

An understanding of the expected volume of migration to Kansas from the various states, while useful, fails to answer the basic questions of regional identity posed at the outset of this study. A Kansas township or county with equal numbers of Yankees, Southerners, North Midlanders, and Europeans would logically have a far different character from a place that was dominated by just one of these culture groups. Clearly, one cannot speculate intelligently about the personality either of the state or of its various sections without a careful examination of exactly where different peoples chose to settle.

A basic theoretical question underlying the issue of regional identity is whether forces that might promote a mixing of peoples on the Kansas frontier were more or less powerful than those that would favor a clustering of subgroups. If we were to accept the standard claims of contemporary government and private promoters, uniformity would be the expectation. Since the passage of the Homestead Act in 1862, land almost had been given away, a generosity that ostensibly would mean nearly equal access for potential settlers. The refusal of the federal government to allocate land in large tracts suitable for group settlement was a related and deliberate attempt to encourage a tightly interwoven settlement fabric. Traditional postwar mobility, at least for the residents of the victorious Northern states, would seem to reinforce this expectation of mixing, as would the growing ease of transportation after 1865. New railroad lines with their regular, advertised schedules and prices would seem to eliminate the need for settlers to travel in large groups. A final democratizing process was the widespread advertising of lands by railroad companies, by the state government, and by numerous other speculators, including information offices set up in many Eastern and European cities.[18]

Despite the officially encouraged expectation of a population melting pot on the frontier, migration theory as well as frontier studies in other states suggest that clustering of the various culture groups would be a more likely prediction for nineteenth-century Kansas, especially for the sections settled by 1865. Although travel books and newspapers told people about the general possibilities of the Western frontier, surviving diaries and map patterns alike argue that specific routes and destinations were products of family and community information networks each operating more or less independently. In other studies this "channelized" migration occurred despite the difficulties of obtaining land in large, contiguous blocks and was greater for some peoples than for others.[19] Such studies lead to the expectation that people who came long distances to Kansas or who felt alienated from the emerging or expected cultural mainstream would be the most likely to settle in clusters. These two categories of people were largely one and the same for Kansas: Lower Southerners, New Englanders, blacks, and the Europeans. The following chapters compare this and other theorizations with the patterns actually established on the land by the varied new citizens of Kansas.

2

The Northeast, 1865

About one-third of Kansas was occupied by the time of the Civil War. The state census of 1865 revealed 142,456 residents, but the zone of moderate population density extended south only to Fort Scott and scarcely beyond the first two tiers of counties west from the Missouri line (see Maps 2.1, 2.2). The middle reaches of the broad Neosho River valley from extreme northern Neosho County upstream to Lyon County held an important outlier of settlement. Rough areas in Wabaunsee and other Flint Hills counties were largely avoided as were several recently vacated Indian lands in Osage, Franklin, and Miami counties. Leavenworth, a transportation focus on the Missouri River as the result of its long-standing military base, was by far the largest urban place, with 15,409 people. Other cities of note included Lawrence, the center of early New England settlement, with 4,424 people, and Atchison, another port on the Missouri, with 3,318.

SETTLERS AND STRATEGIES

The settlement history of the state during its territorial period has been cast solely in terms of the free-state/proslavery issue for so long that it is still difficult for people to accept the more com-

MAP 2.1

*Reference map for eastern
Kansas, 1865.*

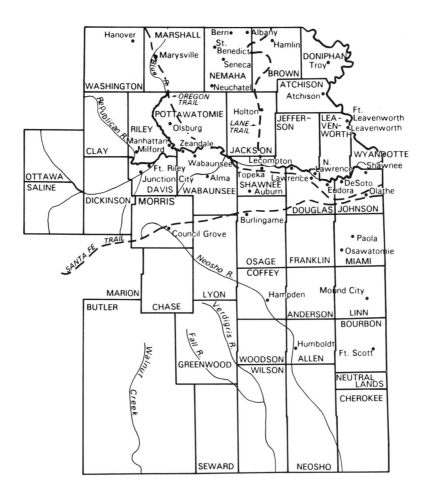

plex truth about motivation. Clearly, though, morality was subservient to greed.[1] White Americans wanted agricultural lands, railroad rights-of-way, and townsites. Their desire was overweening enough by 1850 to extinguish a series of solemn treaties made with the eastern Indians between 1825 and 1843. Some ten thousand people, who had been promised a permanent country of their own in Kansas, were forced to leave.[2] The next phase of this economic struggle pitted white against white, and is reflected in the fierce congressional debates that produced the Kansas-Nebraska Act of 1854. On the national scale these debates involved issues of states' rights, power struggles within the Democratic party, and fears that slavery would limit the economic opportunities in the West for white citizens. Missourians had more immediate concerns. Their state was best positioned to exploit the Kansas frontier, but this right was limited by the existing Missouri Compromise that prevented the extension of slavery into the new land. Some Missourians also feared that a free Kansas would put at risk the future of their own slave properties.[3]

As passed, the Kansas-Nebraska Act seemed to be favorable to Missouri business interests. It

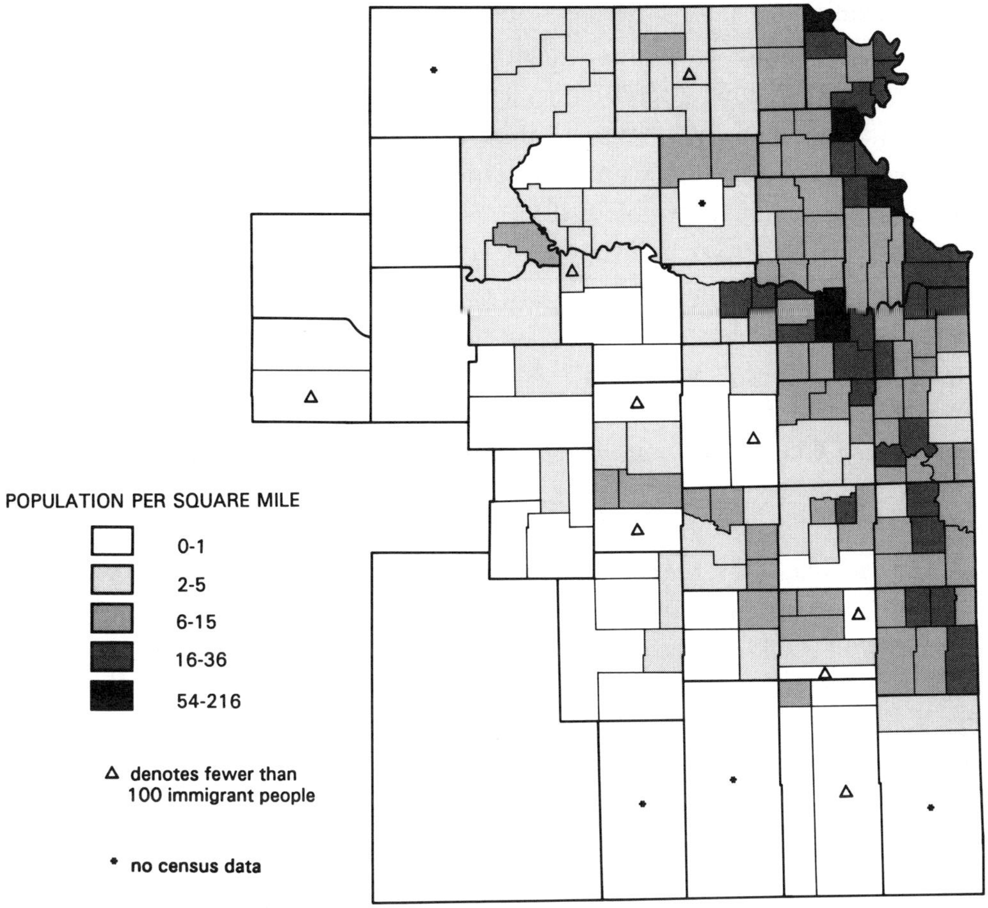

MAP 2.2
Population density, 1865.
Data from Kansas state
census.

POPULATION PER SQUARE MILE

- 0-1
- 2-5
- 6-15
- 16-36
- 54-216

△ denotes fewer than
100 immigrant people

• no census data

granted settlers the right to self-determination on the slave issue, and it created two territories, Kansas and Nebraska, with the unstated but obvious expectation that Kansas would be slave and Nebraska free. Historian James Malin has theorized that Missourians realized that Southerners would be at a disadvantage in the peopling of Kansas. Slave owners would be reluctant to come without a guarantee that a slave code would be passed and also would face risks in adapting slave labor to western crops. From this perspective it was imperative for proslavery Missourians to enter Kansas quickly. Early occupation not only would maximize their own economic gains but also would establish a territorial government sympathetic to the rights of slave owners during the settlement process.[4]

Malin has argued that this preemptive strategy worked during the first year or so of settlement. The Missouri-born people of Kansas Territory elected a proslavery delegate to Congress in 1854 and a proslavery legislature in early 1855. Just as important, Missourians secured most of the good townsites along the Missouri and lower Kansas rivers and made a conscious effort to occupy the scarce eastern timberlands. Possession of the timbered claims, it was argued, would mean control of the adjacent uplands and thus sufficient acreage to build up plantations. Estimates put the ratio of Missourians and other Upper Southerners to Northern and other settlers at two or three to one in March 1855, and the future appeared to be as they had hoped.[5]

The vision of Kansas as a simple westward extension of Missouri was put in doubt by the summer of 1855. The most visible challenge was the Massachusetts Emigrant Aid Company (later the New England Emigrant Aid Company), a group founded for the avowed purpose of recruiting Northern settlers to counter the Southern presence in Kansas. The plan gave hope to some but anxiety to others. Proslavery Missourians cried foul at the intrusion of Eastern influence into Western affairs and sent requests to other Southern states for settlers. These Missourians soon realized, however, that the most likely immigrants to Kansas were neither Yankees nor Southerners, but people from Ohio, Indiana, and Illinois. These states were relatively close at hand, had agricultural systems that could be expected to work in Kansas, and were populous enough to have many young people eager to seek opportunities on a new frontier.[6]

The outcome of this three-pronged immigration in a political sense is a familiar story. As told in terms of the leading personalities of the territorial years, James Lane and most of the other settlers from the Old Northwest sided with Charles Robinson and his fellow New Englanders to ban slavery from the new state. David Atchison and other heretofore vocal Missourians fell silent. This single alliance on the free-state issue masks significant cultural differences between the two Northern groups, however, and raises again the question of settlement geography within Kansas.

If one argues strictly from an economic perspective, the arrangement of at least some of these people may be predicted as a series of concentric rings. Missourians, the closest and most knowledgeable of the potential settlers, would occupy the core area: the Missouri and lower Kansas valleys with an extension southward along their state's western border. Various North-Midland immigrants would arrange themselves next, each located as a function of the time it took for them to hear about Kansas opportunities and to plan and make their journeys. Thus, increasingly faint rings of Illini, Hoosiers, and Ohioans might be expected.[7]

Migrants from New England probably would not follow the ring model. Assuming for them a mixture of economic and political motivation, they could be predicted to cluster tightly in Kansas in order to make their free-state message known, probably preferring cities for this same reason and locations at sites best suited for economic growth. They might be expected to squeeze townsites between existing Missouri ones and to locate upstream on the Kansas River just beyond the limit of its occupation by Upper Southerners.

A series of township-level maps designed to reveal the actual spatial patterns of the new immigrant groups, together with discussion of some cultural distinctions among them, follows. I focus first on the most highly clustered and distinctive of the immigrant groups, the Upper Southerners, the Yankees, the Lower Southerners and blacks, and the Europeans, and then consider the North-Midland settlers, the largest, most mainstream, and most diffuse group.

MISSOURIANS AND OTHER UPPER SOUTHERNERS

The initial push by Missourians into Kansas Territory lasted from 1854 until early 1857. During most of that time they were challenged for dominance in the new land only by Kentuckians and other Upper Southerners, nearly all of whom had lived in Missouri before crossing into Kansas. The goals of securing townsites and timbered lands usually were accomplished by short migrations, often from an adjacent Missouri county. Thus, Leavenworth was founded by businessmen from nearby Weston, Missouri, and Atchison by other Platte County people.[8] It is not surprising that Doniphan and Atchison counties were named after prominent leaders from northwestern Missouri and that Bourbon County bears a Kentucky namesake. As an early historian has described the process, "Almost every gentleman in western Missouri had a claim upon which he had moved, intended to move, or designed to hold."[9]

The distribution of Upper Southerners in Kansas for 1865 resembled the general pattern that had existed for nearly a decade (see Map 2.3). Despite a major immigration by other peoples, Southerners still dominated every county along the Missouri border as well as the Kansas River valley upstream to Topeka. A greater concentration on the northern bank of the Kaw than on the southern was the product of speculation there for the Leavenworth, Pawnee and Western Railroad, the first tracks to ascend the valley.[10] Kentuckians were common in this core area as they were in adjacent parts of Missouri (see Map 2.4).[11] In the southeast, some three thousand overland immigrants from Arkansas were contributors to the surge of Southern settlement, especially in the Neosho and Verdigris valleys (see Map 2.5).[12] Small communities along two major trails produced an additional presence of Southern culture. The most concentrated cluster was at Council Grove and in Morris County generally, the famed last humid-land stop on the journey to Santa Fe. Since the trade route to New Mexico had been initiated by Missourians, it was natural that this key way station would be controlled by them (see Map 2.6). Both of the leading Council Grove promoters, Seth Hays and Thomas Huffaker, were Missourians, and South Midlanders constituted 49 percent of the town's immigrant population.[13] Southerners were prominent early users of the Oregon Trail, too, and lived in modest numbers along its fringes from northern Shawnee County northwest across Pottawatomie and Marshall counties.

Historian Gary Cheatham recently has documented the survival of Southern political sentiment in Kansas into the early 1860s, but notes that by 1864, when the outcome of the Civil War was clear, most of the ardent Confederates had left the state. Peter Abell, one of the founders of Atchison, was among this group.[14] For the most part, though, the immigrants from the Upper

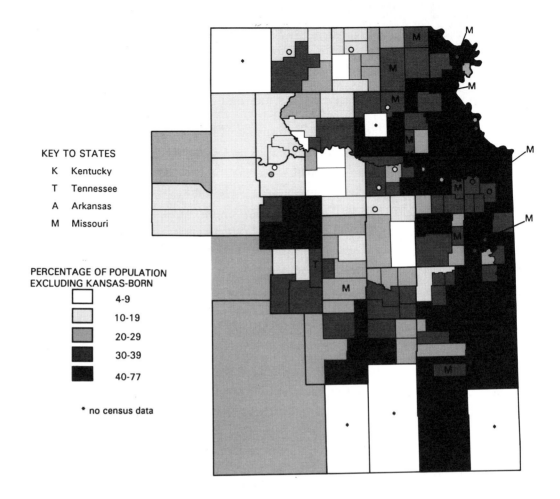

MAP 2.3
Natives of South-Midland states, 1865. Data from Kansas state census. Letter symbols mark cities and townships in which people from a particular South-Midland state constitute 20 percent or more of the immigrant population. For states included in the South-Midland area, see Table 1.1.

KEY TO STATES

K   Kentucky
T   Tennessee
A   Arkansas
M   Missouri

PERCENTAGE OF POPULATION
EXCLUDING KANSAS-BORN

4-9
10-19
20-29
30-39
40-77

* no census data

South stayed on. Scholars have argued that most of these people were not strongly proslavery at the outset and note the practical, rapid shift of their business communities to a pro-Union stance. Leavenworth citizens were the first to convert, by late 1857, and even those in reluctant Fort Scott and Paola had changed by the early part of the war.[15] New immigrants may have hastened these conversions to a degree, but only in rapidly growing Leavenworth did the percentage of Southerners in the population decline markedly (see Table 2.1).

Migration from the Upper South into Kansas nearly ceased for almost a decade, beginning in 1857. Politics certainly was a factor, but it was also important that the choice Kansas sites had already been claimed and that decent agricultural lands in Missouri and Arkansas still remained for the taking.[16] This temporal pause had spatial implications, with few Southerners present in the primary frontier zone of 1857 to 1860 north and west of Topeka. Interest in Kansas from the Upper South quickened again somewhat just prior to the 1865 census. The political climate of Kansas was stable by then and, more important, the frontiers in Arkansas and Missouri no longer offered the

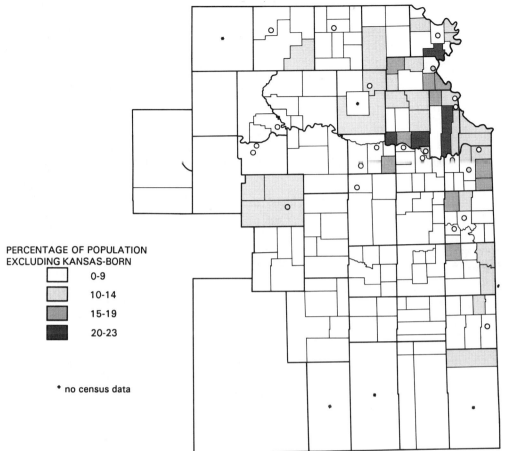

MAP 2.4
*Natives of Kentucky, 1865.
Data from Kansas state
census.*

PERCENTAGE OF POPULATION
EXCLUDING KANSAS-BORN

	0-9
	10-14
	15-19
	20-23

* no census data

quality lands they had a few years before. Southeastern Kansas had become the destination of choice.[17] Its agricultural lands were perceived to be the best available, and they lay near the established paths of Upper South migration into Indian Territory and Texas. Some settlers ascended the upper Arkansas River valley from Tennessee; others came across the Ozark crest from St. Louis to Springfield. Upper Southerners were not the dominant culture in this portion of Kansas, but Missourians and Tennesseans, especially, constituted about one-third of the group that occupied the Neosho, Verdigris, Fall, and Walnut valleys (see Maps 2.6, 2.7). The result was a more heterogeneous mixture here than could be found elsewhere in the new state.

THE YANKEES

From the perspective of the clergy and the business community in New England, the passage of the Kansas-Nebraska bill symbolized the frustration they felt over Southern control of the federal

MAP 2.5
*Natives of Arkansas, 1865.
Data from Kansas state
census.*

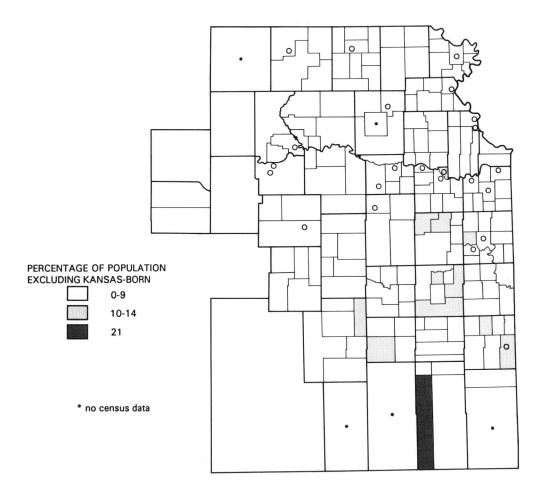

PERCENTAGE OF POPULATION
EXCLUDING KANSAS-BORN

☐ 0-9

▦ 10-14

■ 21

* no census data

government. The bill rescinded the government's pledge that Kansas would be a land for free labor, and it prompted many influential people to action. Some individuals were moved by the moral implications of an extension of slavery, more people by the loss of business and settlement opportunities for themselves and their fellow Northerners, and at least a few by the potential political gains in exploiting the general hysteria. These motives coalesced in the organization of the Massachusetts Emigrant Aid Company in 1854, and its successor, the New England Emigrant Aid Company in 1855. The company planned to place twenty thousand free-state settlers in Kansas and to establish mills and other businesses that would return a profit to investors. Horace Greeley was an early publicist for the effort as was the poet John Greenleaf Whittier. John Carter Brown was named president, and Samuel Cabot, Jr., John Lowell, Charles Higginson, and William Cullen Bryant were among the notables who served on the board of directors.[18]

It is little wonder that such an organization received widespread attention, both positive and negative. Friends of the company have claimed it to be the force that saved Kansas for the Union,

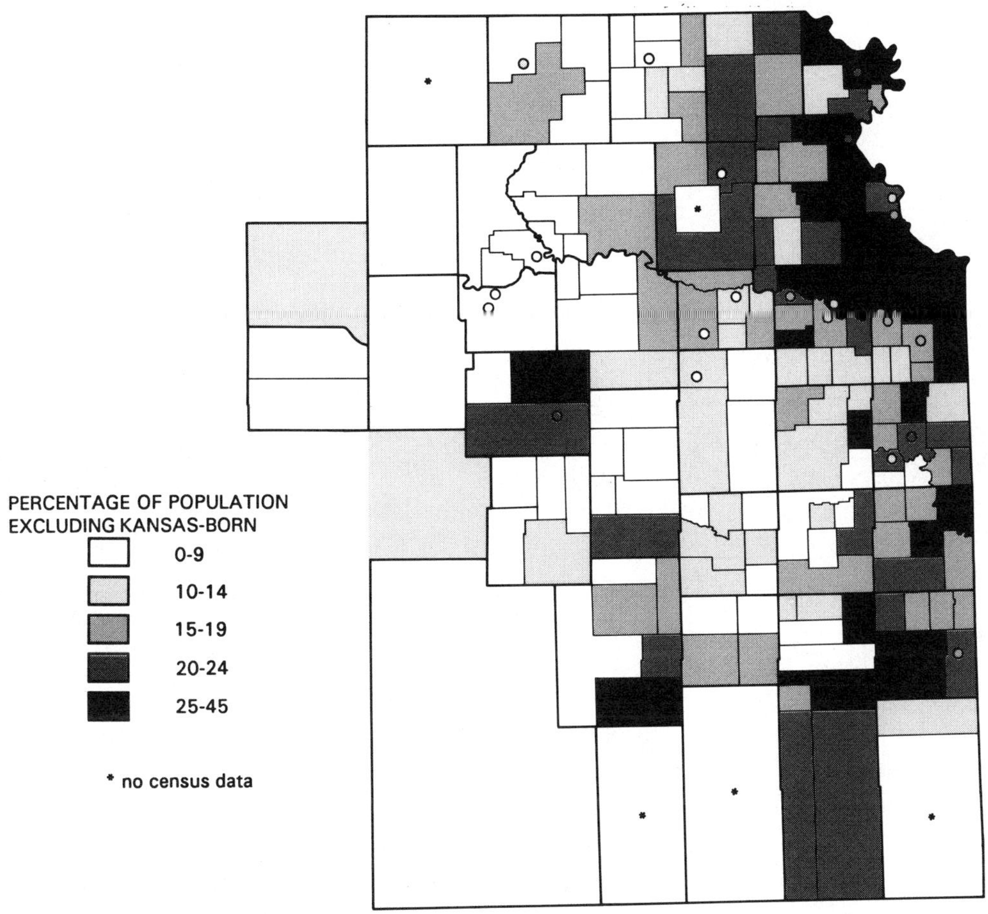

MAP 2.6
*Natives of Missouri, 1865.
Data from Kansas state
census.*

PERCENTAGE OF POPULATION
EXCLUDING KANSAS-BORN

☐	0-9
☐	10-14
☐	15-19
☐	20-24
☐	25-45

* no census data

but detractors hold the group responsible for the bloody guerrilla activities of the late 1850s and early 1860s and even for the Civil War itself. Facts are more difficult to ascertain. Of the twelve thousand settlers from the Northern culture states present in Kansas in 1865, only some two thousand came under company auspices.[19] Moreover, the figure of twelve thousand pales when compared with the total population of the state (see Table 1.1). Still, Massachusetts and New York alone furnished two of the first ten governors of Kansas and five of the eleven most influential early newspaper editors.[20] Yankee influence was heightened by the advantages of education and financial backing over those of the average immigrant, and was aided further by the Northerners' location in a tight geographical pattern astride the major transportation artery formed by the Kansas River valley (see Map 2.8).

The initial party of twenty-nine settlers sent by the company reached Kansas City in late July 1854. Even at this early date they found most of the Kansas borderland either occupied or with title uncertain, pending final removal of Indian groups. Since the New England colony wanted to re-

Table 2.1. *Percentage of Settlers from Selected Culture Areas in Cities of Kansas, 1865 (excluding Kansas-born)*

Collection Unit/Culture Area	State of Kans.	Leavenworth (15,409)[a]	Lawrence (4,424)	Atchison (3,318)	Fort Scott (1,382)	N. Lawrence (977)	Topeka (958)	Paola (704)
New England (Northern)	11	12	23	12	8	10	30	16
North Midland	35	22	29	22	26	32	40	40
Illinois	8	4	4	5	6	10	7	8
Indiana	8	3	5	3	3	6	7	15
Ohio	10	8	11	6	9	9	13	6
Upper South (South Midland)	39	33	29	41	53	47	18	35
Kentucky	7	6	6	12	5	6	3	6
Missouri	19	18	14	21	19	13	7	21
Europe	11	31	18	23	10	9	10	8

Source: Manuscript Kansas state census, 1865.

[a]Parenthetical numbers are total populations.

main cohesive, they traveled "to the first desirable location on the Kansas River to which the Indians had ceded their rights."[21] This place was christened Lawrence on October 1, after the company's major financial backer, but it was known informally as Yankeetown.

The strategy for Lawrence set the tone for later Yankee immigration. The emphasis was on townsites with commercial promise more than on agricultural lands; direct confrontation with Missourians was avoided. Company agents would scout the region and then direct incoming parties of settlers to the chosen spots. In this manner a ribbon of New England settlement was established along the Kansas River upstream from Lawrence (see Map 2.9). Topeka was organized in December 1854 by the final groups to migrate in that year, and Boston (soon to be called Manhattan) was founded by the first company group of 1855. The gap between Topeka and Manhattan was filled in 1856 when a colony from New Haven, Connecticut, decided to settle at Wabaunsee and another group established Zeandale, both in Wabaunsee County. Finally, in 1858, Manhattan people extended the ribbon a bit farther west with the founding of Batcheller (later Milford) on the lower Republican River.[22]

The company policy of securing sites with good commercial potential extended beyond the Kansas River valley. In the spring of 1855, agent Samuel Pomeroy directed a group of ninety settlers from Hampden, Massachusetts, to a location in the middle of the rich Neosho River valley in Coffey County. The previous fall, New York and Pennsylvania settlers under the auspices of the

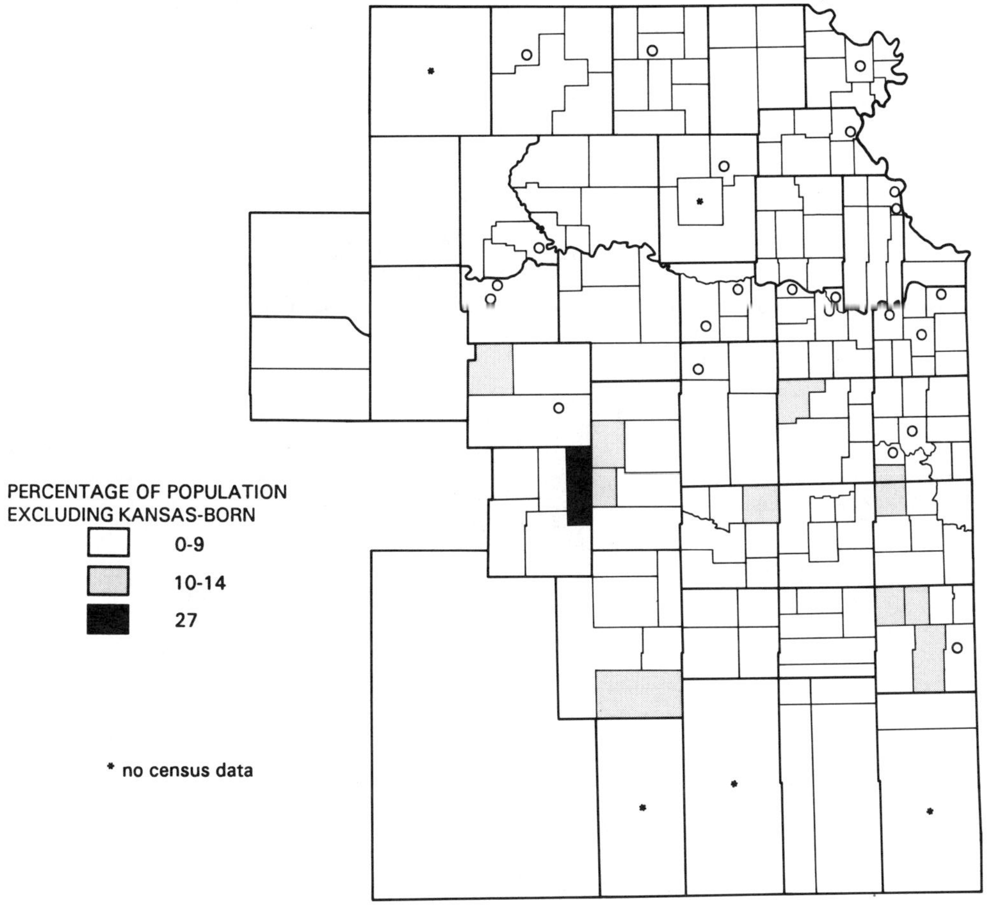

MAP 2.7
*Natives of Tennessee, 1865.
Data from Kansas state
census.*

PERCENTAGE OF POPULATION
EXCLUDING KANSAS-BORN

☐   0-9

▨   10-14

■   27

* no census data

American Settlement Company (a Philadelphia group inspired by the New England company) had organized Council City (later Burlingame) astride the Santa Fe Trail.[23]

A forced change in transportation routes in 1857 produced a series of less ideally located settlements on the uplands of Brown, Nemaha, and Jackson counties. Proslavery people effected a blockade on the Missouri River in late 1856. This led to the establishment of an overland routeway from the railhead at Iowa City, Iowa, into Nebraska and then directly south to Topeka. The Lane Trail, as the route was known, ran across good prairie lands just west of the areas occupied by Missourians.[24] Several small groups from various Northern states decided to establish farming communities near it rather than continue to the Kansas valley. Hamlin (Maine), Albany (New York), and Holton (Wisconsin) derive from this surge of population.[25]

The only Yankee settlement of dubious location was Osawatomie, set amidst Missouri-occupied lands in Miami County. This location was unplanned, the result of a party of New Yorkers deciding to find a townsite on their own after their agent had failed to meet them in Kansas

MAP 2.8

Natives of Northern states, 1865. Data from Kansas state census. Letter symbols mark cities and townships in which people from a particular Northern state constitute 20 percent or more of the immigrant population. For states included in the Northern area, see Table 1.1.

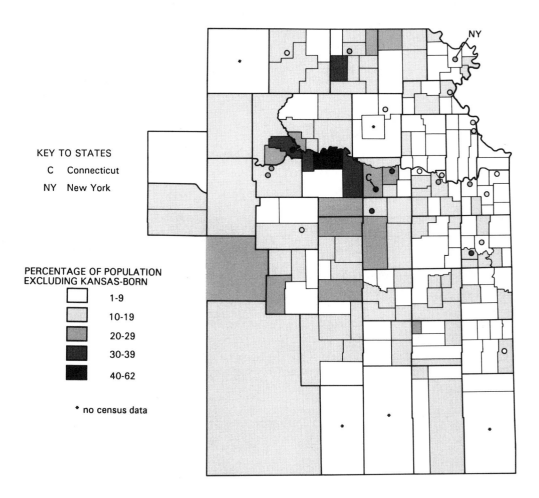

KEY TO STATES

C   Connecticut

NY New York

PERCENTAGE OF POPULATION
EXCLUDING KANSAS-BORN

☐	1-9
☐	10-19
▦	20-29
▨	30-39
■	40-62

* no census data

City (see Map 2.10). The community had an early start (December 1854) but was off the main routes of travel.[26]

The deliberate colonization schemes laid down in the 1850s by the Emigrant Aid Company remained prominent on the Kansas landscape of 1865 (see Map 2.8). Lawrence, as a relatively cosmopolitan city of 4,424 people, still could count 23 percent of its non-Kansas-born population from the Northern culture states (see Table 2.1). This percentage increased to the west: 30 for Topeka, 35 for Burlingame (plus another 20 from Pennsylvania), 52 for Manhattan, and an astounding 62 for Wabaunsee. Along a sizeable corridor from Milford to Burlingame, Yankees constituted one-third or more of the immigrant population. Poorly located Osawatomie maintained its Northern identity as well (30 percent), as did the Brown and Nemaha county settlements. Most of the Hampden colony in Coffey County had dispersed, however, discouraged by the slow pace of commercial development there.

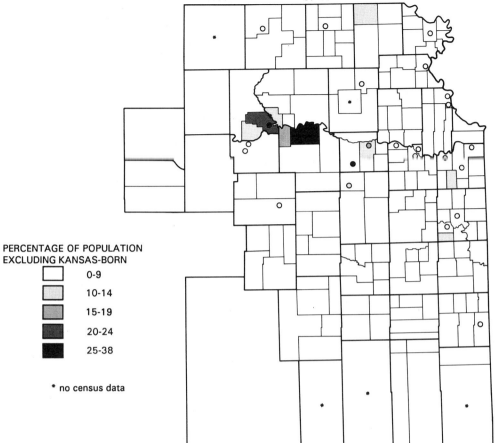

PERCENTAGE OF POPULATION
EXCLUDING KANSAS-BORN

	0-9
	10-14
	15-19
	20-24
	25-38

* no census data

By 1865 Yankee settlers in Kansas no longer felt the need to travel and settle in groups; they constituted about 10 percent of the immigrant population throughout the frontier zone. Perhaps the only surprising aspect of their geography was a presence in Leavenworth and Atchison, the traditional Missouri strongholds. The explanation was business opportunity. Leavenworth, as the largest city in the state by a sizeable margin, attracted entrepreneurs from everywhere. The Yankee presence in Atchison was the product of one of the last investments of the Emigrant Aid Company. Its directors saw potential profit in having a port settlement on the Missouri River, and when a company agent scouted the area for sites in 1857, he found the Atchison town company short of capital and willing to sell a controlling interest in the city. The sale was made and, in a touch of irony, the agent (Samuel Pomeroy) personally bought the local newspaper that had been the leading voice of the proslavery forces only two years before.[27]

MAP 2.10
*Natives of New York,
1865. Data from Kansas
state census.*

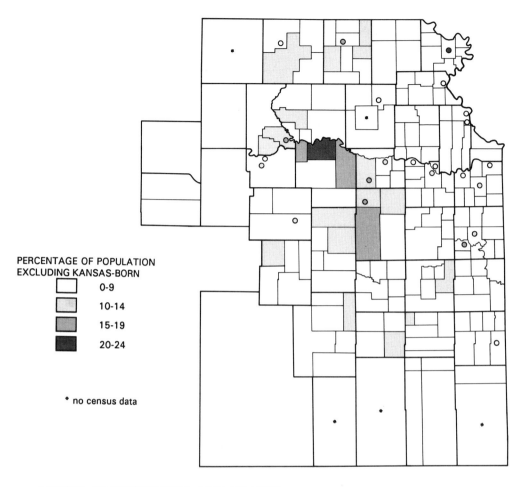

PERCENTAGE OF POPULATION
EXCLUDING KANSAS-BORN

☐ 0-9

◻ 10-14

▨ 15-19

■ 20-24

* no census data

LOWER SOUTHERNERS AND BLACKS

The few Lower Southerners who came to territorial Kansas and stayed to be counted in the 1865 census scattered themselves widely across the landscape. With a single intriguing exception, no town or township had more than 9 percent of its immigrant population from this region, and the vast majority of places had less than 1 percent. Early accounts discuss only one organized colonization attempt from the Lower South. A widely publicized expedition of four hundred men from Alabama, South Carolina, and Georgia was assembled in 1856 by Maj. Jefferson Buford, an effort designed specifically as a moral crusade, a counter to the New England Emigrant Aid Company. Upon arriving in Kansas, though, the men immediately became involved in military activities instead of in business or agriculture. Most of the Buford company are thought to have returned home or otherwise to have left Kansas by 1857, but a few settled just south of Osawatomie.[28] Three adjacent townships there contained a total of forty-eight Lower Southerners in 1865; these people constituted 5 percent of the immigrant population in one township and 9 percent in the other two.

Neosho Falls Township in northeastern Woodson County formed the glaring exception to the otherwise inconsequential presence of Lower Southerners in Kansas. Thirty percent of its immigrant population in 1865 was drawn from this region, particularly from the Seminole Nation, the Creek Nation, Florida, and Georgia. There were 194 people in all, 188 of whom were classified as black. This unusual agglomeration must have been transient, for local accounts only hint of its existence.[29] Black slaves were numerous in both the Seminole and Creek Nations, but it is also possible that these Woodson Countians were misclassified Indians; many Union-sympathizers of several races are known to have come to southern Kansas from the Indian nations even though no Indians are recorded in the 1865 census except in Johnson County.[30] Whatever their race, most of these people were employed as temporary farm workers in the Neosho valley where they were badly needed to relieve the chronic labor shortage of the war years.

Although the Indian nations contributed significantly to the black and other minority population of early Kansas, the vast majority of the state's 12,641 black settlers in 1865 were fugitives from Missouri. The influx began in 1857, once free-state forces had become dominant in Kansas Territory, and it increased rapidly after the beginning of the Civil War. The well-publicized raids of John Brown, James Lane, and other abolitionists certainly stimulated the process, but since many of Missouri's slaves were concentrated in the western counties, escape across the border was fairly easy for them during the chaotic war years. The black population of Missouri decreased by over 41,000 between 1860 and 1863, and enough of the escapees decided to cast their fate with Kansas so that by 1865, 8.9 percent of the citizens of the new state were black. This percentage has never since been matched.[31]

The location of black Kansans was dictated by considerations of transportation and safety. Most of the people were ill-equipped to travel far, yet they needed protection from retaliatory raids by slave owners. Rural border townships with their Missouri-born populations were largely avoided (see Map 2.11). Some settlers ventured as far west as the Neosho valley, but most stayed closer to the Missouri border and clustered instead at urban sites that offered protection. Forts Leavenworth and Scott were obvious havens because of their Union military forces, and the width of the Missouri River was perceived to be an effective barrier against raiders as well. The easternmost of the New England towns, places with reputations for abolition sentiment, were also popular sites.[32]

Eight urban areas contained 56 percent of the state's black population in 1865: Leavenworth (2,455), Wyandotte County (1,504), Lawrence and North Lawrence (1,464), Fort Scott (492), Atchison (432), Mound City (270), Osawatomie (192), and Topeka (170). All of these areas matched one or more of the protection factors noted above, and the assemblage of black settlers within or adjacent to these towns was apparently accomplished with a minimum of tension.[33] Nevertheless, the sizeable presence of Missouri-born blacks necessarily modifies the cultural image of eastern Kansas (see Maps 2.3 and 2.8). If one assumes that the black social system functioned largely apart from that of the adjacent white population, the effective South-Midland influence within the dominant

MAP 2.11
Black population, 1865.
Data from Kansas state
census.

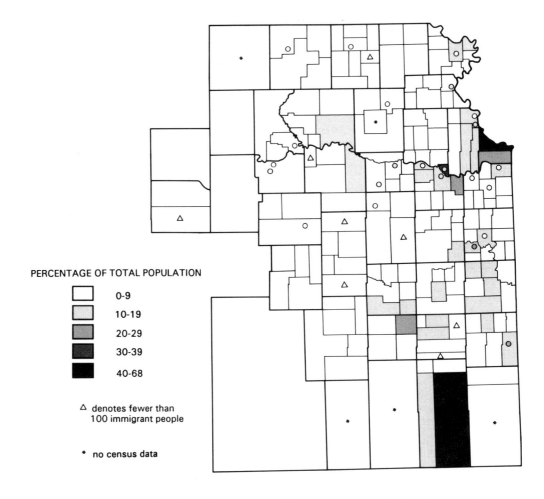

PERCENTAGE OF TOTAL POPULATION

- 0-9
- 10-19
- 20-29
- 30-39
- 40-68

△ denotes fewer than
100 immigrant people

* no census data

white society was smaller than that suggested by Map 2.3; similarly, influences from New England and elsewhere were larger.

THE EUROPEANS

Fueled by a combination of poor harvests, rapid population growth, and desire for social reform, a widespread "America fever" swept across the British Isles and the middle Rhine valley in the 1850s.[34] By 1857 a portion of the resulting emigration had reached the Kansas frontier. Over fourteen thousand German, Irish, English, French, and other foreign-born settlers lived in the state in 1865, adding greatly to the local cultural diversity and constituting nearly 11 percent of the population (see Table 1.1). Surviving documents suggest that these peoples generally opposed slavery, a position that may explain their near absence from Kansas during the proslavery years of 1855 and 1856.[35] Somewhat paradoxically, many of them, especially the Catholics, also were leery of the

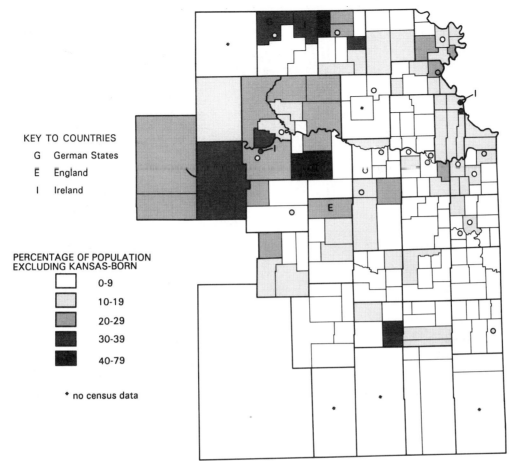

KEY TO COUNTRIES
G   German States
E   England
I   Ireland

PERCENTAGE OF POPULATION
EXCLUDING KANSAS-BORN

0-9
10-19
20-29
30-39
40-79

* no census data

free-state party; they perceived it to be "fanatically abolitionist," too closely identified with the "distinctively Protestant character" of the Emigrant Aid Company.[36]

The geography of the foreign enclaves in early Kansas was determined in large part by time of arrival and by the negative perceptions these settlers held of both Missourians and New Englanders (see Map 2.12). Immigrants from England and British America spread themselves nearly evenly across the state, but the others formed clusters. Some, following a familiar historical pattern, sought anonymity and/or employment opportunities in cities. More than one-quarter of the total European contingent (3,853) lived in Leavenworth, where they constituted 31 percent of the city's non-Kansas-born population. Atchison's population was 23 percent foreign-born, and the number in other major towns ranged between 8 and 18 percent (see Table 2.1). Altogether, 41 percent of the Europeans lived in the immediate vicinity of Kansas' four major cities.

The other major locational strategy was to seek physical isolation on the frontier. These trekkers tended to follow the Kansas valley and other major routes across the territory instead of at-

MAP 2.13
Natives of Ireland, 1865.
Data from Kansas state
census.

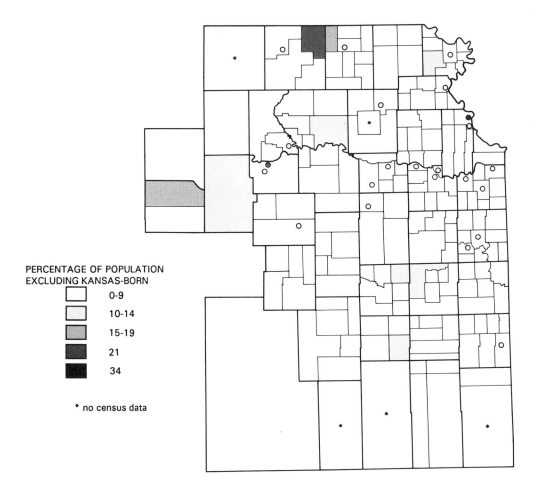

PERCENTAGE OF POPULATION
EXCLUDING KANSAS-BORN

- 0-9
- 10-14
- 15-19
- 21
- 34

* no census data

tempting extended back-country travel, but then they selected land several miles distant from these routes.[37] Through this procedure, holdings were obtained in relatively contiguous blocks at relatively cheap prices; they also provided settings where people could maintain traditional value systems.

Germans and Irish together accounted for nearly two-thirds of the foreign-born Kansans in 1865. They completely dominated the European presence in Leavenworth and in the other major towns, and were the leading rural colonists as well. In the cities, the Irish commonly worked as laborers and the Germans as merchants. Each larger town featured at least one German wholesale grocer, cigar maker, brewer, furniture maker, and newspaper editor; each place had a Turnverein social center as well. Many of the urban Germans were fervent abolitionists and played critical roles in the conversion of the Atchison and Leavenworth communities to the free-state cause.[38]

Beyond the border cities, five thrusts of activity produced a series of significant German and Irish colonies (see Maps 2.13, 2.14). Catholic efforts emanated from a Benedictine priory established

PERCENTAGE OF POPULATION
EXCLUDING KANSAS-BORN

	0-9
	10-14
	15-19
	23
	72

* no census data

at Doniphan in 1857 and moved to Atchison in 1859. The priests there encouraged and provided services for several inland missions, the largest of which were at Wolf River in southwestern Doniphan County and at St. Benedict in northwestern Nemaha County. Both settlements were mixed German and Irish from the beginning, and each contained about 150 people in 1865.[39]

Settlement by German Protestants was less organized than that of their Catholic kin. One of the major centers, in northwestern Marshall and adjacent Washington counties, clustered about an early land claim by G. H. Hollenberg, a founder of Hanover, Kansas. About 110 German-born people were there in 1865, most of them Missouri Synod Lutherans, and this number was about to increase ninefold in the wake of a new railroad into the area from Atchison (the Union Pacific, Central Branch). Several families also settled just south of this concentration, in the Blue River valley.[40]

Farther south, beyond the Yankee settlements along the Kansas River, Gottlieb Zwanziger and other settlers from St. Louis established a second major German Protestant center in the isolated

Mill Creek valley of Wabaunsee County. They laid out the town of Alma in 1857 and lobbied successfully to locate the county seat there. With 160 people in 1865, they constituted 79 percent of the township population and controlled both the city and the county government; such political success for a foreign-born group was unprecedented in Kansas. As their original site prospered, the Alma entrepreneurs sought similar locations along other south-bank tributaries of the Kansas River. Colonies on the West Branch of Mill Creek (Wabaunsee County), on Clark's Creek (Davis and Morris counties), and on Lyon Creek (Dickinson and Davis counties), are, to a degree, extensions of the Mill Creek settlement.[41]

The final two major German colonies in early Kansas, Eudora and Humboldt, stand apart from the others both in location and in motivation. They were products of town companies, groups who sought business opportunity rather than isolation. Humboldt, in the Neosho valley of southwestern Allen and adjacent Woodson counties, was initiated in 1856 by F. M. Serenbets and others in Hartford, Connecticut, and received support from the New England Emigrant Aid Company. Peter Hartig and the other founders of Eudora were from Chicago; they were able to obtain a choice 800-acre site on the Kansas River despite coming in 1857 because Shawnee Indian lands there happened to be on the market at the time. Both of these groups were mixed in religious affiliation, with a Jewish contingent present at Eudora. The Humboldt colony had 73 German-born people in 1865; Eudora had 222 German and German-Swiss settlers.[42]

Besides the Germans and the Irish, only two other national groups formed concentrated settlements in the interior: Swedes in the Blue River valley upstream from Manhattan (fifty-seven people in and near Mariadahl) and Swiss at two Nemaha County sites (forty-six people in and near Bern and Neuchatel). The Swedish group grew from the immigration of John Johnson in 1855, who brought in other family members and named the settlement after his mother. Family also formed the basis for the Swiss groups: Catherine Lehman and her five sons in the case of Bern, and Ami and Charles Bonjour for Neuchatel (the only French-Swiss settlement in Kansas). Although the numbers at the three colonies were small and none of them grew after 1865, Mariadahl residents did help to promote the larger Swedish colonies that came to central Kansas later in the decade.[43]

THE NORTH-MIDLAND MAINSTREAM

The arrival of each group of Missourians, New Englanders, blacks, and Europeans in Kansas was announced with fanfare in the contemporary press. In contrast, the sizeable immigration from Ohio, Indiana, Illinois, and other North-Midland states took place in near silence (see Table 1.1). This indifference was a product of moderate character. In their attitudes toward abolition, states' rights, the Democratic party, and a host of other cultural issues, the North Midlanders were a mixed lot but tended away from the extremism of the other major groups in Kansas; they thus neither angered nor especially pleased these other residents.[44] The North Midlanders did not arrive

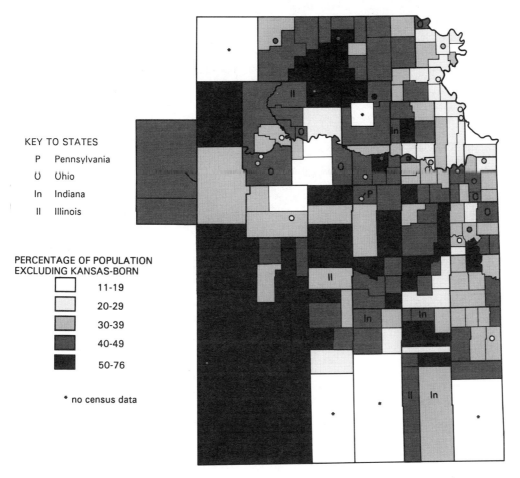

KEY TO STATES

P Pennsylvania
O Ohio
In Indiana
Il Illinois

PERCENTAGE OF POPULATION
EXCLUDING KANSAS-BORN

☐ 11-19
☐ 20-29
☐ 30-39
☐ 40-49
■ 50-76

* no census data

MAP 2.15
Natives of North-
Midland states, 1865.
Data from Kansas state
census. Letter symbols
mark cities and townships
in which people from
a particular North-
Midland state constitute
20 percent or more of the
immigrant population.
For states included in the
North-Midland area, see
Table 1.1.

as early as the Missourians, settle as cohesively as the Europeans, or function as efficiently and methodically as the New Englanders. With the exceptions of the Pennsylvania party that came to Burlingame and an Ohio group that came to Manhattan, they did not immigrate in organized colonies. The movement was by individuals or small groups, and their settlement was biased neither toward urban nor rural destinations. Given these somewhat bland characteristics, North Midlanders were the invisible people of the Kansas frontier.

In keeping with their moderate social temperament, North-Midland peoples dispersed themselves over a broader area than did any of the other culture groups (see Map 2.15). They formed the largest cultural community in most political units, and their numbers fell below 20 percent of the immigrant population in only five townships. North Midlanders constituted the closest approximation to a mainstream that could be found in early Kansas; not only did they mediate among New Englanders, Missourians, and Europeans in culture, but they also performed the same function in space. North of the Kansas River their area of greatest concentration lay in southwest-

MAP 2.16
Natives of Ohio, 1865.
Data from Kansas state
census.

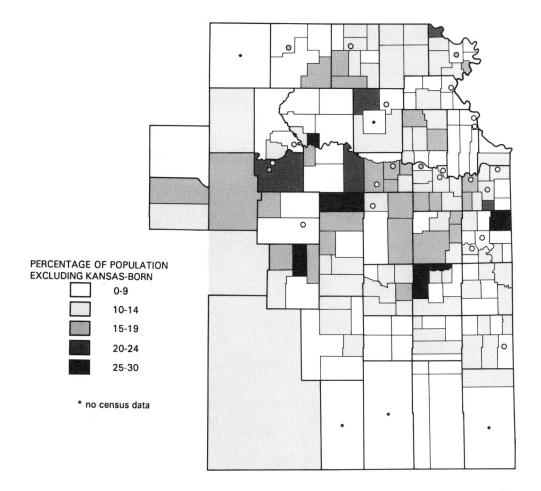

PERCENTAGE OF POPULATION
EXCLUDING KANSAS-BORN

- 0-9
- 10-14
- 15-19
- 20-24
- 25-30

* no census data

ern Nemaha County, a buffer zone to the west of the Missourians, south of the Germans and Irish, and north of the Yankees. Similarly, in southern Kansas they formed the majority of settlers along an irregular zone extending west-southwest from Franklin County, again separating a mix of South-Midland and other peoples to the south and east from Yankees and Germans to the north and west.

North-Midland settlement took the shape of an irregular arc about the core of Missourians and New Englanders. Within this arc, however, the pattern was different from the one suggested by the distance arguments given earlier. Ohio and Pennsylvania natives were the first North Midlanders to arrive in Kansas if one is to judge from their settlement geography (see Maps 2.16, 2.17). Their greatest concentration occurred in a long oval band on either side of the Kansas River settlements. Flanking this band, Indiana-born people created another, broader arc with particular concentration in the Neosho River valley of Coffey and Lyon counties (see Map 2.18). Finally, the destinations of Illini and Iowans formed additional arcs, with the Iowans concentrated in the newest Kansas frontiers such as the Verdigris and Fall river valleys in Greenwood County and in the

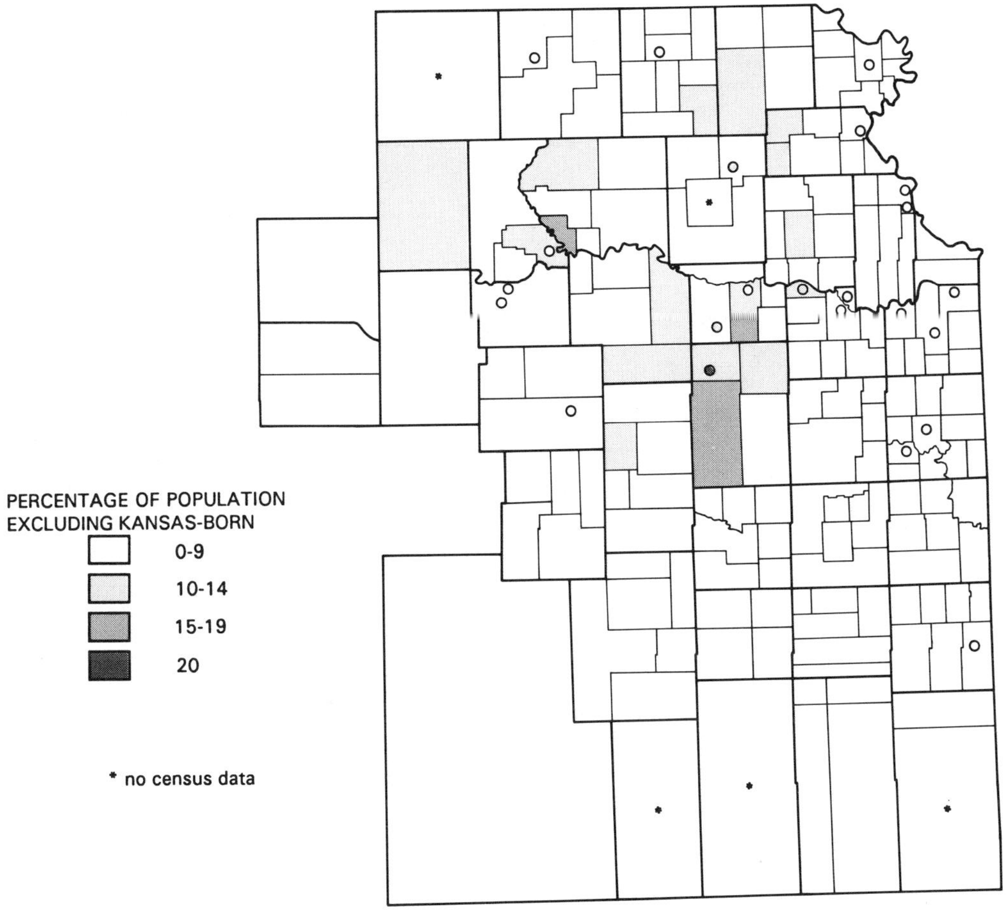

PERCENTAGE OF POPULATION
EXCLUDING KANSAS-BORN
0-9
10-14
15-19
20
* no census data

MAP 2.17
Natives of Pennsylvania, 1865. Data from Kansas state census.

western outposts of Clay and Ottawa counties (see Maps 2.19, 2.20). These patterns make clear that, among the North-Midland states, distance to Kansas was not nearly as important a factor in the timing of emigration as was the stage of their own local economic development. Mature Ohio sent settlers earlier than did frontier Iowa and Illinois.

CULTURE REGIONS

Given the varied but generally moderate culture that contemporary and modern observers alike have attributed to the North-Midland peoples in Kansas, it seems that any attempt to discern culture regions for the state should concentrate initially on the location of the most distinctive peoples. The generalized patterns shown on Map 2.21 are based on this logic and do not contain North-Midland people; it is a striking regionalization.

Upper Southerners, Yankees, and Europeans each formed the dominant culture in certain well-

MAP 2.18
*Natives of Indiana, 1865.
Data from Kansas state
census.*

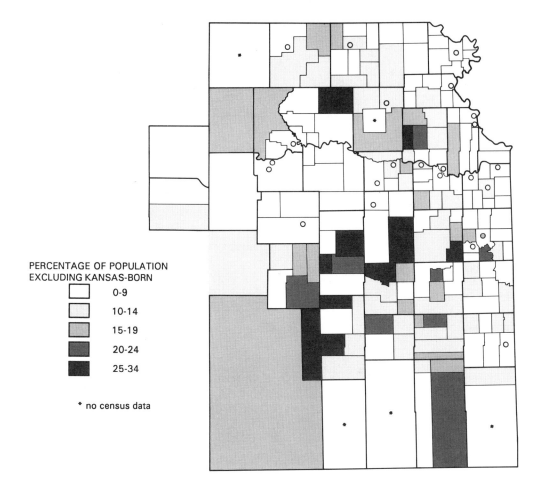

PERCENTAGE OF POPULATION
EXCLUDING KANSAS-BORN

- 0-9
- 10-14
- 15-19
- 20-24
- 25-34

* no census data

defined sections of the state, and Lower Southerners even held sway temporarily in Woodson County. Larger zones, what may be termed the spheres of these respective cultures, surrounded each of the core areas; there the people in question constituted between 30 and 50 percent of the immigrants. Smaller-scale differentiation occurred in the cities and in other places where large numbers of black people lived.

How does one interpret this map of regional cultures? It is interesting to note that virtually no overlap occurs between the spheres of foreign, Northern, and Upper Southern settlement. This suggests that isolation of the three groups from each other was considerable in 1865 and that each traditional heritage could be maintained fairly easily. Such an inference needs to be tempered by remembering that North-Midland peoples are not depicted on this map. Did their buffer culture rapidly mediate between the extremes to create a hybrid society in Kansas, or was the North-Midland role more that of a referee among three antagonists? Thorough analysis of this question

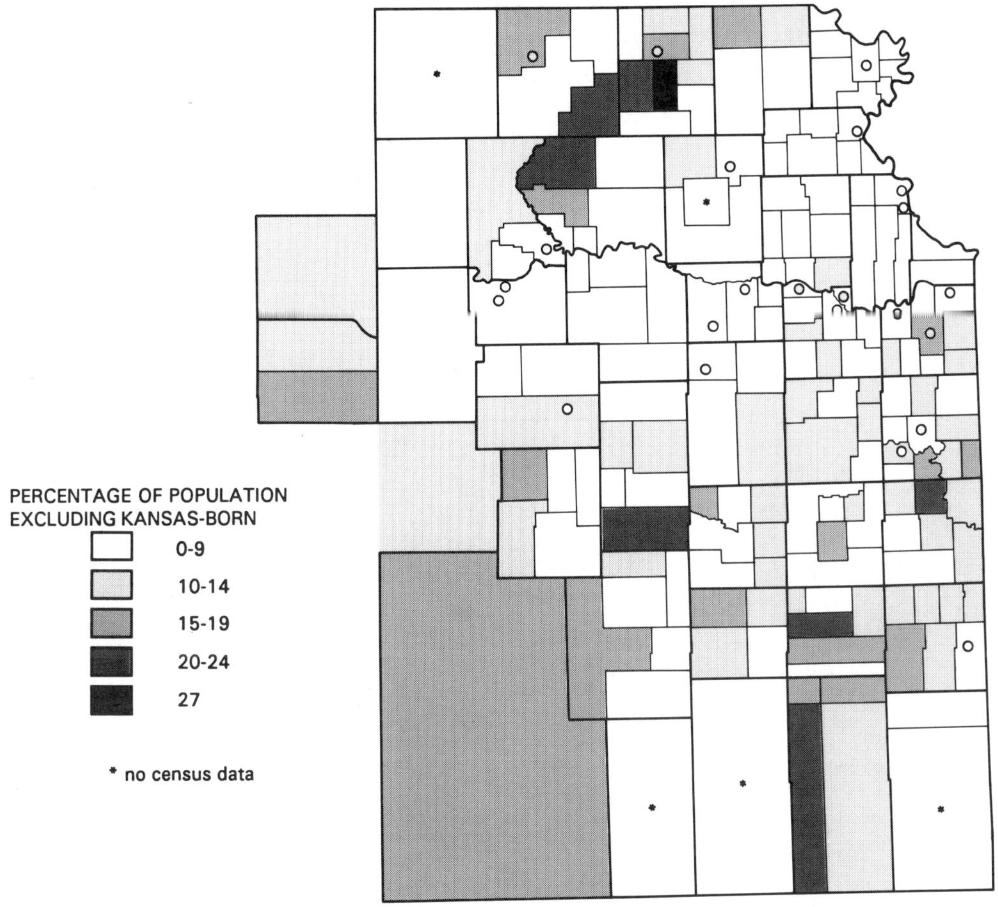

MAP 2.19
Natives of Illinois, 1865.
Data from Kansas state
census.

PERCENTAGE OF POPULATION
EXCLUDING KANSAS-BORN

- 0-9
- 10-14
- 15-19
- 20-24
- 27

* no census data

is daunting, but the issue of cultural distinctiveness deserves assessment in at least a preliminary way. Somewhat arbitrarily, I omit the obviously singular European and black enclaves, for which several good studies already exist, to focus instead on the lesser understood Anglo-American sub-cultures.[45]

Contemporary observers most certainly believed that Yankees and South Midlanders possessed different value systems. These perceived differences formed a major underlying motif for the newspaper stories of the bleeding Kansas era. One example from a North-Midland source will suffice to give the flavor of the two stereotypes:

[Eastern immigrants] come to Kansas for the purpose of instructing the Western people how to build up a model New England state. They are advised, from headquarters, to avoid the use of all Western vulgarisms, and cherish their New England habits and customs. They hear and

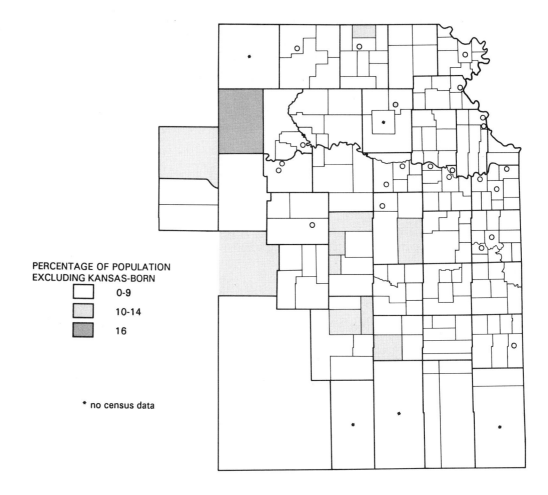

MAP 2.2O
*Natives of Iowa, 1865.
Data from Kansas state
census.*

PERCENTAGE OF POPULATION
EXCLUDING KANSAS-BORN

0-9

10-14

16

* no census data

conceive a great many tales about Western life and manners. . . . They work themselves into a belief that Western men and especially Missourians, are of an inferior order of people, unfit for social intercourse; and unless a man agrees with them in all their peculiar notions about building up a model State, he is charged as a "Missourian"—as this is the worst epithet, in their opinion, they can apply to anyone they dislike.[46]

The portraits drawn of the two groups clearly were exaggerated for political purposes, but each stereotype does have a basis in fact. Consider first some place-name testimony. Townships in the eastern two tiers of counties were named Kentucky, Ozark, Alexandria, Paris (Kentucky), and Potosi (Missouri). In contrast, the principal street in Lawrence was called Massachusetts, and those in Wabaunsee echoed the names of parent New Haven, Connecticut: Grove, Temple, Trumbull. North and South met literally in Marshall County, where an early Southern settlement called Palmetto (Calhoun and Carolina streets) abutted newer, and Northern, Marysville along a half-block

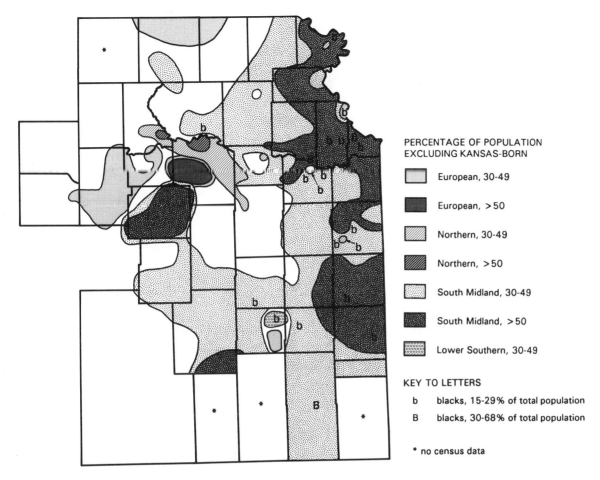

PERCENTAGE OF POPULATION
EXCLUDING KANSAS-BORN

European, 30-49

European, >50

Northern, 30-49

Northern, >50

South Midland, 30-49

South Midland, >50

Lower Southern, 30-49

KEY TO LETTERS

b   blacks, 15-29% of total population

B   blacks, 30-68% of total population

*   no census data

of commercial buildings. One could enter the stores from either the Palmetto or the Marysville side, without having to set foot in the other town, and both communities were able to claim a "main" street.[47]

Although place-names are suggestive of cultural differences, they are hardly conclusive. The stereotypes can be evaluated better by a comparison of Kansas evidence with an abbreviated list of distinctive traits and orientations compiled from dispassionate modern studies:

YANKEES	SOUTH MIDLANDERS
urban settlement	dispersed rural settlement
pro-business	distrust of big business
fastidious	rough-hewn, simple tastes
centralized political power	personal freedom, local political power
organized religion	informal or no religious beliefs

pro-education	anti-intellectualism
permanence	mobility
temperance	hard-drinking
Republican	Jacksonian Democrat
"blue-nosed"	"backward"[48]

Attitudes toward cities and the centralized social institutions associated with urban places are difficult to measure objectively, but the Yankee penchant for settling in cities has already been noted. Early accounts also suggest that their basic concept of what a city should be differed from that of the South Midlander. The clearest statement I have found for Kansas describes a pair of communities in the late 1850s:

> Two different ideas underlaid the founding of Manhattan and Junction City. In the case of Manhattan the original scheme comprehended a finished community; schools, churches, college, libraries and literary societies all existed in embryo, ready to be launched forth at the earliest opportunity. In Junction City a town-site was platted, hotel and saloon started, and the rest was expected to follow by a process of natural evolution. In the one, social, intellectual, and moral needs of the people were anticipated; in the other those needs were left to call into existence the means for their own satisfaction. Manhattan bore the image and superscription of New England—Junction City of the frontier.[49]

Three of the traits said to distinguish Yankees and South Midlanders on the Kansas frontier can be easily quantified: politics, religion, and education. Although a political election necessarily incorporates economic and personal concerns along with cultural ones, and data for religion and education are similarly imperfect measures of culture, the biases in each case are different from one another. Patterns common to the three traits are most likely culturally based.

With regard to politics, the vote on the Wyandotte constitution, October 4, 1859, may be the most appropriate cultural indicator. This election was the final test of the free-state/proslavery issue for Kansas, and it was the only vote in the territorial period not boycotted by some sizeable faction of the electorate. The Wyandotte document was modeled after the constitution in Ohio, a wise compromise choice for the territory, but it nevertheless polarized the people. Democrats opposed adoption not only on the slavery question (which most people had already seen as a lost cause) but also because by defeating the proposal Kansas would remain a territory and thereby in control of appointees made by the Democratic administration in Washington. Republicans characterized the Democrats as border ruffians (i.e., South Midlanders), men without scruples who were pawns of Washington, D.C. The voting was overwhelmingly in favor of the new constitution, 10,421 to 5,530, with majorities in all but Morris and Johnson counties.[50] As expected, though, when county-by-county "in favor" percentages are compared with proportions of the population born in South-

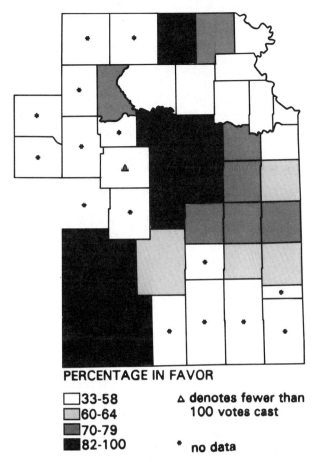

MAP 2.22
*The vote on the
Wyandotte constitution,
1859. Data from Daniel
W. Wilder,* The Annals
of Kansas *(Topeka:
T. Dwight Thatcher
Publishing Company,
1886), p. 227.*

PERCENTAGE IN FAVOR

☐ 33-58
▨ 60-64
▨ 70-79
■ 82-100

△ denotes fewer than
100 votes cast

✳ no data

Midland and Lower Southern states, the correlation is highly negative (r = −.67). Beyond the obvious Yankee/South-Midland dichotomy, the mapped pattern shows that voters in predominantly North-Midland counties such as Nemaha, Lyon, and Osage clearly aligned themselves with those from the New England–dominated places (see Map 2.22).

The common accusation that Missourians were "'down on' schools, churches, and printing offices, and revel in ignorance and filth" can be partially explored through a church inventory taken as part of the 1865 census and through the location of early colleges.[51] The number of churches is not as sensitive a measure of religious affiliation as membership would be, but a ratio of congregations to population may serve as a general indicator of the role of organized religion in people's lives (see Map 2.23). Similarly, a map of four-year colleges founded in 1865 or before, a time when Kansas was still a frontier, would seem to be a reasonable measure of community commitment to higher education (see Map 2.24). Both maps reveal sharp regionalization. Of the South-Midland counties, only Morris had a high ratio of churches per capita, and this figure may even be mis-

MAP 2.23

Churches per 1,000 people, 1865 (asterisk indicates no data). Data from Kansas state census. Shading marks counties in which the ratio is 2.0 or higher.

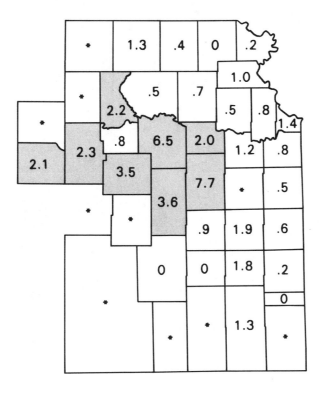

leading since none of that county's four churches had buildings of their own. The Upper South counties were generally the most populous in the state, yet only Atchison possessed a college, and it was a product of Benedictine priests, not of the city's Missouri contingent.

New Englanders, in contrast to the Missourians, were truly committed to the early construction of churches and colleges. The Emigrant Aid Company had a policy against direct aid to religious groups, but company officers and settlers privately established Congregational and Unitarian churches in Lawrence within the first year of settlement, and similar progress occurred in the other Yankee towns. The Emigrant Aid Company freely provided money and building lots for elementary schools and, nearly as quickly, attention was focused on higher education. Amos Lawrence endowed a college in Lawrence in 1855. Two years later, the company donated twenty lots in Manhattan to help start Bluemont Central College, and, in 1858, the state's Congregational ministers advertised for bids for the church-affiliated college that became Washburn, in Topeka.[52] That two of these three institutions became the major public universities in the state is also a direct result of early promotions by Yankee settlers. Of the remaining colleges extant before 1866, the short-lived Western Christian University was also in a New England settlement (Ottumwa, near Hampden); the other three (Baker, Ottawa, and Wetmore) were located in areas of North-Midland influence.

The regionalization of early culture groups in northeastern Kansas has relevance for current as well as for historical issues. The continuing presence of place-names may seem trivial, but the

MAP 2.24
Four-year colleges established in 1865 or earlier. Data from Homer E. Socolofsky and Huber Self, Historical Atlas of Kansas *(Norman: University of Oklahoma Press, 1972), Maps 45 and 46.*

localization of major universities and the state capital in the small New England zone of settlement has had profound consequences for the state's pattern of development. The persistence of attitudes toward temperance, attachment to place, politics, and other cultural values have modern implications, too. Discussion of these traits on a statewide basis, however, seems best postponed until after consideration of the initial patterns of population origin in southeastern, central, and western Kansas.

3

The Southeast, 1885

Kansas in 1885 was a far more complex place than it had been two decades earlier. Census workers counted 1,268,530 people in the state, a total that exceeded the number in 1865 by a factor of nine.[1] The settled area had expanded similarly, reaching almost to the Colorado border in the northwest. Officials calculated the center of the state's surging population to be in the southwest corner of Morris County, a place that had been open prairie just twenty years before.[2]

The complexity of the 1885 scene can be lessened by making a geographical division. Southeastern Kansas was settled under considerably different circumstances than was the central part of the state, and can best be understood on its own terms. The Southeast was the first of the post–Civil War frontiers in Kansas. Its occupation also took place under an unusually heavy shadow of land speculation, as three grant-seeking railroads built through the region nearly simultaneously around 1870. Land titles were uncertain for a decade and, with them, land values. The development of major coalfields in Crawford and Cherokee counties beginning about 1876 added further distinctiveness to the local settlement geography, as did ramifications from a boom in lead and zinc mining at Galena in 1877. Then came the immigration of former slaves at the end of Reconstruction in 1879 and 1880.

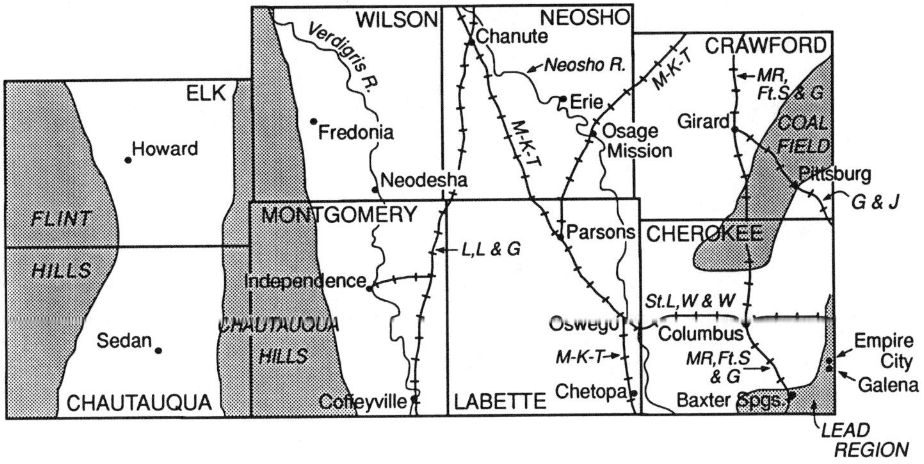

MAP 3.1
*Reference map for
southeastern Kansas, 1885.*

I have arbitrarily defined southeastern Kansas here as the eight counties located directly south of the settled zone of 1865: Chautauqua, Cherokee, Crawford, Elk, Labette, Montgomery, Neosho, and Wilson (see Map 3.1). The region is well watered but has a varied terrain. Early travelers noted with pleasure the rich soils of the broad Neosho and Verdigris valleys but were decidedly less enthusiastic about agricultural opportunities in the dissected uplands that form the western portion of the region. A rugged section of the Flint Hills occupies much of Chautauqua and Elk counties. Just to the east, astraddle the western border of Montgomery and Wilson counties, relatively sterile sandstone soils and a mantle of blackjack and post oak characterize the ten-mile width of the Chautauqua Hills.

All but five townships in the eight-county region exceeded sixteen people per square mile in 1885, and most had far greater densities (see Map 3.2). Parsons, a major division point on one of the pioneering railroads, had 7,245 people. Independence, the county seat of Montgomery County, had 4,115, and Pittsburg, the coal-mining center of the area, had 2,605. The populations of sixteen other towns exceeded 1,000, making this a region approaching economic maturity. The only exception was the cluster of lower density townships in the uplands of Chautauqua and Elk counties. This could be only a reflection of land quality, but it also suggests later-than-average settlement and perhaps occupation by relatively poor people or by those who sought isolation.

SETTLERS AND STRATEGIES

Just as the Kaw valley region in northeastern Kansas had been coveted by Anglo-Americans for years before the government allowed settlement there in late 1854, so the lands of southeastern Kansas were inspected and discussed during the Civil War years and their immediate aftermath. Most of what was to become Cherokee and Crawford counties officially belonged to the Cherokee

POPULATION PER SQUARE MILE

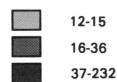

12-15

16-36

37-232

Indian Nation before 1866, and the remainder of the region was largely controlled by the Osage people. Neither group had a large local presence, though, and soldiers moved freely throughout the area along the military road that connected Fort Scott to the north with Forts Gibson and Smith to the south. Raids and counter-raids during the war years had devastated what few improvements had been made on the land, but many soldiers saw potential there. As Eugene Ware, one of these soldiers and later a prominent lawyer and writer in Fort Scott, recalled: "I made up my mind that when the war was over I was going to the Neutral Lands [i.e., the Cherokee-controlled area] and enter up some land, which I afterwards did. It seems that many other soldiers with the experience came to a like conclusion."[3]

Rumors of imminent land cessions by both the Cherokee and Osage peoples encouraged soldiers to come to southeastern Kansas soon after they were discharged. The Cherokee land officially passed to the federal government for sale in 1866 as did an adjacent, equal-sized portion of the Osage holdings in 1867. Both tracts were to be offered for sale at a minimum price of $1.25 per acre, a reasonable if not a bargain price, especially when compared with the amounts asked for equivalent sites in central Kansas where much of the land was controlled by railroads and other large speculators.[4] In anticipation of the cessions and land sales, large numbers of people quietly and unofficially moved into the region after 1865. Over a thousand families were reported on the Cherokee lands at the time of tribal cession in August 1866.[5] A spokesman for the settler association claimed twenty thousand people lived there in 1869.[6]

Attracting people to southeastern Kansas in the late 1860s was never a problem; rather, the issue became how to allot ownership and profits among competing power groups. Settlers wanted land from the government at a minimal price. Railroad companies demanded the same acreage as compensation for laying track. Other speculator groups counted on inside contacts with government officials to deliver choice tracts. The Cherokee and Osage lands became a classic battleground among these forces, pitting a settler "league," the railroad mogul James F. Joy, and a series of corrupt and honest government agents against one another for over a decade.[7]

Although the struggle over ownership of the region reads as high adventure, the details affect the issue of settler origin only indirectly. The important point from the perspective of cultural geography is that potential migrants from many places lacked the early knowledge and/or the financial wherewithal to participate fully in the process. Because railroad companies never gained early control of the region, they could not advertise southeastern Kansas throughout the eastern United States and Europe as was the practice of other railroads on the plains. One result was that the eight counties had only modest numbers of foreign-born peoples in 1885 (see Table 3.1). Another local anomaly was the near absence of formal or informal colonies by any Anglo-American groups.[8] Such group enterprises traditionally had been a way for people from distant places to pool knowledge and resources in order to survive in a new environment. The concept had been important in the settlement of northeastern Kansas in the 1850s and was to be again in the central and western sections of the state in the 1870s and 1880s. New Englanders, Southerners, and Europeans all participated. In the Southeast, though, the early, pervasive, and individualistic presence of veterans from nearby North-Midland states precluded the possibilities for a rich mix of culture groups and settlement forms. One contemporary source claimed that three-fourths of the men in Cherokee and Crawford counties from 1870 were former Union soldiers.[9]

Who were these veterans who constituted the dominant group on the southeastern frontier? They were usually described as poor people who traveled to the region on their own, often by wagon.[10] Over half of them were born in Illinois, Indiana, and Ohio (see Table 3.1), and many had been unsuccessful tenant farmers or laborers in their home states.[11] Generally speaking, they sought cheap land for a new start and lacked the money and political skills to become involved with major speculative activity. By being first on the scene, however, they had their pick of locations, and the fertile, eastern half of the eight-county area offered the widest range of economic opportunities.

Though North-Midland people were the dominant group in southeastern Kansas in the late 1860s and the 1870s, they were not the only participants. New England and other states of the Northern culture area certainly contributed to the Union army, and some of the soldiers from these places saw action in Kansas. Yankees also had had previous first-hand experience with the state during the initial Anglo-American occupance of the 1850s. Despite these ties to Kansas, though, sheer distance would work against large-scale immigration from the Northeast (see Graph 1.3), just as would an intervening frontier opportunity for Northern investors and emigrants in Minnesota.

Table 3.1. *Place of Birth of Southeastern Kansans, 1885*

Collection Unit/Culture Area	No.	(%)	Excluding (by %) Kans.-born	Kans. & Foreign-born
New England (Northern)				
Connecticut	192	(0.1)	0.2	0.2
Dakota	10			
Maine	256	(0.2)	0.2	0.2
Massachusetts	329	(0.2)	0.3	0.3
Michigan	1,372	(0.8)	1.1	1.2
Minnesota	264	(0.2)	0.2	0.2
New Hampshire	143	(0.1)	0.1	0.1
New York	3,693	(2.2)	3.0	3.2
Rhode Island	38			
Vermont	516	(0.3)	0.4	0.5
Wisconsin	953	(0.6)	0.8	0.8
Subtotal	7,766	(4.7)	6.3	6.8
North Midland				
Delaware	85	(0.1)	0.1	0.1
Illinois	25,394	(15.4)	20.8	22.3
Indiana	21,602	(13.1)	17.7	19.0
Iowa	5,927	(3.6)	4.8	5.2
Nebraska	347	(0.2)	0.3	0.3
New Jersey	496	(0.3)	0.4	0.4
Ohio	14,687	(8.9)	12.0	12.9
Pennsylvania	5,001	(3.0)	4.1	4.4
Subtotal	73,539	(44.7)	60.1	64.7
Upper South (South Midland)				
Arkansas	1,076	(0.7)	0.9	0.9
Dist. of Columbia	32			
Indian Territory	291	(0.2)	0.2	0.3
Kentucky	6,885	(4.2)	5.6	6.1
Maryland	544	(0.3)	0.4	0.5
Missouri	12,400	(7.5)	10.1	10.9
North Carolina	1,066	(0.6)	0.9	0.9
Tennessee	3,465	(2.1)	2.8	3.0

Table 3.1. *Continued*

| Collection Unit/Culture Area | No. | (%) | Excluding (by %) | |
			Kans.-born	Kans. & Foreign-born
Virginia	2,167	(1.3)	1.8	1.9
West Virginia	683	(0.4)	0.6	0.6
Subtotal	28,609	(17.3)	23.4	25.2
Lower South				
Alabama	344	(0.2)	0.3	0.3
Florida	12			
Georgia	317	(0.2)	0.3	0.3
Louisiana	234	(0.1)	0.2	0.2
Mississippi	290	(0.2)	0.2	0.3
South Carolina	170	(0.1)	0.1	0.1
Texas	2,043	(1.2)	1.7	1.8
Subtotal	3,410	(2.1)	2.8	3.0
The West				
California	115	(0.1)	0.1	0.1
Colorado	139	(0.1)	0.1	0.1
Idaho	9			
Montana	24			
Nevada	5			
New Mexico	15			
Oregon	50			
Utah	15			
Washington	11			
Wyoming	12			
Subtotal	395	(0.2)	0.3	0.3
Kansas	42,313	(25.7)		
Foreign Countries				
Austria	91	(0.1)	0.1	
Belgium	85	(0.1)	0.1	
British America	1,015	(0.6)	0.8	
Denmark	67			
England	1,624	(1.0)	1.3	

Table 3.1. *Continued*

Collection Unit/Culture Area	No.	(%)	Excluding (by %) Kans.-born	Kans. & Foreign-born
France	253	(0.2)	0.2	
German States	2,468	(1.5)	2.0	
Ireland	1,412	(0.9)	1.2	
Italy	50			
Norway	38			
Russia	55			
Scotland	647	(0.4)	0.5	
Sweden	541	(0.3)	0.4	
Switzerland	120	(0.1)	0.1	
Wales	146	(0.1)	0.1	
Other Countries	29			
Subtotal	8,641	(5.2)	7.1	
Total	164,673[a]	(100.0)	100.0	100.0

Source: Manuscript Kansas state census, 1885.

Note: Southeastern Kansas includes Chautauqua, Cherokee, Crawford, Elk, Labette, Montgomery, Neosho, and Wilson counties.

[a]This total does not include 4,376 residents for whom no place of birth was recorded.

One could predict that the biggest lure for Northerners in southeastern Kansas would be urban investments in railroad and mining towns. Chetopa, for example, the southernmost settlement in Kansas on the Missouri-Kansas-Texas Railroad, was expected by some observers to become "a second Kansas City."[12] The town was positioned in 1870 as the northern gateway to the Indian Territory and as a marketing center for Texas cattle. Such promise was a lure for anyone with money to invest.

The new Kansas frontier would also seem to offer opportunity for certain Upper Southerners. People from this region generally lacked both the money and the political connections to make major investments in the late 1860s, but many of them were close at hand. Their proximity had provided early knowledge of the rich Neosho valley, for they were the dominant group in the scattered Anglo-American population that was recorded on the Osage Reserve in the 1865 census (see Map 2.3). Proximity also meant that they knew about coal deposits on the Cherokee Neutral Lands.[13]

Countering the advantage of juxtaposition was the reality of Civil War devastation in southwestern Missouri. Neosho, only fifteen miles from the Kansas border, had served as the Confederate capital of the state. War had turned neighbor against neighbor, and the resulting burning, looting, and bitterness had severely depopulated most of the region.[14] Fighting continued even after the official end of the conflict. Eugene Ware, who traveled through the Lamar and Carthage area adjacent to the Neutral Tract in 1867, found it to be "practically deserted. . . . The chimneys were standing lonesomely everywhere. Constant talk of murders was heard of, and fights between returning soldiers. It would appear from what they told us that great outlawry prevailed."[15]

Ware and his party had come to southwestern Missouri in search of cheap land; they were not alone. Formerly prosperous counties in that region, ones that had recorded between 5,000 and 8,000 people in 1860, were reduced to about 300 residents apiece by 1865. It was a new frontier in a sense, and veterans from Illinois and Ohio sought out these Missouri lands almost as eagerly as they did the adjacent land in Kansas. Missourians themselves were in turmoil. Many eventually returned to their homesteads; others moved to Texas or to eastern Missouri.[16] Still others decided their best chance for prosperity lay in nearby Kansas. A move across the state line was cheaper than the journey to Texas. It would also offer a new start for a person who held unpopular political beliefs at home or who just wanted to escape painful memories. The likeliest locations for such refugees would be on inexpensive lands away from both the immediate state border and the mainstream of Union veterans, in the hilly, western portion of the eight-county region. Exceptions might occur on mineralized areas, where hopes for economic gain might outweigh all other concerns.

Regardless of whether the migrant to southeastern Kansas in the late 1860s was a poor Illinois farmer, a Missouri refugee, or a New England banker, he or she probably would have heard about mineral deposits in the region. Coal, lead, and natural gas were known before 1870, and zinc ore was found shortly thereafter. These deposits eventually would transform the entire economic, social, and ethnic structure of the area, but transportation inadequacies and a lack of known applications for natural gas and zinc kept speculative interest in local minerals at a minimum until about 1876. The census of 1885 records only the early stages of the mining era.

The main section of the coal belt, in Crawford and northern Cherokee counties, was mined sporadically before the war, with loads being taken overland to Carthage, Missouri, and other settlements as a trade good (see Map 3.1).[17] The decisions of the first railroad through the coal counties indicated that its potential was seen as limited, though. The Missouri River, Fort Scott and Gulf sold its lands there before 1871 at agricultural rates and did not even seek to retain mineral rights.[18]

Lead, zinc, and natural gas discoveries in Kansas initially produced even less economic activity than did coal. The first gas discovery in the area, near Fort Scott in 1865, was ignited to form "the burning well" and was a popular picnic spot for the next two decades. No major industrial uses developed for this fuel in the state until 1893.[19] The problem with lead ores was transportation rather than a perceived lack of utility. Rich deposits near Joplin, Missouri (six miles from Kansas), sat nearly unused for two decades until the more accessible fields in eastern Missouri and Wisconsin were depleted. The arrival of a railroad along the crest of the Ozarks from St. Louis in 1870 initiated major development at Joplin.[20] Kansas deposits, though, were judged as too small and remote for exploitation until 1877, when a major strike in extreme southeastern Cherokee County initiated a boom (see Map 3.1).[21] The nearly simultaneous realization that Kansas coal could be used to smelt zinc led to another frenzy of industrial activity. Its beginning was marked by the opening of the first of several large smelters at Pittsburg in 1879.[22]

PATTERNS OF OCCUPANCE

Contemporary accounts of southeastern Kansas from the 1860s and 1870s speak of settlers coming from a wide variety of places, yet when the writers become specific, the origins noted are usually in one of the North-Midland states. Northern states have a lesser presence, other places none at all. Two biases affect the credibility of these assertions. First, the magazines and journals in which they appeared were nearly all Northern-based, suggesting that the writers themselves may have been regionally prejudiced. Second, the observations were restricted almost exclusively to the towns easily available to travelers, those along the three principal railroad lines; the settlement landscape of Chautauqua, Elk, and Wilson counties thus lay beyond the purview of these writers (see Map 3.1). The former bias may account for the contrast a correspondent for *Scribner's Monthly* saw along the route of the Missouri-Kansas-Texas Railroad. People in Missouri towns, he wrote, "had a grave, preoccupied look, doubtless born of long contemplation of the soil, and of the hard ways of the West," but in adjacent Kansas towns "a sweeping change" had metamorphosed the area "into a transplanted New England."[23]

A comparison of the impressions from the old reports with census data for 1885 reveals some inconsistencies. Although North-Midland people are dominant in both accounts, a strong Upper South presence appears in the official records along with lesser numbers of European settlers and people from the Lower South (see Table 3.1). Together these three groups constituted one-third of the immigrant population of the region. One can understand why the Lower Southerners were not mentioned in the earliest accounts because almost all of them arrived in 1879 or later. They were black refugees from Texas, and their immigration to Kansas was widely reported at that time. Lateness of arrival also may explain some of the inattention accorded foreign-born settlers, many of whom came to work in the coalfields when they were developed after 1876. The lack of acknowledgment for the South-Midland group, though, is more problematic, for they generally were not

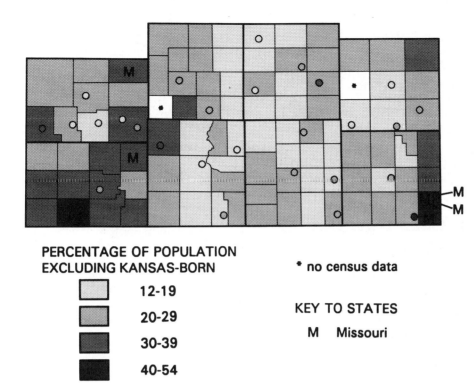

PERCENTAGE OF POPULATION
EXCLUDING KANSAS-BORN

* no census data

	12-19
	20-29
	30-39
	40-54

KEY TO STATES

M   Missouri

MAP 3.3
Natives of South-Midland states, 1885 (southeast Kansas). Data from Kansas state census. Letter symbols mark cities and townships in which people from Missouri constitute 20 percent or more of the immigrant population. For states included in the South-Midland area, see Table 3.1.

late arrivals to the area. Perhaps they clustered away from the railroad lines and larger towns; perhaps they assumed low profiles to escape postwar antagonisms. Either strategy would have kept them away from visiting journalists. Mapping provides a way to clarify these issues.

MISSOURIANS AND OTHER UPPER SOUTHERNERS

The distribution of the Upper South population is strikingly bipolar. One grouping is adjacent to the Missouri border; another is sixty miles to the west, principally in Chautauqua and Elk counties (see Map 3.3). In between, the only outlier is the old town of Osage Mission, now called St. Paul. Not surprisingly, nearby Missourians formed the core in both cases. The secondary states were different, though, with Kentucky in that role in the west and Tennessee in the east (see Maps 3.4, 3.5, 3.6), patterns suggesting that the two clusters have different origins and histories.

The bitterness of feeling between Missourians and Kansans just before and during the Civil War makes any migration of people across the state line in its aftermath a significant event. The county-seat towns of Butler, Harrisonville, and Osceola had been burned by Kansans, and Missourians had instigated a bloody raid on Lawrence. Neither side was quick to forgive.[24] Moreover, Missourians who wanted to emigrate had already developed alternative outlets to the West, including the well-traveled Texas Road and the Oregon Trail.[25]

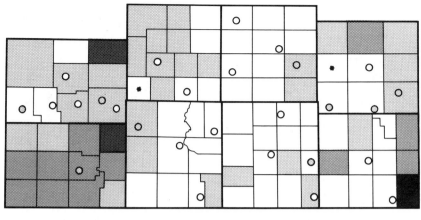

MAP 3.4
Natives of Missouri, 1885 (southeast Kansas). Data from Kansas state census.

PERCENTAGE OF POPULATION
EXCLUDING KANSAS-BORN

* no census data

☐	0-9
▦	10-14
▩	15-19
▨	20-24
■	25-34

My reading of the historical record from southwestern Missouri is that little emigration to Kansas took place in 1865 and the early part of 1866; for Missourians this was a time of homecoming and assessment. Because the war in the West had not ended in any culminating victory or defeat, people were unsure how the society would refashion itself. Any optimism was gone by late 1866, though, especially in the border counties that lay between Kansas City and Joplin. These places had been forcibly evacuated during the war and thus were thoroughly looted. As people tried to rebuild, they found their efforts blocked by partisanship. Southern sympathizers saw themselves so hated and oppressed that they sometimes had to become highwaymen to survive. Radical Unionists were frightened too, but, because they were the best-organized portion of the population, they soon were able to seize local political power. Their tactics were vindictive and brutal. Bands named Vigilance Committee, Regulators, and Advance Guard of Freedom made life nearly impossible for even conservative Unionists. Southern preachers were a special target.[26]

Movements to Kansas began shortly after the election of November 1866, when the radicals became firmly entrenched. The main source areas for the migration are undocumented, but the most devastated peoples lived in the border counties north of Joplin. This region, termed the Burnt District, had been settled a generation earlier largely by Kentuckians.[27] The Kentucky presence in

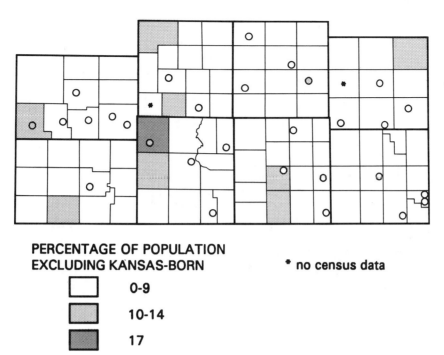

MAP 3.5
*Natives of Kentucky, 1885
(southeast Kansas). Data
from Kansas state census.*

PERCENTAGE OF POPULATION
EXCLUDING KANSAS-BORN   * no census data

[ ] 0-9

[ ] 10-14

[ ] 17

Chautauqua and Elk counties suggests that this area was the principal Kansas destination for the Missouri refugees (see Map 3.5).

Why would Missourians migrate seventy-five miles or more instead of taking closer Kansas lands? The availability of acreage and a fear of conflict with Union veterans are obvious reasons. As many as five thousand people already may have been present in Cherokee and Crawford counties at this time, almost all of them openly Unionist.[28] This argument does not hold for adjacent Labette and Neosho counties, however, where major sections of good land were still available. Price provides the most convincing explanation. Lands in the eastern four counties, the southeastern three-quarters of Montgomery, and the southeastern one-third of Wilson were mostly controlled by railroads and other large speculators. Their asking price ranged between $2.00 and $8.00 per acre, amounts considerably above the traditional preemptive price of $1.25 (see Map 3.7). But west of the angling western boundary of the grant to the Leavenworth, Lawrence and Galveston Railroad was the Osage Reserve, where lands sold for the familiar $1.25. That the trace of the old railroad grant line is mirrored by the distribution of Upper Southerners in 1885 is strong evidence that these hard-pressed people chose their new homesites with finances more than politics or other concerns in mind. A further indication is the lower percentages of Upper Southerners found in the towns

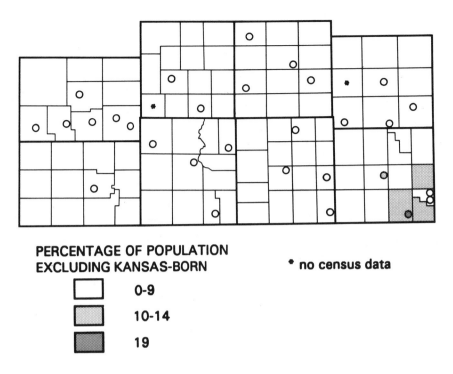

PERCENTAGE OF POPULATION
EXCLUDING KANSAS-BORN   * no census data

[ ] 0-9

[▨] 10-14

[■] 19

of Chautauqua and Elk counties than in the surrounding townships; these Southerners had little money to invest in urban speculation.

If migration to Chautauqua County was the norm for Missourians coming to Kansas, the second concentration of Upper Southerners, in southeastern Cherokee County, becomes an anomaly. The explanation here is not early migration but a later, well-documented one tied to a major mineral discovery: a lead deposit found on the banks of Short Creek in 1877. Despite border politics, Missourians controlled this site. They were the lead experts, with years of experience at nearby Joplin, and they boomed not only Galena and Empire City, the twin towns along Short Creek, but also Baxter Springs and other camps.[29] An observer in 1883 described these places as all tributary to "the great city, Joplin, around which they cluster and upon which they are in a large part dependent."[30] The presence of Tennessee natives in this section of Kansas is further proof of a Joplin origin (see Map 3.6) since they had been the principal group to settle the lead mining district in the late 1840s.[31] Some of them became pioneers for a second time in 1877.

Osage Mission, the third and smallest concentration of Upper Southerners in southeastern Kansas, has a prewar origin. It began in 1847 to serve the role its name suggests and, because it was the only Anglo-American settlement in the region, it became home to some Indian traders. These, like the staff of the mission, were largely Upper Southerners, part of the group who initiated the rich interchange between Missouri and Texas along the Texas Road.[32]

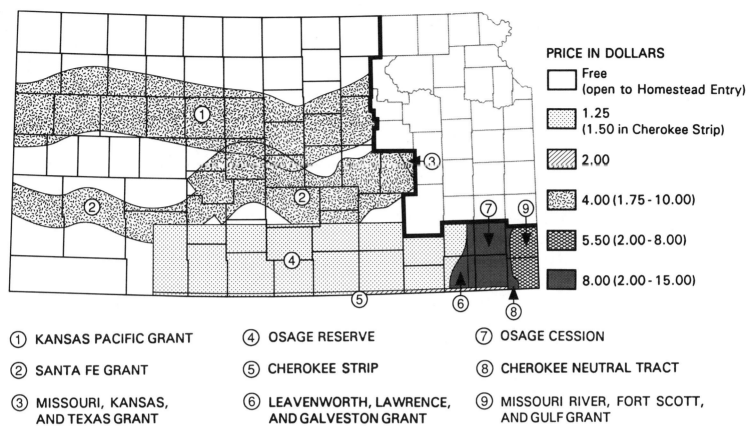

PRICE IN DOLLARS

☐ Free
(open to Homestead Entry)

▨ 1.25
(1.50 in Cherokee Strip)

▨ 2.00

▨ 4.00 (1.75 - 10.00)

▨ 5.50 (2.00 - 8.00)

■ 8.00 (2.00 - 15.00)

① KANSAS PACIFIC GRANT

② SANTA FE GRANT

③ MISSOURI, KANSAS,
AND TEXAS GRANT

④ OSAGE RESERVE

⑤ CHEROKEE STRIP

⑥ LEAVENWORTH, LAWRENCE,
AND GALVESTON GRANT

⑦ OSAGE CESSION

⑧ CHEROKEE NEUTRAL TRACT

⑨ MISSOURI RIVER, FORT SCOTT,
AND GULF GRANT

MAP 3.7
Average land prices, circa 1875 (southeast and central Kansas). Data from Fourth Annual Report of the Kansas State Board of Agriculture, 1875 *(Topeka: George W. Martin, 1876), pp. 665–70, and from Richard Sheridan,* Economic Development in South-central Kansas, Part IA: An Economic History, 1500–1900 *(Lawrence: University of Kansas School of Business, 1956), p. 82.*

EUROPEANS AND BLACKS

In contrast with the rather large but mostly unheralded presence of Upper Southerners in southeastern Kansas, a much smaller immigration of European and black settlers was widely reported. Part of the reason for the attention was the greater cultural distinctiveness of these latter peoples, of course, but the circumstances of their arrival were unusual, too. Most of the Europeans came to work in the underground coal mines near Pittsburg that developed rapidly after 1876. Black settlers arrived in two waves of migration, one from Tennessee in 1875, and another from Texas, Louisiana, and Mississippi in 1879 and 1880. Three formal colonies were established in the region by or for these people.

Europeans constituted 5 percent of the regional population in 1885 (see Table 3.1). More than a thousand each came from the German states, England, Ireland, and British America. Outside of the coalfields, they were widely scattered; only one township had a population with 20 percent foreign-born (see Map 3.8). The Europeans had arrived in most of these places in the late 1860s

MAP 3.8

Natives of European and other foreign countries, 1885 (southeast Kansas). Data from Kansas state census.

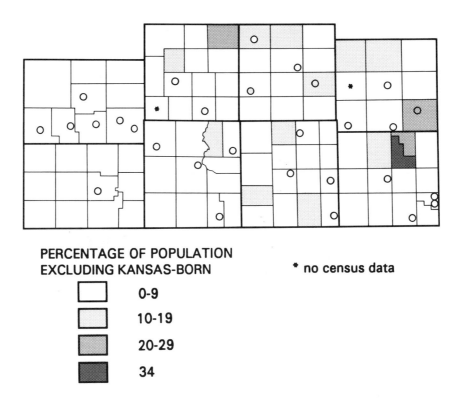

PERCENTAGE OF POPULATION
EXCLUDING KANSAS-BORN

* no census data

☐ 0-9

☐ 10-19

▨ 20-29

■ 34

with the first wave of Union veterans.[33] They settled on good lands (often purchased from the railroads) and tended to avoid the larger urban centers.

The Swedes were the most clustered of the Europeans. Though only 541 strong, they were the principal foreign group in the tier of townships along the northern border of Crawford, Neosho, and Wilson counties. A Baptist colony came first, in 1868, supplemented the next year by a larger Lutheran group led by C. J. Eklund and Swan Swanson. Of this latter group, at Vilas in Wilson County, an observer said simply that "they have made that locality bloom and prosper."[34] Another concentration of a single nationality was at Osage Mission and its surrounding township, where 112 Irish resided. Neither of the county histories notes their presence, but the mission itself would have been an attraction since it was Catholic and sponsored schools that were open to non-Indian children.[35]

The two mining areas in the region present a sharp contrast to one another in the origins of their populations. The lead district, dominated by Upper Southerners, attracted almost no European settlers; the coalfields, less than twenty miles away, had nearly an inverse composition. This difference was not lost on early writers, who sometimes invoked it as an explanation for why laborers in the coal camps became unionized and those in the lead camps did not.[36] Mining conditions

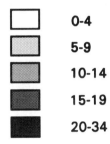

PERCENTAGE OF TOTAL POPULATION

☐	0-4
▨	5-9
▨	10-14
▨	15-19
■	20-34

provide a more convincing argument for both the ethnic and the union differences, however. Early lead mining was a small-time, even part-time activity, and its "poor man's camps" appealed to local farmers who wanted a way to earn money during the winter. Most coal mining, in contrast, was big business, with labor needs larger than the adjacent farming population could supply.[37]

The 1885 census was taken as the coal industry was increasing rapidly in scale. Although Italians, Slovenes, and Austrians would soon come to Crawford and Cherokee counties in large numbers, they were insignificant in 1885. Germans and English each constituted over one-quarter of the 2,115 Europeans who resided in the core townships of the mining district (the shaded areas on Map 3.8). Irish and Scottish immigrants together accounted for another quarter of the total and Welsh, French, and Belgian settlers another tenth. Studies have strongly associated these groups, except for the Irish, with the underground mines.[38] German participation is probably overstated by the census numbers, though, since some of these people had settled in the area as early as 1868, before the mining activity had begun.[39]

Fewer blacks than Europeans lived in southeastern Kansas, but they were even more concentrated (see Map 3.9). With only 3 percent of the regional population (5,569 total), they constituted more than one-third of the populace in Baxter Springs and 21 percent of Parker Township in Mont-

Table 3.2. *Place of Birth of Blacks in Selected Cities and Townships of Southeastern Kansas, 1885 (by %)*

Collection Unit	No. Excluding Kans. and Unknown Nativities	Ky.	La.	Miss.	Mo.	Tenn.	Tex.	All Other Places
Chautauqua County								
Little Caney Twp.	111	19	20	17		12	4	28
Cherokee County								
City of Baxter Springs	318	15	1	1	4	55	2	22
City of Columbus	206	3	3	3	2	82	1	6
Crawford Twp.	107	17		2		40	30	11
Crawford County								
City of Cherokee	110	18	7	9	20	26	9	11
Labette County								
City of Chetopa	247		2	2	5	6	59	26
City of Oswego	327	2	4	2	5	20	38	29
City of Parsons	808	8	3	2	8	6	52	21
Oswego Twp.	106	4	1	2	6	6	62	19
Richland Twp.	78	8	3	1	3	10	56	19
Montgomery County								
City of Coffeyville	150	7	1	5	5	15	45	22
Parker Twp.	130		2	2	1	4	59	32

Source: Manuscript Kansas state census, 1885.

gomery County. On the county level, Labette had 2,138 black residents, 7 percent of its total population; 967 of these were in Parsons.

The general clustering along the southern two tiers of townships suggests a common origin for these migrants and a single strategy for settling. This assumption of simplicity is challenged, however, when one looks at places of birth (see Table 3.2). The majority of the black residents of Cherokee and Crawford counties were from Tennessee; those in Labette, Neosho, and Montgomery counties came mostly from Texas; and Chautauquans were born in a variety of Southern places. These data also make it clear that the black Kansans of 1885 were different from the Missouri-born group who had sought refuge in the state during the war years and who had made up most of the minority population in 1865.

Tennesseans were the first of the new black immigrants to arrive. They were part of a spontaneous popular movement in the Nashville area that began as a quest for affordable land. Leaders were discouraged by high prices in Tennessee and ultimately recommended removal to the Kansas frontier. One leader, Benjamin "Pap" Singleton, visited Cherokee County in 1873 and by 1875 had collected funds to purchase a thousand acres from the Missouri River, Fort Scott and Gulf Railroad, four miles from Baxter Springs.[40] The Singleton Colony, as it became known, "prospered," according to early reports.[41] The land was fertile, the colonists had come with at least minimal amounts of capital, and Singleton and other leaders escorted the migrants along an easy river and rail route through St. Louis and Kansas City. Though the colony was adjacent to the lead district that opened shortly after their arrival, few blacks were employed in the mines.[42] Farming was the original emphasis of the colonists, but this soon began to change; by 1885 the nearby towns of Baxter Springs, Cherokee, and Columbus had sizeable numbers of Tennessee-born blacks (see Map 3.9 and Table 3.2).

Historians look upon the immigration of black Tennesseans to Kansas in the 1870s as something of an anomaly, since the Upper South was not awash with racial tension during the Reconstruction process. Violence was very much a part of Reconstruction in the Lower South, however, especially after 1878 when politicians began to dismantle the rights of black citizens in the name of economic development. In Louisiana, Mississippi, and Texas, especially, life for them became very uncertain.[43]

"Kansas fever" was one of the products of racial terror. In March 1879 a rumor spread along the lower Mississippi valley that any black person who wanted to move to Kansas would be given free transportation and land. Extreme versions had General Sherman leading the migration with outright gifts of five hundred dollars per family. Though none of these stories were true, the myth gave people the will to escape the social and economic crisis that surrounded them. The journey was a form of religious experience, a modern-day exodus, with St. Louis as the equivalent of the Red Sea and Kansas as the promised land of Canaan.[44]

Approximately six thousand "exodusters" came to Kansas in the few months when the fever was at its highest. Most of those from Louisiana and Mississippi entered the state through the Kansas City gateway.[45] Texans, though, went to the railheads of the Missouri-Kansas-Texas line at Denison and Sherman, and thus came into Kansas in Labette County (see Map 3.10). Goodwill generally prevailed in the entry towns of Chetopa, Oswego, and Parsons, but facilities and supplies were taxed.[46] An obvious solution was to get the people on the land where they might be self-sufficient. Some of the immigrants ventured out on their own, scattering over the Neosho valley townships north of Oswego, but others moved to one of several colonies set up by white sponsors. Two of these were in southeastern Kansas.

The Little Coney settlement in southeastern Chautauqua County was one of two communities sponsored by the Kansas Freedmen's Relief Association (see Map 3.9). This group sent fifty-six families there from Topeka in 1881, a mixture of exodusters and some black immigrants from Ken-

MAP 3.10
*Natives of Lower
Southern states, 1885
(southeast Kansas). Data
from Kansas state census.
For states included in the
Lower Southern area, see
Table 3.1.*

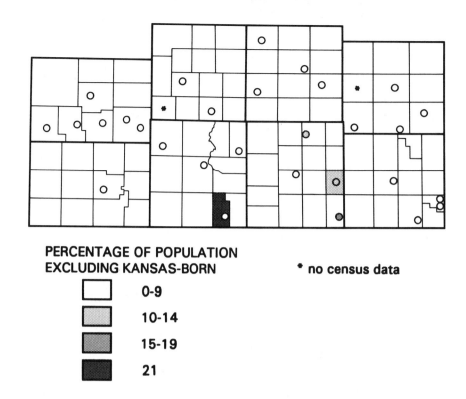

**PERCENTAGE OF POPULATION
EXCLUDING KANSAS-BORN**   *** no census data**

☐ 0-9

▨ 10-14

▨ 15-19

■ 21

tucky and Tennessee who had arrived slightly earlier. A visitor the next year reported that racial prejudice was minimal but that farm results were mixed.[47] The second colony in the region was initiated by Daniel Votaw, a white Quaker attorney from Montgomery County who had become active in the refugee aid movement. In 1881 he purchased 160 acres in the Verdigris valley just north of Coffeyville, which he subdivided into twenty lots. Most of the settlers there were Texans, who moved from Labette County (see Maps 3.9 and 3.10). Here too the farming results were mixed, with floods being the chief problem.[48]

YANKEES AND NORTH-MIDLAND PEOPLES

Contemporary observers believed that the emerging character of southeastern Kansas was shaped primarily by Union veterans from the Northern and North-Midland states. "They have exerted a power vastly out of proportion to their number," claimed the historian of Wilson County. "Always standing for law and order, exemplifying loyalty, toleration and charity, they have strengthened good government, promoted fraternity and bettered the character of society and citizenship."[49]

The gushing words of John Gilmore are hard to evaluate, but certainly in terms of numbers

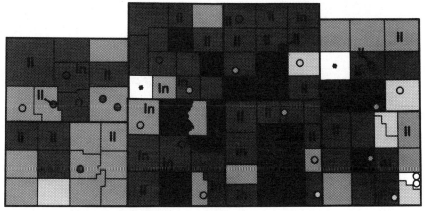

MAP 3.11
Natives of North-Midland states, 1885 (southeast Kansas). Data from Kansas state census. Letter symbols mark cities and townships in which people from a particular North-Midland state constitute 25 percent or more of the immigrant population. For states included in the North-Midland area, see Table 3.1.

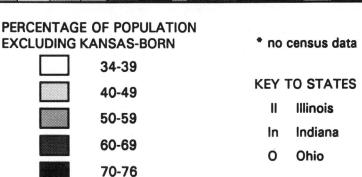

PERCENTAGE OF POPULATION
EXCLUDING KANSAS-BORN

☐	34-39
☐	40-49
☐	50-59
☐	60-69
☐	70-76

* no census data

KEY TO STATES

Il   Illinois

In   Indiana

O   Ohio

and location, the veterans were positioned for influence. North-Midland peoples did it with sheer numbers. If natives of Kansas are excluded, the 61,683 settlers from Illinois, Indiana, and Ohio made up over half of the regional population in 1885 (see Table 3.1). They also arrayed themselves evenly across the landscape. North Midlanders formed a majority of the population in all townships but seven and exceeded 70 percent of the total in eighteen (see Map 3.11). The numbers of Yankee immigrants were much more modest, at 7,766, but their concentration in cities suggests a disproportionate influence along the lines described by Gilmore (see Map 3.12).

The urban orientation of Yankees in the region can be seen by a comparison of their overall percentage with their frequency in the larger cities (see Table 3.3). In no case was their urban percentage lower than their general one. Although I did not collect the data on occupation and property to evaluate the often-made claim that Yankees were frontier capitalists, their overall geography is consistent with such an assertion. Residents of neither of the two towns with the lowest percentages, Erie and Galena, had been successful early in their recruitment of a railroad (see Map 3.1). Any careful observer of the time could see that Erie would become tributary to Chanute and therefore was no place in which to make investments. Galena, although an active center, was solidly under the control of business people from Missouri.

The distribution of North-Midland settlers is best understood by a comparison with the pat-

MAP 3.12
*Natives of Northern
states, 1885 (southeast
Kansas). Data from
Kansas state census. For
states included in the
Northern area, see Table
3.1.*

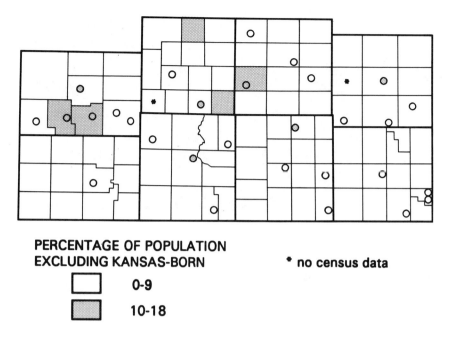

PERCENTAGE OF POPULATION
EXCLUDING KANSAS-BORN   * no census data

☐ 0-9

▨ 10-18

Table 3.3. *Percentage of Settlers from Selected Culture Areas in Cities of Southeastern Kansas, 1885
(excluding Kansas-born)*

Collection Unit/ Culture Area	Region	Parsons (7,245)[a]	Independence (4,115)	Pittsburg (2,605)	Cherryvale (2,601)	Oswego (2,511)	Girard (2,410)	Chanute (1,911)	Coffeyville (1,813)
New England (Northern)	6	10	12	8	9	7	10	7	8
North Midland	60	50	60	46	64	52	65	64	55
Illinois	21	18	15	19	23	18	27	20	19
Indiana	18	13	19	10	19	13	15	17	14
Ohio	12	10	15	9	12	12	12	17	10
Upper South (South Midland)	23	20	19	22	19	26	17	15	24

Source: Manuscript Kansas state census, 1885.

Note: Southeastern Kansas includes Chautauqua, Cherokee, Crawford, Elk, Labette, Montgomery, Neosho, and Wilson
counties.

[a]Parenthetical numbers are total populations.

terns of other peoples. The lowest North-Midland percentages are in the lead district with its Upper South majority, in the coal areas with their mixed populations, and in the colonies and other clusterings of black immigrants (see Map 3.11). The dominance by natives of Illinois, Indiana, and Ohio within the broad North-Midland stream is consistent with the general observation that places settled forty to fifty years previously are usually primary contributors to a frontier.[50] Illinois and Indiana fit this time frame ideally in 1870. Land values in the Military Tract of west-central Illinois, for example, rose from an average of ten dollars per acre in 1850 to forty dollars in 1870.[51] When one couples this inflation with the traditional postwar mobility of veterans and the first-hand views that many of them had had of Kansas, it is no surprise that thousands came to claim this good and inexpensive land.

The distribution of rural settlers from each of the three states is generally similar one to another, and Illinois and Ohio people spread themselves especially evenly across the landscape (see Maps 3.13, 3.14, 3.15). Local historians make no mention of the concentrations of Ohioans in two townships of Neosho County, but the single highest incidence of Illini, in Sheridan Township in south-central Crawford County, is the result of the only Anglo-American colony recorded for the region. This was Beulah, a grouping of "several hundred" Methodist immigrants who had pur-

Table 3.3. *Continued*

Collection Unit/ Culture Area	Chetopa (1,629)	Osage Mission (1,508)	Fredonia (1,427)	Galena (1,378)	Erie (1,337)	Howard (1,302)	Baxter Springs (1,240)	Sedan (1,151)	Neodesha (1,095)	Cherokee (1,003)
New England (Northern)	7	7	7	6	6	10	7	8	11	7
North Midland	45	48	67	34	70	65	42	64	57	52
Illinois	8	17	21	12	27	17	13	19	13	22
Indiana	11	15	21	9	20	20	11	22	18	10
Ohio	16	9	14	7	12	14	9	11	16	11
Upper South (South Midland)	24	30	21	51	21	17	40	23	22	29

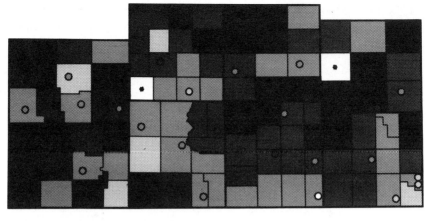

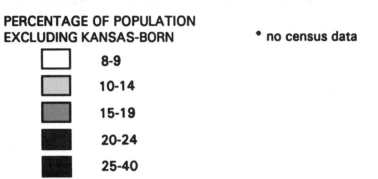

**PERCENTAGE OF POPULATION
EXCLUDING KANSAS-BORN**   * no census data

☐	8-9
◻	10-14
◼	15-19
◼	20-24
◼	25-40

chased land from the Missouri River, Fort Scott and Gulf Railroad.[52] The group boosted the immigrant population of the township to 40 percent Illini.

Immigrants from the three major North-Midland states differentiated themselves somewhat in their orientation to cities. None of these peoples were as urban-minded as were the Yankees, but Ohioans were more so than the Illini, and the Illini, in turn, more than the Hoosiers (see Table 3.3). Ohioans were present in Independence, Chanute, Chetopa, and Neodesha in percentages notably higher than their overall one. Illini occupied a similar position in Girard and Erie, but Indianans did so nowhere. In contrast, Indianans were notably underrepresented in seven cities, Illini in five, and Ohioans in only four.

A full assessment of the rural-urban continuum within the North-Midland contingent is impossible to make from nativity data alone, but it seems reasonable that typical settlers from Ohio would have more money to bring with them for business investments than would those from Illinois, simply as a function of the relative ages of the two states and the time available for capital accumulation. Ohioans, in this light, might be seen as blends between Yankee entrepreneurs and Illinois yeoman. The position of Indianans in this scenario seems incongruous at first, given the physical location of the state between Ohio and Illinois. The rural bias and implied relative capital

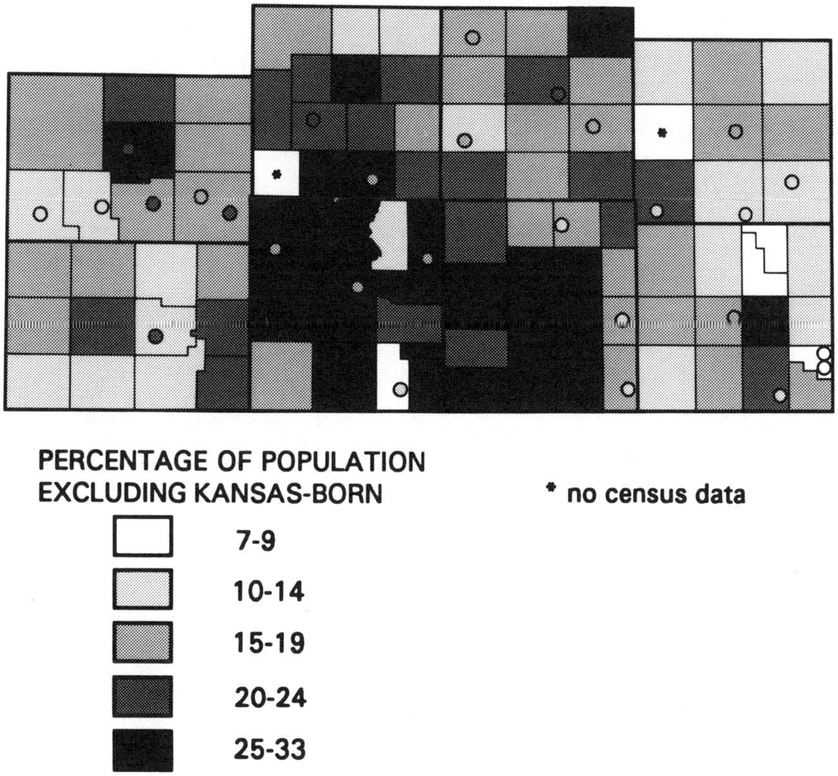

PERCENTAGE OF POPULATION
EXCLUDING KANSAS-BORN
* no census data
7-9
10-14
15-19
20-24
25-33

MAP 3.14
Natives of Indiana, 1885 (southeast Kansas). Data from Kansas state census.

deficiencies, however, are what one would predict given the relatively late development of that state and the strongly rural, self-sufficient character ascribed to its early population.[53]

CULTURE REGIONS

The Union veterans who poured into southeastern Kansas in the late 1860s and early 1870s established a uniform culture over most of the region. By 1885 these people saw themselves as progressive and their society as mature. Their agriculture was well developed; their railroad hub, Parsons, had established linkages not only with Kansas City and Topeka but also with Fort Worth and Chicago; and their coalfields were proving to be much richer than previously thought. In fact, entrepreneurs had just completed construction of a fourth big smelter at Pittsburg and were ready to crown that place as "the premier zinc city of the United States."[54] Republican politics was taken for granted.

Increased development of the coalfields in the 1890s, particularly the large-scale introduction of foreign-born laborers, would soon transform the character of Cherokee and Crawford counties. New foods, new religions, and even new political orientations would emerge.[55] Coincidently, just

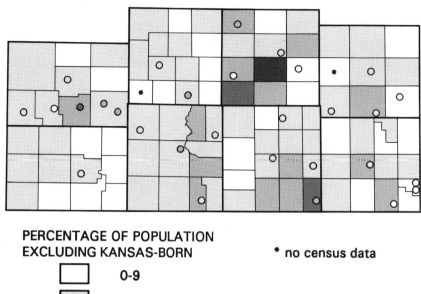

**PERCENTAGE OF POPULATION
EXCLUDING KANSAS-BORN**

* no census data

☐ 0-9

▨ 10-14

▨ 15-19

▨ 20-24

■ 25

to the west, the first big natural gas field to be developed in the United States would transform Chanute, eastern Wilson County, and all of Montgomery County into industrial centers of note.[56] The scene in 1885 was calm and undifferentiated by comparison (see Map 3.16).

Concentrations of black Texans in Oswego, Chetopa, and near Coffeyville formed the most distinctive culture in the region. Although only a few examples of outright racial segregation apparently occurred at the time, and although these black Kansans voted the straight Republican ticket, the differences were clear. The Texans grew cotton, to name only one obvious example, and felt separate enough to start their own newspapers in the Votaw Colony and in Parsons.[57]

The Tennessee blacks at Baxter Springs did not stand so far apart from their immediate surroundings as did the Texans. This corner of Cherokee County was the exception to the rule of overall regional dominance by North-Midland culture. It was solidly Upper Southern in tone, and its populace included many white Tennesseans as well as black immigrants. For all practical purposes, the mining camps there were an extension of Missouri ideas across the border, strong on the concept of individualism and low on enthusiasm for organized religion and formal education.[58]

Little cogent commentary about life and values in the zone of South-Midland culture focused

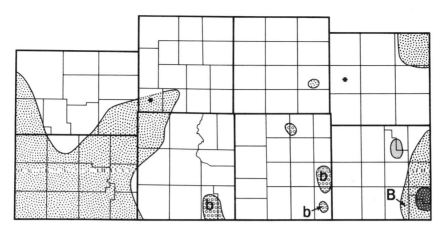

MAP 3.16
*Generalized nativity
regions, 1885 (southeast
Kansas). Data from
Kansas state census. Areas
left blank are generally
those in which people
from North-Midland
states form the dominant
immigrant group.*

PERCENTAGE OF POPULATION
EXCLUDING KANSAS-BORN

- European, 30-49
- South Midland, 30-49
- South Midland, > 50
- South Midland plus
  Lower Southern, 30-49

KEY TO LETTERS

b blacks, 15-21%
   of total population

B blacks, 34%
   of total population

* no census data

on Chautauqua County exists for this time period. Still, the area was distinctive. Upper Southern people constituted 32 percent of Chautauqua's immigrant population and reached a peak of 49 percent in Hendricks Township along the southern border. This general area has long borne the nickname of the Little (or Kansas) Ozarks, but it is unclear whether the reference is to terrain, to culture, or to both. Similarly, it is an open question whether the relative lack of railroads and other economic development there in 1885 should be attributed more to physical isolation or to the traditional predilection of Upper Southerners for dispersed settlement and their distrust of urban entrepreneurs.[59] Since the strong Upper Southern presence in Chautauqua County actually extends westward across the whole of southern Kansas (as the next chapter will document), a more thorough evaluation of this issue is best deferred for the moment.

4

The Central Plains, 1885

Between 1865 and 1880, Kansas attracted immigrants at a pace unmatched anywhere else in the country. Paul W. Gates, the historian who has studied this process most closely, called the movement "astonishing" and saw it as a product of "Kansas fevers" breaking out in settlements as near as Iowa and Illinois, and as far away as Russia.[1] The raw numbers are impressive enough (a growth from 107,206 people in 1860 to 996,096 in 1880), but an image of the farming frontier pushing westward one hundred miles a year during peak periods conveys the excitement of the time even better.[2] Many thousands of people gambled their futures on a place they knew only through advertisements and perhaps through letters from friends who had migrated the year before.

The well-watered lands of southeastern Kansas attracted the bulk of immigrants to the state in the immediate postwar years. Space there was limited, though, and by 1870 most people turned their attention westward to the immense plains area that lay beyond Junction City and Council Grove. From the perspective of physical geography, little differentiated one part of this region from another. Four parallel streams flow across most of the northern half before coming together to form the Kansas River. Two of these, the Solomon and the Republican, offered settlers unusually wide and inviting valleys. Southern Kansas features the Arkansas River, another natural east-west

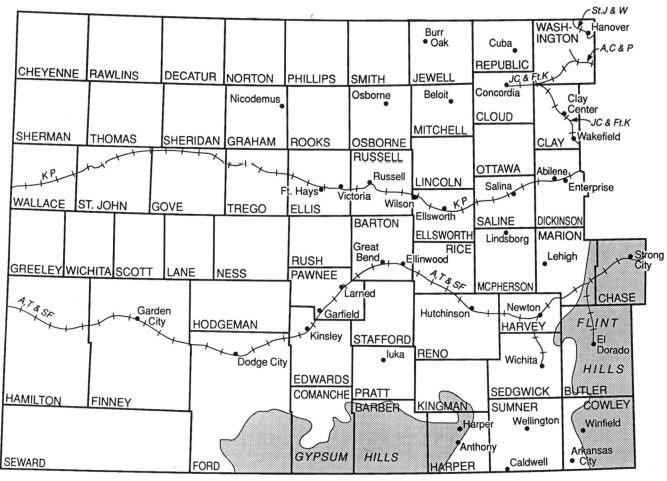

MAP 4.1
Reference map for central and western Kansas, 1885.

routeway that had good possibilities for settlement. Rough land is limited to two major locales: the Flint Hills, an elongated north-south band of limestone escarpments about forty miles wide, and the Gypsum or Red Hills, a region of mesas and canyons that dominates most of present-day Barber, Comanche, and Clark counties (see Map 4.1). In contrast with southeastern Kansas, no mineral resources of consequence were known to exist at the time.

Despite its rather uniform physical environment, potential settlers after 1867 never saw central Kansas as homogeneous. The first of two major railroads, the Union Pacific, Eastern Division, reached Salina in the spring of that year on its way westward from Junction City to Denver. It was completed across the state by the fall of 1868. Four years later, workmen in southern Kansas laid the final rails for the main line of the Atchison, Topeka and Santa Fe, which extended from its namesake Kansas cities through Newton and then along the Arkansas River to the Colorado border and beyond (see Map 4.1). These two railroad companies deliberately built far ahead of the settlement frontier and, as compensation for their financial investment in the future, the federal government awarded them alternate sections of land within an area ten to twenty miles wide on either side of their tracks.

The railroad activity divided central and western Kansas into three distinct bands of land, paralleling one another east and west across the state (see Map 3.7). Of these, observers were confident that the central sector would become the most prosperous. It contained both railroads, and thereby enjoyed a transportation advantage that would speed the commercialization of agriculture and help incipient industry to thrive. Investments in this sector, although probably more expensive than elsewhere, would almost assuredly hold greater potentials for profit. In 1885, twelve years after completion of the Santa Fe across the state, these two railroads remained unchallenged as transportation arteries for the western two-thirds of Kansas.

Costs and availability of land within the railroad belt and its two flanking zones were paramount considerations for potential immigrants to postwar Kansas. Initial discussions around most family hearths probably centered on the Homestead Act, for this law was recent (1862) and promised 160 acres of land for only a small filing fee and residence on that land for five years. Such a "free" offer would have had even greater appeal in the years immediately following the economic panic that gripped the nation in 1873. Unfortunately, acreage open to entry under the full provisions of the new statute was not universally available.[3] In Kansas, such tracts were highly localized in, and therefore characteristic of, only the northernmost of the three major east-west bands of land (see Map 3.7).

Migrants knew that special rules pertained to the railroad belt, but often were shocked to discover that the Homestead Act applied to scarcely any of the big swath of land across south-central Kansas. This southern band largely coincided with the 6,250 square-mile Osage Reserve. Tribal leaders had ceded the tract to the federal government to be sold for the benefit of the tribe. The price, eventually set at $1.25 per acre, had been standard for public land before 1862. It was not unreasonable except when contrasted with the lands available for free across the northern tier of the state.[4] The cost differential between northern and southern locations was made even greater in 1873, when settlers on the public domain in the north learned that they could enter on a second free 160 acres under terms of the newly passed Timber Culture Act. That people recognized the relative costs of land acquisition in the two sections of the state is evident on a map of population density. The frontier line in 1885 was about one hundred miles farther west along the Nebraska border than it was on the old Osage lands (see Map 4.2).

Complexities of land availability and cost were greatest in the central belt. Alternate sections of land within the railroad grants had been retained by the government, and these were available for homesteading. Before 1879, though, most individuals could claim only eighty acres of such land.[5] The alternative was to buy tracts from one of the railroads or from private speculators. No acreage restrictions were involved with such purchases, but the price was steep. The better lands of

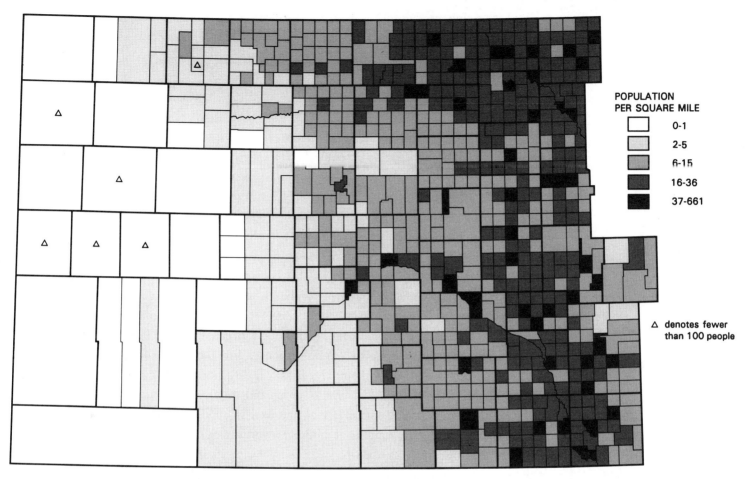

POPULATION
PER SQUARE MILE

0-1
2-5
6-15
16-36
37-661

△ denotes fewer
than 100 people

MAP 4.2
*Population density, 1885
(central and western
Kansas). Data from
Kansas state census.*

the Santa Fe sold for five to six dollars per acre in the early 1870s, and prices averaged about four dollars over the entire two grants (see Map 3.7).[6] Credit availability helped to ease the financial burden to a degree, but a county-by-county mapping of the state for 1875 showed that most settlers avoided the railroad offerings until comparably located government lands had been taken.[7]

Three revisions to the Homestead Act also had important implications for the settlement geography of the three belts of land. Before 1866 and after 1876, veterans of the Confederate armed forces were not allowed to file claims under its provisions.[8] The 1866 date was no factor for Kansas, but over one-third of the state was still unoccupied in 1876. Veterans of the Union forces, in contrast, were given special inducement to come to the public lands. Beginning in 1870, each soldier was allowed to select up to 160 acres within the railroad grants (the zone in which everyone else was still restricted to eighty acres).[9] Two years later these veterans were given the right to count up to four years of their military service toward the five-year residency requirement needed to secure title.[10] This 1872 ruling was significant in that titles were a prerequisite before land could be mortgaged, and mortgages, in turn, were an important way to obtain the capital needed to keep a new farm or business solvent.

SETTLERS AND STRATEGIES

The thrust of settlers into central Kansas before 1885 occurred in two distinct surges. A series of grasshopper invasions and a national financial crisis ended the first wave after 1873. Boom times returned in 1877 and lasted for four more years until an extended drought began to take a toll on settler enthusiasm. Nothing in the contemporary literature indicates that these fits and starts affected the overall pattern of immigration, although people who came from the eastern states after 1876 were possibly poorer than earlier migrants. A study of contemporary newspaper accounts suggests that financial failures in the older Midwest and elsewhere after the panic of 1873 produced much of the surge to Kansas in the late 1870s.[11]

Surviving memoirs and other accounts imply that personal contacts underlay most of the decisions to migrate. This mirrored the experience of a few years earlier in the southeastern part of the state. The central Kansas situation was different, though, because of the railroads. Officials with both the Santa Fe and the Kansas Pacific (as the Union Pacific, Eastern Division, was renamed in 1869) felt compelled to sell many of their grant lands quickly, not only because of a need to raise immediate capital but also to ensure a flow of crops and other products over their lines. They became the major promoters of the state, in fact, and were so effective at it that the Kansas legislature saw no need to appropriate significant monies for this activity until 1875.[12]

Who were the most likely candidates to come to this postwar frontier? The amendments to the Homestead Act discussed above obviously favored Northern and North-Midland peoples, and railroad advertising strategies targeted much the same audience. Kansas Pacific officials began their national sales promotion with the establishment of land offices at St. Louis, Chicago, Buffalo, and New York City (along with Topeka and Denver).[13] More detailed information exists on the strategy of the Santa Fe executives. Their first major effort came in 1875 as an attempt to refute adverse publicity that had accompanied the grasshopper outbreaks of the previous year. Over two hundred editors accepted invitations to tour the state in the company of Gov. Thomas Osborn and U.S. Senator John J. Ingalls. The hometowns of these editors reveal a highly focused marketing plan: primary attention to Illinois, Indiana, Ohio, and eastern Iowa, with secondary emphasis in northern Missouri, Michigan, and Wisconsin (see Map 4.3).[14] This pattern persisted throughout the decade. Railroad officials concentrated their agents in these same seven states, and the composition of a massive, subsidized excursion for prospective buyers in 1878 was reported: Illinois, 172; Iowa, 154; Indiana, 79; Wisconsin, 33; Ohio, 28; Michigan, 26; Pennsylvania, 17; New York, 15; Missouri,

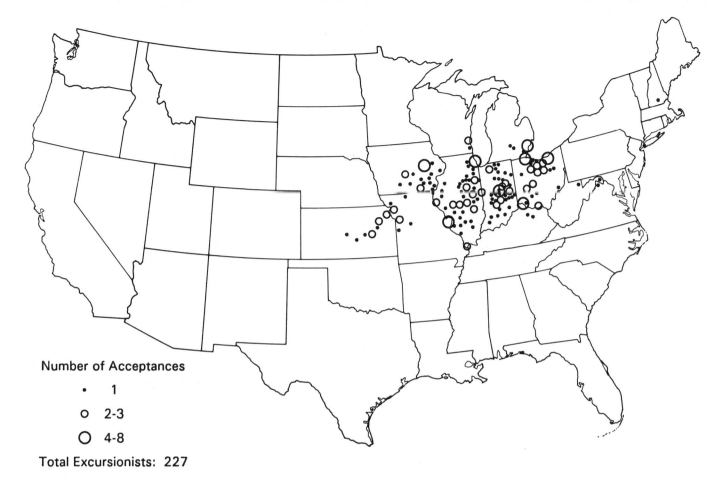

Number of Acceptances

- • 1
- ○ 2-3
- ◯ 4-8

Total Excursionists: 227

14; California, 1; and Virginia, 1.[15] Another tour for editors was arranged in 1877, this time limited to Illini alone.[16]

    Contemporary descriptions of the new frontier population suggest that the promotional targeting by the railroads and the restrictions and incentives written into the homestead laws had their desired effect. One writer who toured the region praised the lace curtains and the shelves of books he saw and concluded that "this very family might be from New England, since New England invented Kansas, and has sent her thousands of citizens; but, more likely they are from some state not farther east than Ohio."[17] Nearly every observer also associated the new Kansas with the Grand Army of the Republic, including one writer who estimated that the state contained "over a hundred thousand soldiers."[18] According to two compilations of the various colonies organized in eastern states for the move to Kansas, twenty-nine of fifty-one major non-European settlements in the region were from North-Midland states (Ohio, 11; Pennsylvania, 8; Illinois, 7; Iowa, 2; Indiana, 1). People in the Northern states generated fifteen parties (New York, 7; Wisconsin, 3; Connecticut,

MAP 4.3
Newspaper editors who participated in an excursion to lands of the Santa Fe Railroad, 1875. Data from Kansas in 1875: Strong and Impartial Testimony to the Wonderful Productiveness of the Cottonwood and Arkansas Valleys *(Topeka: Atchison, Topeka and Santa Fe Railroad Company, 1875), pp. 2–3.*

2; Michigan, 2; Massachusetts, 1), and the remaining seven originated in the Upper South (Kentucky, 5 [including two black groups]; Maryland, 1; Tennessee, 1).[19]

Most press reports identified two exceptions to the hegemony of Union veterans from the Northern and North-Midland states. They noted a small, all-black town in Graham County called Nicodemus but treated it mostly as a curiosity. Several colonies of North-European immigrants elicited sustained and in-depth analysis: Swedes in McPherson County, English in Clay County, Bohemians in Ellsworth County, and Germans in Barton County. Even more ink was devoted to two German-speaking groups who had emigrated from Russia: Catholics in Ellis and Rush counties and Mennonites in Marion, McPherson, and Harvey counties. Altogether, census workers recorded over sixty-four thousand foreign-born settlers in central Kansas for 1885, 15 percent of the non-Kansas-born population (see Table 4.1). These highly clustered and therefore highly visible Europeans were largely another product of the two land-grant railroads. Agents had carefully pursued these peoples (and just as carefully avoided South and East Europeans) and arranged for transportation and escort service to their new homes. In the case of the Mennonites, Santa Fe officials even went so far as to memorialize the Congress to have the group exempted from military service.[20]

A close examination of surviving contemporary reports raises several suspicions that the emergent cultural geography of Kansas in the 1870s was more complex than suggested in typical journalistic accounts. The major differences in land availability and cost among the three east-west belts are reasons enough for doubt. Evidence that the expensive railroad tracts were passed over by early land seekers adds to the possibilities for variation as does the eventual sale of many such acres to several different European groups. Finally, reportage about the frontier in central Kansas suffered from the same geographical bias that was noted for the Southeast. A large majority of writers viewed the landscape only as they saw it from the window of a railroad car; whatever was going on in extreme northern or extreme southern Kansas was nearly invisible to the nation.

Predictions for the settlement geography of the state in 1885 are perhaps best made by considering each of the three east-west belts in turn. The central railroad zone, as the place with the most opportunities for economic growth, could be expected to have the most complex pattern. People with money would want to be there, of course, and this would suggest a relatively high concentration of New Englanders and other people from prosperous sections of the Eastern seaboard. The central belt also would be the most likely spot to find capital investments from the United Kingdom and other European nations. Through these ventures, perhaps, would come some monied settlers from the same places.

North-Midland people also would probably find the railroad belt attractive. Some would have money to invest. Far greater numbers would be drawn by the land benefits accorded Union soldiers, especially a chance to get 160 acres of obviously valuable government land near the Kansas Pacific or Santa Fe tracks for almost no money. Finally, European groups who selected Kansas as a new

Table 4.1. *Place of Birth of Central and Western Kansans, 1885*

Collection Unit/Culture Area	No.	(%)	Excluding (by %) Kans.-born	Excluding (by %) Kans. & Foreign-born
New England (Northern)				
Connecticut	1,162	(0.2)	0.3	0.3
Dakota	200			0.1
Maine	1,523	(0.3)	0.4	0.4
Massachusetts	2,374	(0.4)	0.6	0.7
Michigan	7,798	(1.4)	1.9	2.2
Minnesota	1,863	(0.3)	0.4	0.5
New Hampshire	797	(0.1)	0.2	0.2
New York	20,541	(3.8)	4.9	5.8
Rhode Island	314	(0.1)	0.1	0.1
Vermont	2,386	(0.4)	0.6	0.7
Wisconsin	8,459	(1.6)	2.0	2.4
Subtotal	47,417	(8.8)	11.3	13.4
North Midland				
Delaware	300	(0.1)	0.1	0.1
Illinois	65,391	(12.1)	15.6	18.5
Indiana	44,465	(8.2)	10.6	12.6
Iowa	39,767	(7.3)	9.5	11.2
Nebraska	4,213	(0.8)	1.0	1.2
New Jersey	2,061	(0.4)	0.5	0.6
Ohio	51,957	(9.6)	12.4	14.7
Pennsylvania	30,823	(5.7)	7.4	8.7
Subtotal	238,977	(44.1)	57.1	67.5
Upper South (South Midland)				
Arkansas	912	(0.2)	0.2	0.3
Dist. of Columbia	99			
Indian Territory	144			
Kentucky	14,977	(2.8)	3.6	4.2
Maryland	2,139	(0.4)	0.5	0.6
Missouri	27,677	(5.1)	6.6	7.8
North Carolina	2,272	(0.4)	0.5	0.6
Tennessee	5,758	(1.1)	1.4	1.6

Table 4.1. *Continued*

Collection Unit/Culture Area	No.	(%)	Excluding (by %) Kans.-born	Excluding (by %) Kans. & Foreign-born
Virginia	5,564	(1.0)	1.3	1.6
West Virginia	3,261	(0.6)	0.8	0.9
Subtotal	62,803	(11.6)	15.0	17.7
Lower South				
Alabama	385	(0.1)	0.1	0.1
Florida	40			
Georgia	570	(0.1)	0.1	0.2
Louisiana	283	(0.1)	0.1	0.1
Mississippi	647	(0.1)	0.2	0.2
South Carolina	340	(0.1)	0.1	0.1
Texas	954	(0.2)	0.2	0.3
Subtotal	3,219	(0.6)	0.8	0.9
The West				
Alaska	1			
Arizona	35			
California	309	(0.1)	0.1	0.1
Colorado	610	(0.1)	0.1f	0.2
Idaho	23			
Montana	14			
Nevada	52			
New Mexico	75			
Oregon	190			0.1
Utah	50			
Washington	57			
Wyoming	48			
Subtotal	1,464	(0.3)	0.4	0.4
Kansas	123,187	(22.8)		
Foreign Countries				
Austria	1,118	(0.2)	0.3	
Belgium	241		0.1	
Bohemia	2,334	(0.4)	0.5	

Table 4.1. *Continued*

Collection Unit/Culture Area	No.	(%)	Excluding (by %) Kans.-born	Kans. & Foreign-born
British America	7,367	(1.4)	1.8	
Denmark	1,249	(0.2)	0.3	
England	6,802	(1.3)	1.6	
France	662	(0.1)	0.2	
German States	16,852	(3.1)	4.0	
Hungary	357	(0.1)	0.1	
Ireland	4,718	(0.9)	1.1	
Netherlands	426	(0.1)	0.1	
Norway	888	(0.2)	0.2	
Russia	8,909	(1.6)	2.1	
Scotland	2,143	(0.4)	0.5	
Sweden	8,126	(1.5)	1.9	
Switzerland	1,481	(0.3)	0.4	
Wales	360	(0.1)	0.1	
Other Countries	323	(0.1)	0.1	
Subtotal	64,356	(11.9)	15.4	
Total	541,423[a]	(100.0)	100.0	100.0

Source: Manuscript Kansas state census, 1885.

Note: The region of central and western Kansas includes Chase County, the tier of counties from Washington to Cowley, and the area westward from this tier.

[a]This total does not include 19,342 residents for whom no place of birth was recorded. Among them are all the people in Comanche, Greeley, Hamilton, and Wichita counties. Percentages may not total exactly because of rounding.

home most likely would choose railroad land. Aliens were eligible for farms under the Homestead Act once they had declared their intentions to become citizens, but many of these people were unfamiliar with the nuances of the law. Railroad agents had recruited most of them and could offer the large blocks of land that many sought.[21]

The band of counties two tiers deep across northernmost Kansas was isolated, but nearly all of it was open to homestead entry. It was rich farming country and included the wide valleys of the Republican and Solomon rivers. Probable settlers there would seem to be a mixture of Northern and North-Midland peoples, drawn largely from the western sections of these culture areas where fewer people had the capital reserves necessary to play in the higher stakes games of speculation that characterized the railroad belt. Iowans should be common in north-central Kansas, Upper Southerners and Europeans rare.

If the northern band of land was somewhat isolated, the southern one was even more so. As land entries under the Homestead Act were forbidden under terms of the Osage treaty, so was the gratuitous award of any land to railroads. Potential settlers thus knew that transportation would be slow to develop. Much of the country also was broken terrain: the Flint Hills to the east and the Gypsum Hills to the west (see Map 4.1). Without the lure of free land to attract Union veterans, of railroad towns to entice Northern investors, and of expensive advertising to tantalize European farmers, south-central Kansas was left to people who had limited options and/or those who saw special opportunity in this particular environment. Many North-Midland people would fall into these categories, but Upper Southerners would seem to be an especially good match for the place. The heavy overall Union atmosphere in central and northern Kansas would have repelled those settlers with Confederate backgrounds; so too the biased land laws. In contrast, the southern part of the state already had a strong Upper Southern presence, especially in nearby Chautauqua County. The biggest attraction of these hilly lands, though, was the cattle business. The area was well grassed and lay on the main trails between Texas and the Kansas railroads. Upper Southerners, with cattle trailing deeply ingrained in their regional culture, would be good bets to seize this opportunity.[22]

Census workers in 1885 found that 57 percent of the 418,236 people who had moved to central Kansas had been born in North-Midland states (see Table 4.1), a ratio comparable to that found on the slightly earlier frontier in the southeastern counties. The contributions of other culture groups to this newest borderland were altered somewhat (cf. Table 3.1). The percentage of Yankees had risen from 6 to 11, and that for Europeans from 7 to 15. Southerners were less influential overall but still 16 percent of the total mix. The question remains, though, of the actual cultural geography created by these peoples.

MISSOURIANS AND OTHER UPPER SOUTHERNERS

In a region so pro-Union that a majority of its counties are named after officers and other members of the Grand Army of the Republic, it is not surprising that migrants from the Upper Southern states would cluster together for mutual support.[23] Many of these people came to a group of counties in north-central Kansas focused on Phillips, Rooks, and Graham (see Map 4.4). Much larger numbers selected lands on the old Osage Reserve south of the Santa Fe grant; there Southern-

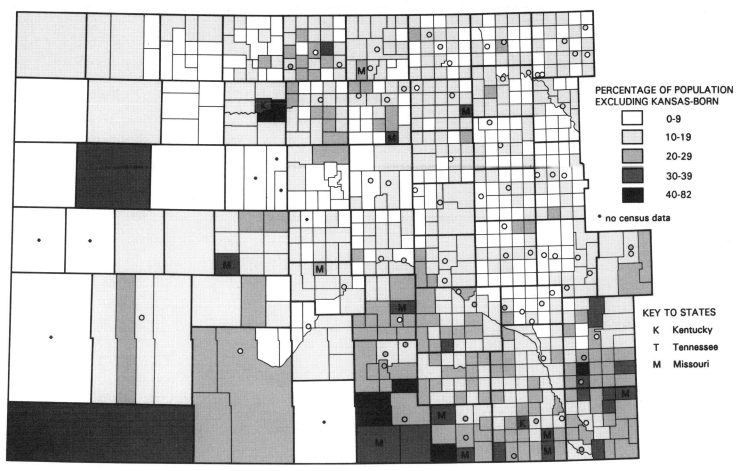

ers routinely made up one-third of the population in most townships. Black as well as white settlers were part of the overall South-Midland mix; blacks outnumbered white Southerners in two of the rural counties (Graham and Hodgeman) and were important contributors in several of the larger cities.

The presence of white Southerners in north-central Kansas runs counter to expectations. What would they be doing in a place where Confederate veterans could not make a homestead entry and where they would be surrounded by people with Northern values? Closer inspection proves the question to be academic. Although these settlers indeed were from South-Midland states, they were not Southern in cultural background. One clue is the mix of states present: these "Southerners" were almost entirely Missourians, not a blend of Missourians with people from Kentucky and Tennessee as was the case in most other areas of South-Midland settlement in Kansas (see Maps 4.5, 4.6, 4.7). This circumstance suggests a source area for these settlers in far northern Missouri, the only part of that state with a North-Midland heritage.[24]

MAP 4.4
Natives of South-Midland states, 1885 (central and western Kansas). Data from Kansas state census. Letter symbols mark townships in which people from a particular South-Midland state constitute 20 percent or more of the immigrant population. For states included in the South-Midland area, see Table 4.1.

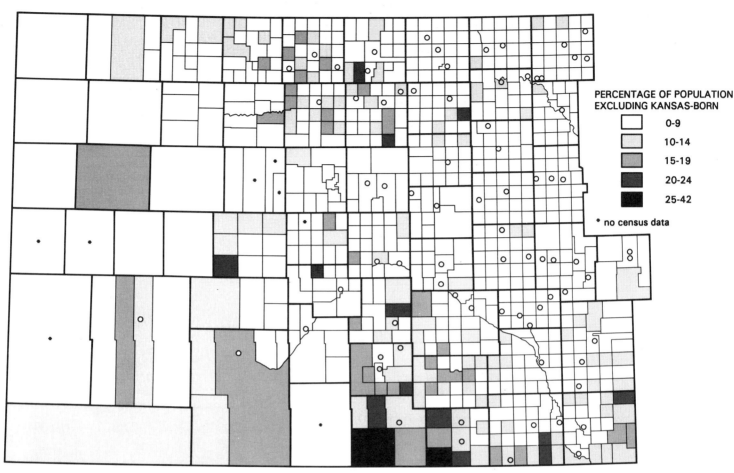

PERCENTAGE OF POPULATION
EXCLUDING KANSAS-BORN

☐ 0-9
▨ 10-14
▤ 15-19
▨ 20-24
■ 25-42

* no census data

MAP 4.5
*Natives of Missouri, 1885
(central and western
Kansas). Data from
Kansas state census.*

Biographical histories compiled for Rooks and Osborne counties provide details of this migration. Of the forty-seven early residents of Rooks County listed as born in Upper South states,
thirty-nine were from Missouri. Veteran status, where noted, was Union. Twenty-five of these
thirty-nine came from the three northernmost tiers of counties in the state and four others from
solidly pro-Union German communities.[25] For Jackson Township in southeastern Osborne
County, eleven of the twenty-two pioneer Missouri families recorded came from these same three
tiers of counties. Eight others were Unionists from Hickory County, on the Ozarks border, who
followed one another west in a classic example of chain migration.[26] The scarcity of northern Missourians in Kansas east of Osborne County is probably a matter of timing. Many of the Missouri
counties near the Iowa border were themselves in the pioneer stage as recently as the 1850s and
would have had few, if any, surplus people to send to the frontier of Washington or Clay County
in the late 1860s.[27]

The congeries of Missourians, Kentuckians, and Tennesseans who came to the lands south of

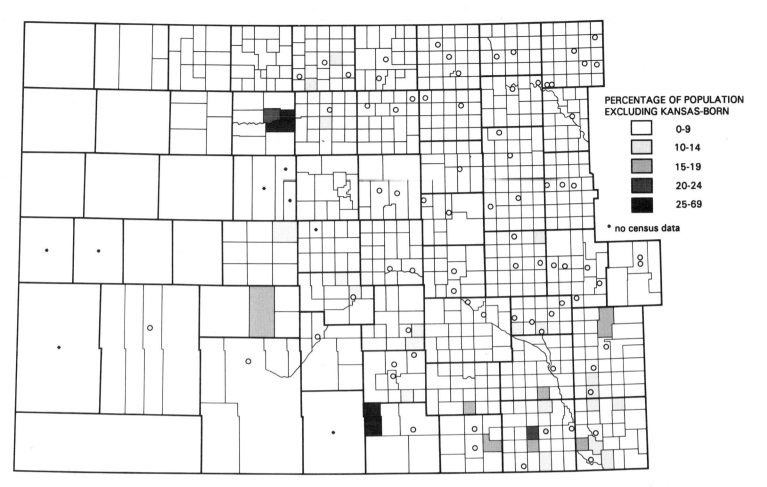

PERCENTAGE OF POPULATION
EXCLUDING KANSAS-BORN

☐	0-9
▨	10-14
▦	15-19
▨	20-24
■	25-69

* no census data

MAP 4.6
*Natives of Kentucky, 1885
(central and western
Kansas). Data from
Kansas state census.*

the Santa Fe grant seems to have been classically South Midland in culture. The nature of the lands selected is one indication of this. Even though tracts in the Osage Reserve sold for $1.25 per acre, regardless of topography, and South-Midland people were among the first Anglo-American settlers to enter this part of Kansas, they concentrated themselves in areas of broken terrain. One can see this pattern in nonrailroad portions of the Flint Hills: in southern Butler County and in the rougher, eastern portion of Cowley County (see Maps 3.7, 4.1). It is even clearer in the Gypsum Hills. Noncensus information for Comanche County implies that the percentage of Southerners there in 1885 was even higher than that recorded for adjacent portions of Barber County.[28] Local history suggests that such hilly acreage was deliberately sought; the reason was cattle.

The idea that the Western cattle industry has Southern roots may still be new to some people, but its truth has been firmly established by revisionist scholars. Upper Southerners were an important part of this heritage. Kentucky was home to the first major trans-Appalachian herding culture, and this tradition was extended to central and to southwestern Missouri in the 1820s and

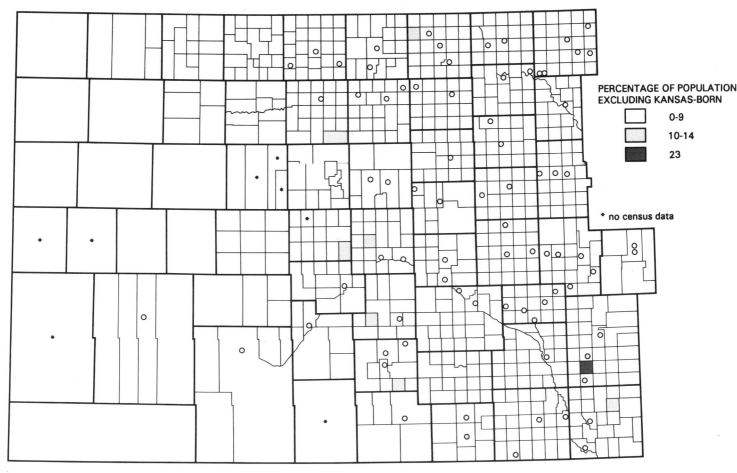

PERCENTAGE OF POPULATION
EXCLUDING KANSAS-BORN

☐ 0–9

▨ 10–14

■ 23

* no census data

MAP 4.7
*Natives of Tennessee, 1885
(central and western
Kansas). Data from
Kansas state census.*

the 1830s. Cherokees brought the industry to what is now northeastern Oklahoma at about this same time, and they had built up a herd estimated at 240,000 head by 1860.[29]

In retrospect it seems almost inevitable that a major cattle industry would develop in south-central Kansas and that people from the Upper South would be major players in its implementation. The quality of pasturage on the big-bluestem prairie in the Flint Hills had been well known since at least 1867 when drovers from Texas exploited it on their way to the railhead of the Kansas Pacific at Abilene. Similar success had been predicted early for the Gypsum Hills range based on its high density of buffalo.[30] To capitalize on this bounty, the Kansas Pacific and (after 1872) the Santa Fe railroads offered shipping facilities no more than a few tens of miles to the north. Cattle, a third component, also were easily available. Four major trails from Texas passed directly through the area, and settlers could assemble herds from stragglers and other animals. Permanent local ranches existed as early as 1867 in Butler County and 1872 in Barber County.[31]

The involvement of Upper Southerners in the history of Kansas ranching deserves extended study, but many facts and stories suggest its importance. War refugees from the traditional cattle center of southwestern Missouri formed one of the major pioneer groups in the eastern portion of the southern Flint Hills (see Map 3.4). South-Midland people also were instrumental in the establishment of the early drives from Texas to the north, including that most famous drover, Tennessean Jesse Chisholm.[32] Drovers, refugees, and other such people not only had the experience to see the potential of the grassy Kansas hillsides but they also faced little competition for them. Most settlers from the northern states had other priorities in mind.[33]

A pattern emerges. John Teter, the first major stockman in Butler County, was a native of West Virginia. Three of the four ranchers featured in the biographical section of an early history of Barber County also were South Midlanders: C. C. Mills from East Tennessee, W. O. Mize from Kentucky, and Wylie Payne from Missouri. These connections probably explain why the first graded cattle in Barber County were driven in from Missouri (1873) and why later improvements there came via bulls imported from Kentucky.[34]

The cattle industry in south-central Kansas actually extended beyond the state's border. Just to the south, the Cherokee Outlet contained six million acres of excellent grass that had never been used by the tribe. Informal leasing arrangements there in the 1870s evolved into two major ranching empires: the Comanche Cattle Pool (cofounded by Barber County's Wylie Payne) and the Cherokee Livestock Association. Both groups marketed through Kansas towns. Anthony and Harper, in Harper County, drew most of the Comanche Pool's business along with other Gypsum Hills trade; Caldwell, in Sumner County, was headquarters of the Cherokee company.[35] The population mixes in these specialty cities bore further witness to the linkage between South-Midland and cattle culture. The percentages of Southerners there not only were substantially larger than the regional average, but they also exceeded those of the surrounding townships (see Table 4.2).

Ranching was unchallenged westward from central Sumner County until about 1878.[36] A new wave of settlers then began to establish farms on the more level tracts. These people were of mixed origins, but the overall effect was to dilute the South-Midland presence. The percentage of Southerners in Barber County, for example, fell from forty-eight in 1875 to thirty-four in 1885. The process was slowest in Comanche County, the heart of the Gypsum Hills, where in 1882 "nearly all" of the population was reportedly still engaged in stock raising.[37]

BLACKS AND OTHER SOUTHERNERS

The lure of free homesteads and other economic opportunities in central Kansas attracted black as well as white settlers. In fact, given the popularity of eastern Kansas as a haven for former slaves, one might have expected a large black presence in the west. Movement was hampered, though, by a lack of money and by intervening opportunities for settlement in Kansas City, Topeka, Parsons, and other cities where an immigrant might find not only a job but also a supportive

Table 4.2. *Percentage of Settlers from Selected Culture Areas in Cities of Central and Western Kansas, 1885 (excluding Kansas-born)*

Collection Unit/ Culture Area	Total for Region	Wichita (16,023)[a]	Wellington (6,346)	Newton (5,128)	El Dorado (4,573)	Hutchinson (4,251)	Winfield (4,183)	Salina (4,009)	Clay Center (3,830)	Abilene (3,516)
New England (Northern)	11	13	10	13	13	12	11	14	17	13
North Midland	57	57	60	52	62	57	64	44	48	62
Illinois	16	18	22	12	20	17	19	12	15	13
Indiana	11	14	13	12	12	13	17	6	8	6
Iowa	10	6	6	4	5	6	6	3	4	5
Ohio	12	12	12	14	18	15	16	12	11	14
Upper South (South Midland)	15	17	24	16	18	20	18	17	12	14

Collection Unit/ Culture Area	Arkansas City (3,328)	Concordia (3,002)	Harper (2,769)	McPherson (2,530)	Dodge City (2,446)	Anthony (2,132)	Beloit (2,003)	Caldwell (1,970)	Washington (1,822)
New England (Northern)	13	18	8	12	12	10	20	11	18
North Midland	60	55	65	59	48	53	54	50	58
Illinois	20	19	21	18	14	18	12	18	11
Indiana	11	8	14	8	10	10	9	9	8
Iowa	8	11	9	9	6	6	16	6	15
Ohio	16	10	15	14	12	10	10	9	12
Upper South (South Midland)	20	11	22	14	18	29	13	28	13

Collection Unit/ Culture Area	Minneapolis (1,779)	Clyde (1,770)	Marion (1,691)	Peabody (1,588)	Ellsworth (1,584)	Larned (1,507)	Nickerson (1,503)	Great Bend (1,499)
New England (Northern)	19	19	15	16	14	14	15	16
North Midland	54	53	56	60	50	60	58	48
Illinois	12	17	19	16	9	19	17	13
Indiana	8	7	9	12	9	8	13	5
Iowa	9	8	6	5	8	5	7	8
Ohio	16	12	14	14	14	16	14	15
Upper South (South Midland)	13	10	16	14	12	15	14	15

Source: Manuscript Kansas state census, 1885.

Note: The region of central and western Kansas includes Chase County, the tier of counties from Washington to Cowley, and the area westward from this tier.

[a]Parenthetical numbers are total populations.

social network. Thus only 4,920 black settlers lived in central and western Kansas in 1885, less than 1 percent of the regional population.

Despite their small numbers, the black settlements in the west were well known. This was primarily because of two frontier colonies: Nicodemus in Graham County and the Hodgeman County settlement, one hundred miles to the south (see Map 4.8). Greater numbers of black immigrants actually lived in the larger cities of the region, especially in Wichita, but contemporary white observers largely ignored these people (see Table 4.3).

The ventures at Nicodemus and in Hodgeman County are related to one another, and both, in turn, are indirect products of the earlier promotional efforts of Benjamin "Pap" Singleton. Singleton, as was discussed in the last chapter, saw Kansas as a source of affordable land for blacks from Tennessee and Kentucky. His activities led not only to colonies in rural eastern Kansas but also to a sizeable congregation of relatively prosperous blacks at his staging center of Topeka. In 1877, two promoters from Graham County, W. R. Hill and W. H. Smith, perceived this pool of Topekans as potential settlers for a speculative townsite called Nicodemus that they had just platted on the South Fork of the Solomon River. Hill (a white man) and Smith (a black man) planned to make this town an all-black venture and to pair it with an all-white one (Hill City) twelve miles farther upstream.[38]

The idea of Nicodemus had appeal. Like the town's probable eponym, the first African slave to buy his freedom in America, Nicodemus offered a chance for blacks to take charge of their own destiny. Smith and Hill marketed their venture with circulars and public talks. After recruiting 30 colonists from Topeka, they went to Lexington and Georgetown, in Kentucky, where they convinced another five hundred people to migrate in late 1877 and early 1878. A smaller group came from Missouri along with scattered individuals from Mississippi and elsewhere. Nicodemus was reported to have between six hundred and seven hundred people by late in 1878, making it the largest settlement in the state north of the Kansas Pacific tracks and west of Beloit.[39]

The recruitment activity for Nicodemus inspired another group of Kentuckians to form their own mutual-aid colony in Kansas. These people sent John Thomas, a Baptist minister, to select a site, and then in the spring of 1878, 107 of them immigrated to the middle of the newly organized Hodgeman County. Fifty more settlers joined them in 1879, about the time that the first arrivals had decided to concentrate on farming instead of building a town.[40]

The sites of Nicodemus and the Hodgeman colony were similar in that both were on public land open to homestead entry yet reasonably close to railroad stations. They were decent locations, but both settlements had the misfortune to be implanted just as a series of droughty years hit the region. Optimism was not entirely exhausted by 1885, but the populations had shrunk from the peaks of six years earlier. Census workers recorded 465 black residents in Graham County (16 percent of its population), and Hodgeman County had 137 for 8 percent. Nicodemus Township was 91 percent black, however, and adjacent Wild Horse Township 32 percent black, making a notable

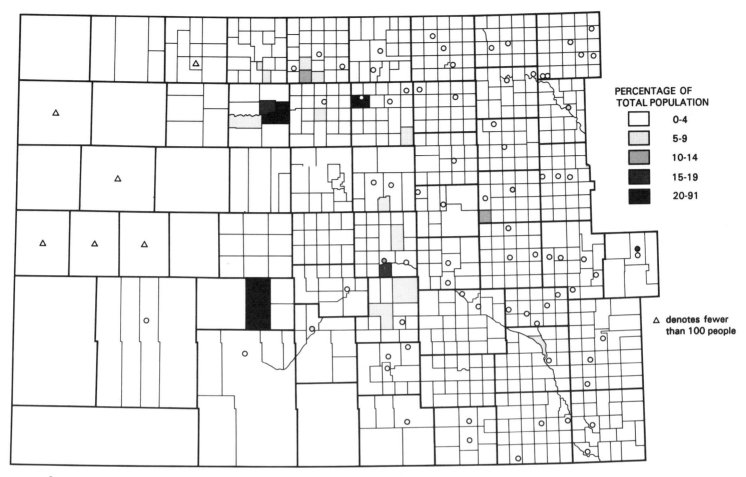

PERCENTAGE OF
TOTAL POPULATION

☐	0-4
▨	5-9
▦	10-14
■	15-19
■	20-91

△ denotes fewer
than 100 people

MAP 4.8
*Black population, 1885
(central and western
Kansas). Data from
Kansas state census.*

cultural island on the Kansas scene. Center Township in Hodgeman was 21 percent black (see Map 4.8).

Historians of Nicodemus blame its stagnation not only on drought, but also on a scarcity of potential settlers moneyed enough to invest in the townsite. Promotion of Hill City to a white clientele became a more lucrative venture for Hill and Smith. Nicodemus residents themselves also turned down at least one chance for growth. They officially dissolved their town company in 1879 rather than face pressure to absorb large numbers of the destitute exodusters who were pouring into eastern Kansas from the Lower South at that time. The Nicodemus colonists argued that they were barely able to keep themselves alive. They also reasoned that the presence of the extremely poor and uneducated Mississippi blacks would harm the greater cause of black colonization in the state.[41]

The same kind of gradual, planned migration from the Upper South that produced Nicodemus brought at least a few black settlers to every county in central Kansas. Those with money

Table 4.3. *Place of Birth of Blacks in Selected Cities and Townships of Central and Western Kansas, 1885 (by %)*

Collection Unit	No. Excluding Kans. and Unknown Nativities	Kentucky	Mississippi	Missouri	South Carolina	Tennessee	Texas	All Other Places
Barton County								
City of Great Bend	148	1	3	4	50	29		13
South Bend Twp.	30	13		13		30		44
Chase County								
City of Strong City	113	29	1	12	1	34	6	17
Graham County								
Hill City Twp.	45	69				22		9
Nicodemus Twp.	209	77	4	5		7		7
Wild Horse Twp.	71	70	1	17		3		9
Harvey County								
City of Newton	201	74	1	4	1	7		13
Hodgeman County								
Center Twp.	98	70		3	1	6		20
Saline County								
City of Salina	176	6	46	36		3		9
Sedgwick County								
City of Wichita	434	18	7	23	1	11	4	36

Source: Manuscript Kansas state census, 1885.

usually bought or rented farms.[42] The others, a majority, concentrated in the larger cities along the Kansas Pacific and the Santa Fe rail lines, where they held a variety of jobs, including working as porters and brakemen on the trains (see Map 4.8).[43] Topeka, at the junction of the two railroads, served as a point of dispersal. Along the Kansas Pacific, Salina had 279 black residents (7 percent of the total population), Abilene 161 (4 percent), and Ellsworth 78 (4 percent). Santa Fe towns attracted slightly greater numbers, led by Wichita with 554 (3 percent of the total population). Newton had 228 black residents (4 percent), Great Bend 180 (12 percent plus another 46 people in adjacent South Bend Township), and Strong City 143 (15 percent).

Nativity data show only one instance of a major exoduster settlement in the region: at Salina (see Table 4.3). The white citizens of both Wichita and Hays are known to have denied residence to groups of these refugees sent from Topeka by the Kansas Freedmen's Relief Association.[44] Other cities may have done likewise. The Salina community reluctantly accepted the group intended for Hays even though they had to raise money to release the immigrants' baggage from impoundment by the Kansas Pacific.[45] The presence of seventy-four people from South Carolina makes the black contingent in Great Bend unique, but I have found no information on whether this migration was part of the exoduster experience.

Racial tolerance was apparently more common than not in central Kansas, especially once fear of a continued invasion from the Lower South had passed. Blacks were few enough so as not to be perceived as a threat to the white majority, and problems of the frontier were usually more pressing than issues of prejudice. The newspapers in Kinsley and Larned covered local affairs in Hodgeman County without mention of racial labels, and black men were elected to countywide office in both Graham and Hodgeman counties.[46]

Besides the South Carolinians in Great Bend and the Mississippians in Salina, the only other concentration of Lower Southerners in the region was ninety-three white Georgians who settled in two adjoining townships (both named Salt Creek) along the border between Lincoln and Mitchell counties. Local histories shed no light on this group, but they made up 22 percent of the population in the Mitchell County township, and their identity there was strong enough that a rural school was named Georgia.[47]

THE EUROPEANS

A strong European presence was one of the most widely reported characteristics of the central Kansas frontier. Contemporary observers were naturally attracted by interesting distinctions of language and behavior, but the amount of coverage was much greater than that generated by a fairly similar percentage of Europeans (15 versus 13) on the 1865 frontier of the state. The absence of the Civil War as competition for newspaper space was one reason for the discrepancy, of course. Another was a much larger total number of European immigrants in 1885. The official count for the region was 64,356, and even this impressive number understated the true situation considerably (see Table 4.1). Many, perhaps one-third, of the people who were perceived as foreign actually were second-generation immigrants. If their numbers are added to those for the native Europeans, the ethnic component in the region comes to about 20 percent of the total. The most important factor in the Europeans' visibility, though, was geographic; their major settlements were tightly clustered and located along the well-traveled main lines of the region's two major railroads (see Map 4.9).

The degree of correspondence between European communities and the grant lands of the Kansas Pacific and the Santa Fe is remarkable. A count of townships and cities with 40 percent or more of their populations foreign-born shows that fifty-one of the sixty-one occurrences, or 84 percent, are in the railroad belt (compare Maps 3.7 and 4.9). This figure rises even higher as the focus is

PERCENTAGE OF POPULATION
EXCLUDING KANSAS-BORN

- [ ] 0-9
- [ ] 10-19
- [ ] 20 20
- [ ] 30-39
- [ ] 40-99

* no census data

KEY TO COUNTRIES

A Austria
B Bohemia
C Canada
E England
G German States
H Hungary
R Russia
S Sweden
Z Switzerland

sharpened. Forty of the forty-five places with more than half of their populations foreign-born are in this zone (89 percent) as are fifteen of the sixteen where the percentage exceeds 75 and all six of those with 90 percent or more born abroad.

Such correspondence is not coincidence; railroad officials worked hard to attract these people. Their efforts, though, are only partial explanations for why so many Europeans chose to undertake the long trans-Atlantic migration to the Kansas prairies in the 1870s and 1880s. Steamship companies joined the railroads in the recruiting process. Both modes of transportation had begun to come into their own in the 1860s, and officials realized that revenues could be increased by making the immigration experience as painless as possible. The process was well tuned by the end of the German wars for unification in 1870, complete with reliable emigration commissions and information bureaus.[48]

The means of the mass movement are easier to document than the reasons for it. Certainly the democratic institutions and abundant public lands in America acted as bright lures, especially as

MAP 4.9
Natives of European and other foreign countries, 1885 (central and western Kansas). Data from Kansas state census. Letter symbols mark cities and townships in which people from a particular foreign country constitute 20 percent or more of the immigrant population.

they were touted to exist in Kansas and the other frontier states of the time. The other issue concerned conditions at home: Europe in the 1870s was in the midst of a major demographic, social, and economic upheaval. Though conditions varied from place to place, health improvements, rapid industrialization, and an end to feudalism had proved to be mixed blessings. With their benefits came rapid population growth, a growing realization of social inequalities, failing local economies, and political tension.[49]

Many people moved from farms to cities as a means of coping with changing conditions, but no one was sure if the new industrial centers could absorb the influx. Emigration was another alternative and an especially attractive one for those people who wanted to remain as farmers and for those who faced political or religious prejudice. This choice, of course, was emphasized by the railroad and steamship agents. Trips to Australia, Brazil, or Canada would be easy, but the United States garnered the lion's share of the emigrants, partly because their agents offered the most persistent sales pitch. One Kansan, Carl B. Schmidt of the Santa Fe Railroad, was acknowledged to be among the best at this trade.[50]

Since conditions over most of Europe favored emigration in the 1870s, it is initially surprising to find that the mix of people who actually came to Kansas was heavily skewed toward a few nationalities and toward even fewer ethnic groups. This circumstance was largely the product of selective recruiting. According to historian David Emmons, conventional American wisdom held that certain nationalities made better farmers than did others. The English, Scots, and Welsh were included in the favored group; the Irish were not. On the continent, Scandinavians were judged to be good potential colonists and the Germans even better ones. Opinion was mixed on the French (whether from Europe or from Canada) but was generally negative on Italians and other South Europeans.[51]

Kansas Pacific officials, through their National Land Company, could afford to be selective in their European recruitments because their main line was completed relatively early (1868), in the midst of the general postwar boom. They sent land commissioners only to England, Scotland, Wales, Sweden, Norway, Denmark, and Canada.[52] Santa Fe officials, four years later, targeted these same places and also Belgium, France, Bohemia, and especially Germany. German settlers, in fact, were sought not only in Germany but also in the eastern United States, Switzerland, Austria, Moravia, Russia, and elsewhere. Russia proved to be an extremely lucrative source.[53]

THE GERMANS

Germans ultimately became by far the largest European contingent on the central Kansas frontier. Even without direct recruitment from Kansas Pacific agents, their numbers reached nearly seventeen thousand in the 1885 census, 26 percent of the total from overseas (see Table 4.1). To this figure, one realistically should add the immigrants from Austria, Hungary, Switzerland, and Russia, for nearly all of these peoples were either ethnic Germans or at least German speakers. With these countries included, the German contribution rises to 45 percent of the European total, but even this figure is incomplete. It still does not include literally thousands of second- and third-generation Germans from Pennsylvania, Ohio, and other states who also came to Kansas at this time.[54]

Germans in Kansas were distinguished not only by their numbers but also by their extremely dispersed pattern of settlement (see Map 4.10). Barton County forms a visible core, but significant concentrations exist far to the east and the west, and both inside and outside the railroad grant lands. The pattern suggests that Germans came to Kansas over a fairly long period of time and that they had more varied backgrounds and motivations than most other European immigrants to the state. Both observations are true. They came from Prussia and Wurttemberg, Hanover and Bavaria—all sections of the realm—and they tended to emigrate as individuals or in small family groups rather than as large colonies.[55] Some were ardent Lutherans, others Catholics, and still others freethinkers and Pietists. Their dispersion throughout Kansas was also a function of their tendency to use older German settlements in the eastern states as way stations for several weeks to several years on their way to the frontier. German communities in Kansas thus rarely were pure in terms of place of origin within Germany; religion and/or economic status were more important predictors of their new spatial affiliations.[56]

Germans were always the largest European group in nineteenth-century Kansas. In the early days, most of them had been fervid free-staters, and many had located on the western fringes of settlement, away from border raids and Missouri immigrants. Extensions from two of these communities appear prominently on Map 4.10. Southeastern Dickinson County, in the upper valley of Lyon Creek, was pioneered by a loose-knit but large group of Germans from Watertown, Wisconsin. They came over a fifteen-year period beginning in 1857, seeking not only cheap land but also an escape from winters they judged to be too long and snowy. Methodists concentrated in the lower valley, Lutherans upstream.[57] The Lyon Creek people developed close connections to New Basel, a nearby and contemporary German-Swiss community (see Map 4.11). New Basel was isolated and never grew, but one of its pioneers, Christian Hoffman, founded the industrial city of Enterprise in 1868. His mill at Louden's Falls, on the Smoky Hill River, attracted the bulk of its workers from the Lyon Creek and the Swiss settlements. The townspeople, excluding native Kansans, were 24 percent German- or Swiss-born in 1885. Herington, an important railroad town founded in extreme southeastern Dickinson County in 1884, attracted other people from these same rural areas.[58]

The second German community that dates from the territorial period centers on the city of Hanover, in northeastern Washington County. Settlement in that county began in 1857 when Gart H. Hollenberg, a German-born entrepreneur, built a supply station for travelers on the Oregon Trail. As his store and ranch prospered, Hollenberg gradually transformed himself into "a sort of local squire": a member of the state legislature and an active promoter of regional business. He saw

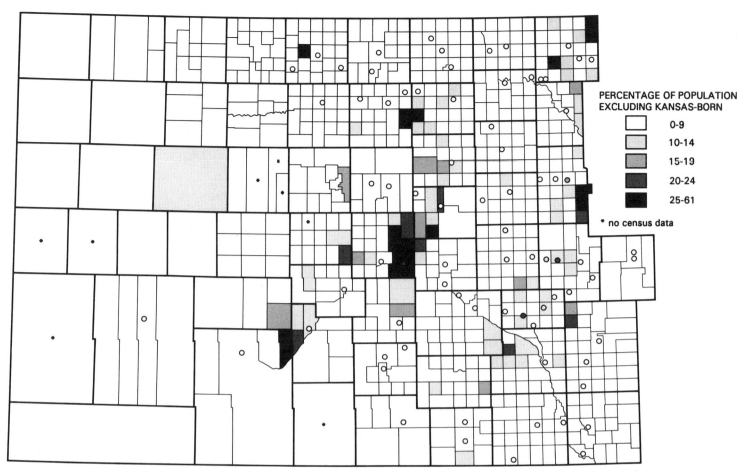

PERCENTAGE OF POPULATION
EXCLUDING KANSAS-BORN

0-9
10-14
15-19
20-24
25-61

* no census data

MAP 4.10
Natives of German states, 1885 (central and western Kansas). Data from Kansas state census.

a chance to develop an urban center in 1869 in anticipation of the region's first railroad, the St. Joseph and Western (see Map 4.1), and Hanover was the result. He platted it where the tracks would descend into the valley of the Little Blue River and named it after his birthplace. When he was also successful in making the town a division point on the new railroad, rapid growth was ensured. German settlers came from Leavenworth and elsewhere, and, by 1872, they were solidly in control of the community.[59]

Hanover was unique in 1885 Kansas, "a real German city" with aspirations for industrial stature. It had a public square, a brewery, a brickyard, and two rail lines. Despite these achievements, though, the population was only 979 (30 percent German-born, excluding native Kansans). Economic stagnation had set in shortly after the death of the town patron in 1874, while he was on a trip to Germany in search of new immigrants. With Hollenberg's death, the religious character of the area changed as well; new immigrants tended to be Catholic rather than Lutheran, a change

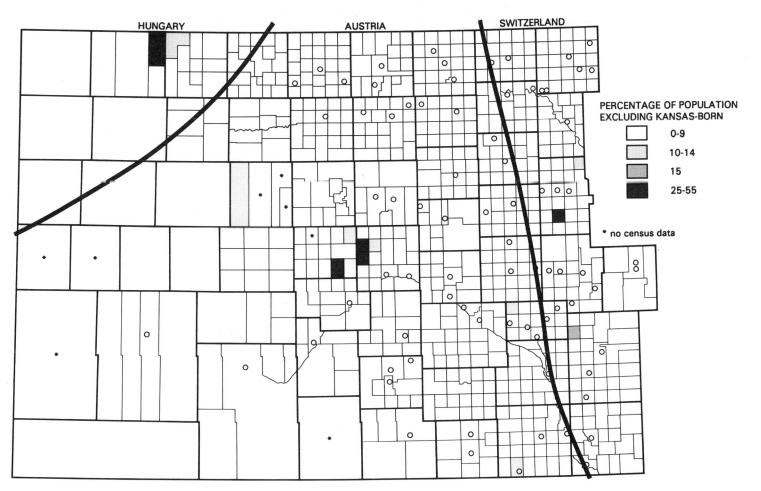

PERCENTAGE OF POPULATION
EXCLUDING KANSAS-BORN

☐	0-9
▨	10-14
▩	15
■	25-55

* no census data

MAP 4.11
*Natives of Austria,
Hungary, and
Switzerland, 1885
(central and western
Kansas). Data from
Kansas state census.*

that began through the successful recruiting of a local priest. It was augmented by a policy of Louis Fink, Bishop of Kansas, who encouraged Catholic immigrants to cluster so as to gain cohesion and to ease pressure on overworked missionaries. The Hanover area grew as a result of this policy, but the presence of new Irish and Czech Catholics (along with German ones) gradually eroded the ethnic purity of the town.[60]

Four German settlements of note were founded during the speculative heyday of railroad grant lands, but away from these heavily promoted sections of central Kansas. All are near the state's northern border, where they appear as rather isolated ethnic islands in a sea of North-Midland and Northern settlement. From east to west, they are the Linn-Palmer community in southwestern Washington County, the Tipton group astride the line between Mitchell and Osborne counties, the Stuttgart colony in Phillips County, and the Hungarian-Germans in Rawlins and Decatur counties (see Maps 4.10, 4.11). A common factor in these four clusterings was a pioneer group who came from an older German community in the United States. This familiarity with American ways, including the homestead laws, probably explains the willingness and ability of these peoples to pioneer in the relatively unknown and unadvertised northern counties.

The cluster in Washington County began in 1871 when two brothers, William and Christian Hornbostel, moved overland from the large German colony in Concordia, Missouri. They scouted true frontier sites in Sedgwick County and elsewhere but decided to buy previously owned land in Washington County because of its high-quality grass. The brothers then served as a magnet for other Germans, first from their old home area of Concordia and Cole Camp, Missouri, then from Illinois, and then directly from overseas. Almost all these people were Lutherans. The group gradually bought out older settlers, including some French Canadians, and grew in size to about eight hundred people. Because so many came from Missouri, the shadings on Map 4.10 understate their presence considerably.[61]

Tipton can be viewed as a smaller-scale version of Hanover. A charismatic Prussian, Frederick Sackoff, was president of the town company. He came to Kansas from northeastern Iowa in 1872 and brought several families with him. Their initial success soon attracted several hundred additional farmers and business people, many of them from the Rhineland.[62] The area was termed "wealthy" by one observer in 1883 and was said to have a "widespread" reputation as a German center.[63]

Stuttgart, in Phillips County, was the smallest of the four northern settlements. Many of its founders were from Wurttemberg, site of the original Stuttgart, but knowledge of Phillips County came from the older Kansas German community in Marshall County, which the pioneers used as a way station. Four families moved to Phillips County in 1872, but numbers stayed small until the Rock Island Railroad came in 1887. Soon thereafter, entrepreneurs founded the village of Stuttgart, and the local German population reached its maximum of about four hundred.[64]

The settlers in the isolated Beaver Creek valley of Decatur and Rawlins counties had no connections with the other three German clusters in northern Kansas. They were from Sopron, a colony of ethnic Germans in extreme northwestern Hungary, and had come on the Burlington and Missouri River Railroad to Crete, Nebraska, in the mid–1870s. They found prices for farmland in southeastern Nebraska more expensive than they could afford, but heard that good homesteading land was still available some two hundred miles to the west. The first families, including Mathias and Tekla Hafner, made the overland trek by wagon in 1876 and 1877. They were pleased with the site, wrote to their friends and former neighbors, and by 1885 the ethnic community numbered 336. The trip westward became easier in 1880 when the Burlington extended its rails to McCook, twenty miles north of the settlement, but the route remained a Nebraska rather than a Kansas one. This orientation continued when a Burlington feeder line was extended up the Beaver valley, and it is still so today.[65]

The corridor of the Kansas Pacific Railroad is not readily visible on Maps 4.10 or 4.11. This is not because German peoples were hesitant to locate in what clearly was going to be a prosperous section of the state but because railroad officials in 1868 and the years immediately following were so confident of this prosperity that they did little to recruit German colonists from overseas or elsewhere. Laissez faire was the general policy on the Kansas Pacific lands.[66] Many ethnic Germans from Pennsylvania and Ohio joined their North-Midland brethren in Dickinson, Saline, Ellsworth, Russell, and Ellis counties, but clusters of native Germans evolved in only three locations. Two of the three were composed largely of Hanoverians, a people who tended toward compact settlements more than other Germans: Lutherans in the Saline River valley at Sylvan Grove (Lincoln County) and Catholics at Walker (Ellis County). Each community numbered about two hundred.[67]

The largest German group in the Kansas Pacific corridor, and the only one to obtain direct assistance from the railroad, was a Baptist community in southwestern Ellsworth County. In exchange for eighty acres of land, church leaders agreed to publicize in their national journal that a colony was forming here, and settlement began in 1878. People came initially from Green Garden, Illinois (hence a local township name), and then from abroad, for a total of about five hundred. Lorraine, the main town, was somewhat isolated and developed a reputation for social and economic self-sufficiency; this cohesion was needed in 1957 when residents had to rebuild after a major fire.[68]

Officials with the Santa Fe Railroad took a decidedly more aggressive approach to the promotion of grant lands than did their counterparts with the Kansas Pacific. They had little choice. The Santa Fe lagged four years behind its rival in laying track. More significantly, the completion of its main line in 1872 was followed almost immediately by national financial panic in 1873 and, in Kansas, by the infamous grasshopper year of 1874. Massive advertising began immediately after these catastrophes, and officials decided to target Germans for special recruitment. This decision probably was an easy one, based not only on the reputation of Germanic peoples as good farmers but also on their avoidance by promoters of the Kansas Pacific lands.

Santa Fe officials chose Carl B. Schmidt, a Saxon who had come to Kansas in 1868, to be their general agent in charge of European immigration. He seemed born for the job. Schmidt crossed the Atlantic an amazing thirty-seven times in the course of his work, and through his efforts Kansas "soon became as familiar to the households of the German peasant as that of Canaan was to the Israelites in bondage." Schmidt brought some sixty thousand German-speaking people to the state and settled most of them within the boundaries of the Santa Fe grant. In this effort, he probably did more than any other individual to influence the emerging cultural geography of the state.[69]

One of the Santa Fe's early endeavors was the promotion of lands in Marion, McPherson, and Harvey counties among German peoples in Pennsylvania and other eastern states. The idea was to establish initial clusters of acculturated Germans who, in turn, might help the direct immigrants from Europe to cope with economic and social realities in America. Mennonites became a special target, beginning with a sale of 5,000 acres in Marion County to M. W. Keim and his brethren of Johnstown, Pennsylvania.[70] Another large block went to Christian Krehbiel and others from Sommerfield, Illinois: 18,000 acres near Halstead, in Harvey County.[71] These nuclei worked as planned. They were important not only in the decisions of large Mennonite congregations from Russia to immigrate here but also for an assortment of others from Germany proper.[72]

By 1885 the railroad towns of Halstead, Newton, and Hillsboro had emerged as significant German centers in the Mennonite district. Halstead was especially important in the early years, home to Bernhard Warkentin's mill on the Little Arkansas River and to a major Mennonite newspaper. Two of Schmidt's recruiting successes also loomed prominently in the general area. A prosperous group of West Prussian Mennonites from the Vistula delta had come to northwestern Butler County in 1876. Just south of them, but maintaining a social distance, was a Swiss Mennonite congregation from Canton Bern.[73]

Schmidt was sensitive to religious differences among his recruits. To parallel the Mennonite concentration in Marion and Harvey counties, he encouraged German Catholics toward an area just northwest of Wichita. German Americans again served as the pioneers, this time a hundred families originally from Trier who had tired of winters in Minnesota. They established their church at St. Mark, which eventually became the spiritual focus for some thirteen hundred immigrants spread over two counties (see Map 4.10); Rhinelanders, Alsatians, and Westphalians were common. The large size of this colony was a product of the joint efforts of Schmidt, who recruited, and of Bishop Louis Fink, who encouraged compact settlement.[74] Visitors judged the community to be "very prosperous" by 1885, and its people "fervent" about their ethnicity and their religion.[75]

Barton County was Schmidt's third major focus for German settlement. This was to be a mixed colony, a place he called Germania. He initiated colonization in 1873, making Ellinwood the principal town. Soon there were "500 families of every religious denomination from all parts of Germany, Austria, and Switzerland."[76] Later-arriving individuals and small groups arranged themselves nearby, wherever good land could be found. The pattern gradually assumed a circular shape, with a large marshland known as Cheyenne Bottoms forming an open center in the middle of the county (see Maps 4.2, 4.10, 4.11). Northeastern Barton County, near Odin, became home to about six hundred Moravian Catholic Germans from near Brno. Another Moravian Catholic group dominated in the northwest, around Olmitz (their old village name). They were of mixed ancestry, with some names German and some Czech, but the census taker in 1885 chose to call most of them Austrian. South of Olmitz, Albert became the focus for three hundred East Frisian and Hanover settlers, mostly Lutheran. To complete the circle, in 1880 Schmidt placed four hundred Baptists from Hanover and Prussia just across the Arkansas River from Ellinwood, in northern Stafford County.[77]

West of Germania the population density in 1885 fell off rapidly, but several colonies of German recruits chose to locate there, presumably valuing cultural isolation over other factors. A small group of Congregationalists came to northern Pawnee County, some Catholic Alsatians to south-eastern Hodgeman County, and some Lutheran Saxons to northeastern Ford County.[78] Two more substantial colonies also chose this tri-county area. The largest, at Windhorst in Ford County, was a collaborative effort between Schmidt and the Aurora Colonization Society of Cincinnati. About four hundred people came from all over Germany, beginning in 1878. They were mostly nonfarmers, but devout Catholics, and managed to persist despite experiencing a total crop failure in their first season. The final group, in extreme western Edwards County, is notable as the only German colony on Santa Fe land recruited by an agent other than Schmidt. Lawrence Offerle brought some one hundred people there from Geneseo, Illinois, and named the post office after himself.[79]

THE RUSSIAN-GERMANS

Important as Germania and St. Mark were to Schmidt and to Kansas as a whole, they generated nothing close to the plaudits accorded two other German-speaking groups: the so-called Russian-Germans. Ultimately thirty-three thousand strong, their numbers obviously were a factor in the acclaim.[80] Another was the high visibility of their settlements: compact units along the main lines of the region's two principal railroads (see Map 4.12). Propaganda also played a role. The first of the Russian groups to migrate, Mennonites from near the Black Sea, came in the summer and fall of 1874. This event directly followed two disasters in public relations for the state: grasshoppers and economic depression. Even though outsiders sometimes described the new arrivals as "quaint and unimaginative," Kansas publicists touted their coming as auspicious. The finest farmers in all of Europe have chosen Kansas, went their litany; you should, too. Historians say that the strategy worked.[81]

The Russian-born people who came to Kansas were ethnic Germans whose ancestors originally had moved to Russia during the reign of Catherine the Great (1762–1796). Catherine had needed reliable settlers for two annexations to her realm: the middle Volga region during the 1760s and the Crimea during the 1780s. For the first, she recruited a mix of Catholic and Lutheran peoples from the poorer states in southern Germany, which had been devastated by the Seven Years' War; for the second, she enlisted Mennonites from the Vistula delta, who were unhappy with their new Prussian ruler. Both groups enjoyed prosperity for a century, and by 1870 they numbered about 300,000.[82]

The stimulus for the mass immigration of the Russian-German groups to North America usually is said to be the withdrawal of a long-standing exemption from Russian military service. Suspicions of an imminent, more general erosion of their ethnic autonomy, a need for more land, and internal religious controversy were perhaps equally important reasons. At any rate, in 1873 Carl Schmidt learned about a reconnaissance delegation that the Mennonites had sent to the United States and made arrangements to take them on a week's tour of Santa Fe properties; soon afterward

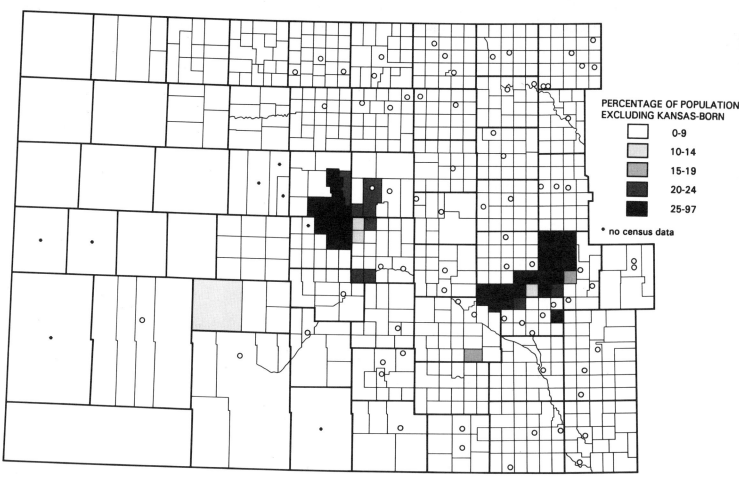

PERCENTAGE OF POPULATION
EXCLUDING KANSAS-BORN

0-9
10-14
15-19
20-24
25-97

* no census data

MAP 4.12

Natives of Russia, 1885 (central and western Kansas). Data from Kansas state census.

he sold them land in Marion County on favorable terms. Some four thousand new immigrants were in the state by the end of 1874. Three years later, following a lengthy personal recruiting trip to Russia, Schmidt reported the total to be eight thousand. Eventually, about fifteen thousand Mennonites came to Kansas, almost all within the bounds of the Santa Fe grant, and Schmidt was hailed as their Moses. This number, impressive as it is, could well have been higher had not fears of another grasshopper outbreak induced some of the congregations to opt instead for Nebraska, the Dakotas, and Manitoba.[83]

Carl Schmidt also deserves credit for bringing the Volga Germans to Kansas. He showed their delegation acreage near Larned, just beyond his Germania colony, but leaders decided that this tract was both too sandy and too expensive.[84] They turned instead to the nearby agent for the Kansas Pacific, Adam Roedelheimer. He was able to offer them black-soiled, upland acreage at a reasonable price ($2.00 to $2.50 per acre), and so they bought land north and south of an incipient

English colony in eastern Ellis County. The Volga Germans were poorer than their Mennonite kin, and they began their migration two years after the first large arrivals of the Mennonites. These circumstances, together with a general revival of Kansas fever among eastern Americans in the late 1870s, meant that the Volga colonists avoided celebrity status during their early years.[85]

Although the Russian-Germans saw themselves as German to the core, Kansans perceived them as quite distinctive from other German immigrants. Since the Russians long had lived in isolated colonies, they retained customs from the eighteenth century and initially had only minimal dealings with their neighbors. The first of their colonists in Marion County attracted much comment in the press by opting to reside in an agricultural village rather than each family living on their own farmland. This practice of village residence was also the norm with the Volga people in Ellis County. Both groups had distinctive crops, distinctive ovens, and distinctive accents. Where their colonies abutted existing German settlements, as at Walker in Ellis County, social intercourse usually was minimal. Most Kansans came to label the new immigrants as "Rooshians."[86]

Despite the uniformity generally perceived by outside writers, the two major clusters of early Russian-German settlement actually contained considerable internal variety. Most of their Kansas communities were direct transfers of people from single villages in Russia. Close observers thus could see that accents varied from place to place, religious practices were not all the same, and relative social status was a matter for debate. Within the Volga group, for example, settlers at Catherine, northeast of Hays, were seen as "proud city folk" by residents of the five other early villages. The people at Schoenchen were drawn from the same Russian village as those at Liebenthal, but since they could not agree with the others on the location for their new home in Kansas, they founded a separate town.[87] Religious divisions among the Volga Germans reproduced themselves geographically. With the exception of Liebenthal in extreme northern Rush County, Catholic settlers established all of their early villages in Ellis County (Catherine, Munjor, Pfeifer, Schoenchen, and Victoria). Lutherans and other Protestants arranged themselves in an arc from southern Russell County through northwestern Barton County, and into northeastern Rush County, with foci on the towns of Milberger, Otis, and Bison. Their numbers were about one-third those of their Catholic neighbors, but the groups were similar in degree of isolation and general conservatism.[88]

The twenty or so Mennonite colonies varied more along a liberal-conservative continuum than did the Volga Germans, a variation that was (and is) reflected in religious and spatial subdivisions. People in the most liberal contingent, the General Conference Mennonites, lived in four core areas arranged as a loose half-ring around the important railroad city of Newton (see Maps 4.10, 4.12). Directly north of Newton, at Goessel in Marion County, was the large Alexanderwohl congregation. Counterclockwise from Goessel, major groups lived at Moundridge in McPherson County (a colony from the old Polish province of Volhynia, now in Ukraine) and at Buhler in Reno County (a Black Sea group like the one at Alexanderwohl). The eastern arm of the arc was formed by the

Prussian and Swiss settlements already noted. As a central point, Newton and North Newton gradually became the economic and cultural focus for the General Conference groups, including the site of Bethel, their church-supported college. A fifth General Conference settlement, related to the Moundridge group, was located in an outlier position at Pretty Prairie in southern Reno County.[89]

Mennonite Brethren and Krimmer Brethren, decidedly conservative groups who merged in 1960, clustered in Marion County. One of their congregations, under Jakob Wiebe, created the first Russian settlement in Kansas, at Gnadenau, and their strength remains in this area. Hillsboro, just north of Gnadenau, is the modern focus, long-time home to their college (Tabor), publishing house, and general headquarters. Holdeman Mennonites, the most conservative and smallest of the major groups, are actually a Kansas creation. In 1878, John Holdeman converted a group of Volhynian immigrants to his strict philosophy. These were an extremely poor people initially, who were looked down upon by other Mennonites for their lack of agricultural skills. They survived their first years in Kansas largely through charity on tiny forty-acre plots just south of Canton in southeastern McPherson County. Some of this original, semiostracized group decided to move away from Canton, the Holdeman influence, and the other Mennonites; they ventured along the Santa Fe tracks to Pawnee Rock, in southwestern Barton County, where they lived in boxcars while desperately working to acquire capital. Ultimately both Volhynian settlements prospered, and the Pawnee Rock group became associated with the General Conference.[90]

Although the major thrust of the Russian-German immigration was completed by 1885, people continued to arrive until after the turn of the century. Newcomers initially bought land near the older centers and thereby made many townships almost totally Russian-German in character. Already by 1885 the non-Kansas-born population in the city of Lehigh (Marion County) was 81 percent Russian and that for the surrounding township 94 percent; in Ellis County, the percentages for Catherine and Herzog Townships were 89 and 97, respectively. Later arrivals, mostly those after 1885, together with young people from the core counties, founded many new communities in western Kansas and beyond.

One Russian settlement stood completely apart from the others, both geographically and culturally: Beersheba, a Jewish colony on Pawnee Creek in Hodgeman County (see Map 4.12). Beersheba was one of several short-lived attempts by the German-American Jewish community in the early 1880s to sponsor agricultural havens for the first wave of refugees from czarist pogroms. A Cincinnati group guided sixty settlers to government homestead land just north of the Santa Fe grant in 1882. They helped the colonists to file their claims, provided a resident superintendent, and even purchased implements and livestock. Despite this support, the colony declined sharply after 1885. The settlers preferred other careers to farming, and most of them moved to Dodge City and elsewhere to become merchants.[91]

Though dwarfed in scale by the composite mass of German immigrants, Scandinavian settlers were the second-largest European contributor to the central Kansas frontier of 1885. Over ten thousand were present, with Swedes representing 79 percent of the total (see Table 4.1). The numerical dominance of the Swedes as well as their settlement pattern in the state are both products of timing. As a result of improved health practices, all the Scandinavian countries had experienced large population increases in the early decades of the nineteenth century. This had led to financial hardships by midcentury, since industrial jobs were few and new agricultural land scarce. The crisis came first to Sweden, in the form of a crop failure and local famine in 1867 and 1868. Annual emigration by the tens of thousands began almost immediately.[92]

Many of the Swedes who came to the United States soon found themselves in Chicago listening to their kinspeople, railroad agents, and others describe the choices available for farmsteads. The closer frontiers in Iowa, Minnesota, and Nebraska attracted most of the attention, but Kansas had its proponents, too. Kansas had received some good publicity in the 1850s from the only Swedish-American newspaper of the time and had a small, but successful, Swedish colony dating from that decade located just north of Manhattan, in the Blue valley (see Map 2.12). Those people who decided to look at the Kansas frontier seriously around 1870 were drawn first to Junction City, which was on the Kansas Pacific line and near the old Blue valley settlement. It also was the gateway to good homestead land in the Republican valley and to equally good, unsold railroad land just a county or two to the west. The Swedes took both options.[93]

The first cluster developed in central Dickinson County (see Map 4.13). Lars Jaderborg had come to this section of the Smoky Hill valley early, in 1858; impressed with the land, he wrote letters to his friends. Over three hundred people eventually came, most of them taking eighty-acre homesteads within the Kansas Pacific grant but some buying railroad property. This group became known as the Enterprise Swedes even though the town of Enterprise (just to the west of the Swedish holdings) was founded slightly after Jaderborg's arrival by German-Swiss people. Still, the possibility for industrial jobs at the mill in Enterprise did help to attract Swedes to the area.[94]

The main thrust of Swedish immigration to Kansas was fostered by cooperative land companies, not by individuals such as Jaderborg or by agents of the Kansas Pacific. These companies, intended as temporary ventures, were formed by immigrants who, having made their way individually to Illinois, would join together to search for farming sites and to secure favorable land prices and transportation rates. Three such groups, all created in 1868, came to Kansas. Representatives from one, the Scandinavian Agricultural Society of Chicago, purchased twelve sections of private land along the Republican River in Republic County. The other two companies bought adjoining properties from the Kansas Pacific in southern Saline and northern McPherson counties. The

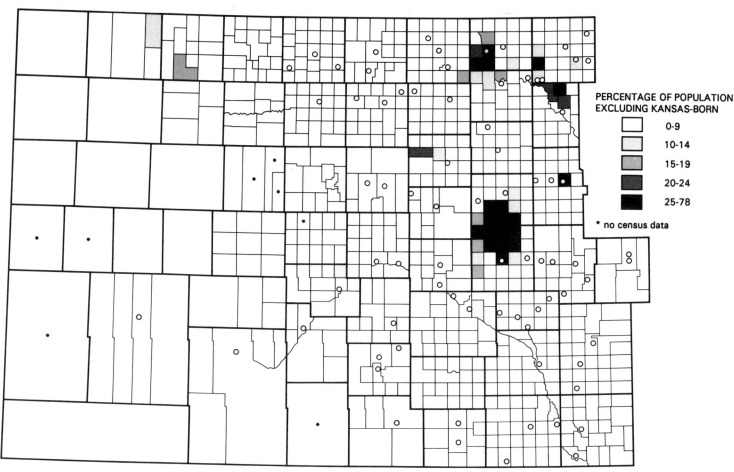

PERCENTAGE OF POPULATION
EXCLUDING KANSAS-BORN

- 0-9
- 10-14
- 15-19
- 20-24
- 25-78

* no census data

MAP 4.13
*Natives of Scandinavia,
1885 (central and western
Kansas). Data from
Kansas state census.*

13,160 acres of the First Swedish Agricultural Company (a Chicago group) encompassed the future sites of Lindsborg and New Gottland. The towns of Fremont, Marquette, Salemsborg, Assaria, Falun, and Smolan would soon give character to the 14,080 acres purchased by the Galesburg Land Company just northwest, west, and southwest of the Lindsborg site. Within ten years, Swedish dominance was nearly complete over a diamond-shaped tract whose dimensions, thirty miles by twenty-five miles, were those of a typical Kansas county (see Map 4.13).[95]

The Galesburg Company disbanded immediately after individuals had secured their own pieces of land, but the First Swedish Company endured for nine years and was responsible for laying out the city of Lindsborg in 1869. The main role played by each company, though, was the creation of an ethnic center large enough to attract other immigrants. Over forty-five hundred Swedish-born people lived in Saline and McPherson counties in 1885; when second-generation Swedes are included, the total rises to nearly eight thousand. Lindsborg served as the economic and cultural focus of the general community from the beginning, home to the first church and, after 1881, to Bethany College. The pioneers were a poor and sincerely religious group, with a Pietist minister, Olof Olsson, setting the tone. They banned saloons but otherwise wanted to participate fully in the American economy. The result was a clean, industrious settlement where assimilation in language, education, and politics was pursued almost from the beginning. Both Olsson and another early leader, Carl Swensson, became active in the Republican party at the state level.[96]

The cooperative settlement in Republic County was more isolated than the Lindsborg colony during the early years, and its growth also was hampered by an Indian scare shortly after its founding. Still, about fourteen hundred Swedes and two hundred Norwegians came, creating the second-largest Scandinavian concentration in the state. The immigrants included a Swedish minister from Bucklin, Missouri, and seventeen families from his congregation. The founding Scandinavian Agricultural Society created a central town called New Scandinavia (now Scandia) and owned a mill there, but most of the society's members preferred life in the country. In 1885 only 12 percent of the town's population (excluding native Kansans) had been born in Sweden or Norway.[97]

The last major group of Swedish settlers with ties to the early dispersion center at Junction City occupied lands near the Republican River in Clay and Washington counties. Because the valley proper of the lower Republican was a great transportation artery and thus a mixing area for peoples, the more concentrated enclaves of Swedes and other ethnic groups occurred on tributary streams. The most prominent of these, at Brantford in Washington County, dates from 1869 and grew at the expense of both Lindsborg and New Scandinavia. Its founders had rejected McPherson County because of its sandy soils and Republic County because they feared a recurrence of the Indian raids of 1868. They liked the black soils around Dry Creek, bought out the original settlers, and enlisted enough friends and relatives to make a settlement of about five hundred people.[98]

Despite the location of Enterprise and Lindsborg on the Kansas Pacific grant, railroad recruitment actually played a remarkably small role in bringing Scandinavian settlers to Kansas. A long tradition of cooperative enterprises in Europe seemingly made it natural for these people to band together when necessary and thus to create communities on their own terms. The Lindsborg settlers approached the Kansas Pacific officials to buy, rather than the other way around, and by 1870 enough Swedes were in the state so that new immigrants did not have to rely on railroad agents or other strangers for advice. Probably as a result of these circumstances, the several efforts of Santa Fe promoters to create Swedish colonies came to little; only two appear on the map for 1885.

The most successful of the Santa Fe efforts was New Andover, in southwestern McPherson County and adjacent Rice County. It began in 1870, with early settlers drawn from an older Swedish center in Andover, Illinois. Although the colony was fairly close to Lindsborg, the New Andover people oriented themselves more toward Hutchinson, where a second Santa Fe settlement existed. Ultimately about three hundred Swedes came to New Andover and two hundred to the Hutchinson area. Two other Santa Fe attempts at colonization, Burns in Marion County and Garfield in Pawnee County, attracted no more than a hundred immigrants from abroad. Significantly, Carl Schmidt chose to ignore them in his reminiscences.[99]

Ten years and some 150 miles separate the core Swedish settlements in Kansas from two outposts in the northwest: at Lund in Decatur County and at Enne in Rawlins County (see Map 4.13). Both had links with Nebraska, in a manner similar to the ties of the Hungarian Germans there, as well as with the older Swedish settlements in Kansas. Several people at Lund came from Enterprise, many at Enne from Republic County. The immigration total of the two places was about one hundred by 1885.[100]

Whereas the few Norwegians who came to Kansas associated themselves closely with the Swedes, the Danes kept more to themselves. Three small Danish settlements appear on Map 4.13, all founded in 1869 but each one quite distinctive. The largest group, under the leadership of C. Bernhardt, founded the town of Denmark in Lincoln County. These people were members of an intellectual and ardently nationalistic faction of the Danish Lutheran church, the Grundtvigian. They craved isolation so as to maintain Danish ways and pioneered several cooperative enterprises in Lincoln County, including a successful creamery. The colony attracted about four hundred settlers, many coming from Iowa, but the lack of a railroad stymied economic growth in the late 1880s.[101]

Jamestown, in northwestern Cloud County, was home to a Danish Baptist colony of about three hundred people. Its leader, Niels Nielson, had been one of the first Baptists in Denmark. He and his followers emigrated in the face of intolerance from the state Lutheran church. Though physically close to the Republic County Swedes and Norwegians, the Jamestown colonists remained separate until after the death of Nielson in 1887. The third and smallest Danish settlement, at Greenleaf in Washington County, was unplanned. Olaf Pearson, a Swede on his way to Kansas, induced a group of Danes he met on the immigrant ship to try the state; they happened to find land near Greenleaf and grew to a community of about one hundred.[102]

THE ENGLISH AND THE IRISH

Over fourteen thousand immigrants from England, Ireland, Scotland, and Wales came to the central Kansas frontier, a total that exceeded even that of the Scandinavians (see Table 4.1). The Irish, like the Swedes, came because of economic desperation, but the others moved more in the hope of bettering already reasonable lives. Their rates of emigration, in fact, have been correlated with the amounts and sites of British overseas investment. The American plains were a prime location in this regard during the last half of the nineteenth century.[103]

Kansas enjoyed its greatest popularity in Great Britain during the 1870s. A widely read travel account, William H. Dixon's *North America* (1867), praised the state as the "most perfect" section of the prairies. Upper-class capitalists saw potential for adventure and for the breeding of livestock; ordinary farmers liked the assertion that "labour in Kansas has high value." Beginning in 1872, interest was high enough to support a London newspaper concerned almost entirely with the prospects for immigrants to the plains frontier. Railroads, of course, offered discounted fares and easy credit to all comers.[104]

The impressive numbers of British citizens who pioneered on the plains sometimes take modern Kansans by surprise, for these immigrants were nearly invisible. The only one of their early colonization plans to receive much local publicity failed after a few years.[105] More important, assimilation into American life was so easy that most of these settlers saw little advantage in staying close to their fellow countrymen. The 2,143 Scots in central Kansas dispersed themselves so widely that they reached no more than 6 percent of the population in any city or township (calculated without Kansas-born residents). The 360 Welsh did achieve the benchmark of 10 percent once (in Harvey County), but the much larger Irish (4,718) and English (6,802) contingents reached this plateau only six times apiece (see Maps 4.14, 4.15).

Just as good reasons exist for the dispersal of British settlers, so do arguments for their concentration in the railroad belt. They were courted by the agents as educated, desirable settlers; they knew capitalist ways and often had money to invest; and they preferred the immediate land titles they could get through purchase over the more extended process of "proving up" homestead entries.[106] Kansas Pacific officials set up a recruitment office in London, and Santa Fe people did the same in Liverpool; from these efforts came two major colonization schemes, both on Kansas Pacific land.

The first colony, Wakefield, was a joint venture headed by John Wornald of Yorkshire and the Reverend Richard Wake, a Methodist minister who had moved to America in 1854. Wake, an advocate for settling English agricultural laborers in the American West, met Wornald in 1866 while recruiting in England, and they discussed possibilities for a colony in Kansas. Three years later, an investment company had been assembled and Wake negotiated the purchase of 32,000 acres from the Kansas Pacific for $102,000. The tract was on the Republican River in Clay County, sixteen miles upstream from Junction City.[107]

Promotion for Wakefield was aimed at poor English tradesmen. The first contingent of seventy-seven colonists came in the fall of 1869, and several hundred more arrived over the next four years, each buying land from the company. The colonists put a clear ethnic stamp on the place, naming townships Athelstane and Exeter and their own city after Wornald's hometown in Yorkshire. They did not have great economic success, though, as their limited farming experience was tested by a drought in 1870, bad economic conditions in 1873, and grasshoppers in 1874. The land company officially dissolved itself in 1873, but by then the local character had been firmly established in an

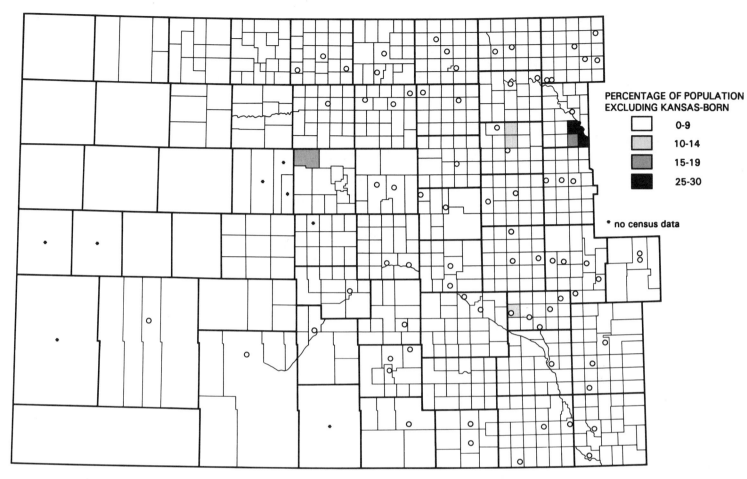

PERCENTAGE OF POPULATION
EXCLUDING KANSAS-BORN

0-9
10-14
15-19
25-30

* no census data

MAP 4.14
*Natives of England and
Wales, 1885 (central and
western Kansas). Data
from Kansas state census.*

English mold. Even today, the Kansas and Yorkshire Wakefields maintain a sister-city relationship.

The second British colony on Kansas Pacific land was so short-lived that its residents had dispersed by 1885; still, it bears mention because the scheme was one of the most publicized in Kansas history. George Grant, a Scottish entrepreneur, bought 25,245 acres in eastern Ellis County in 1872, envisioning a sheep and cattle empire, with capital to come from British investors. Kansas Pacific officials cooperated by building a new siding at Grant's headquarters (called Victoria), along with an elaborate depot. Despite the fanfare, no more than three hundred colonists ever came. The publicity, in fact, was a vain attempt to overcome the financial and grasshopper disasters that hit Kansas just after the Grant purchase. The colony was moribund by 1876 when the Volga Germans decided that the Scottish pastures might make good wheatfields.[108]

The shading that appears in northwestern Ellis County on Map 4.14 has nothing to do with the Grant Colony but denotes the Cochran Ranch, several thousand acres in the broken lands

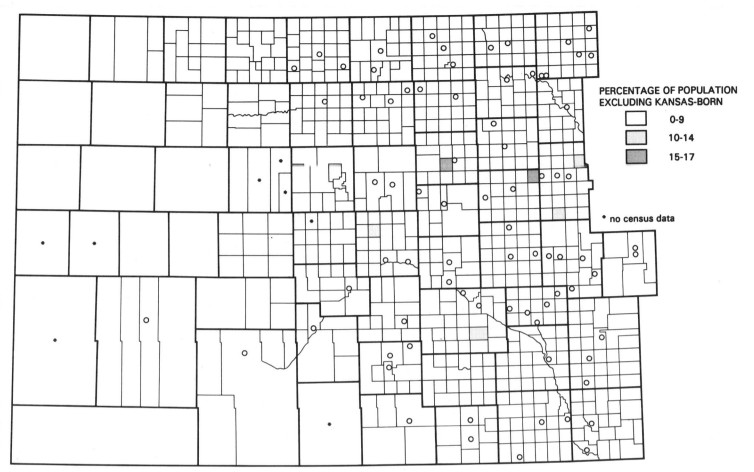

PERCENTAGE OF POPULATION
EXCLUDING KANSAS-BORN

☐ 0-9
▨ 10-14
▩ 15-17

· no census data

along the Saline River. Robert Barnes and his nephew Al Barnes purchased the initial acreage in 1882 and then invited a dozen or so other English cattlemen to help expand the business. These families established the only totally rural Episcopal church in Kansas, St. Andrew; it still survives.[109]

Neither local histories nor accounts of English colonization in Kansas mention the 102 English-born people who were living in two townships of Ottawa County during 1885. The proximity of this small agglomeration to the Wakefield Colony, though, suggests that a connection existed between the two clusters. The Ottawa townships lie just north of the Kansas Pacific grant, and may have been sought out by Englishmen who lacked the money to buy Wakefield lands. The final concentration shown on Map 4.14, at Burrton in Harvey County, is Welsh. It was an unplanned, unadvertised assemblage, an extension down the newly built Santa Fe tracks from a sizeable Welsh population in Emporia. The group never numbered more than a hundred and was mostly rural, but they did organize a Presbyterian church in Burrton in 1873.[110]

MAP 4.15
Natives of Ireland, 1885 (central and western Kansas). Data from Kansas state census.

Despite the legendary poverty of Irish immigrants to the United States, those who came to central Kansas frequently located within the railroad belt (see Map 4.15); this tendency is easily explained. "A considerable proportion" of railroad laborers in the state were of Irish descent, and railroad lands had been endorsed in a popular 1873 handbook for Irish immigrants.[111] The book included a long, open letter from Bishop Louis Fink of Kansas, in which he judged these accessible and reasonably priced tracts as "by far preferable to out-of-the-way homestead lands."[112]

Kansas Pacific acreage proved to be especially popular for Irish settlers. Although some people in the early 1870s claimed "there is no Sunday west of Junction City and no God west of Salina," the early and continuous presence of missionaries along this railroad probably helped to encourage and stabilize settlement there.[113] Originally, the western outpost was the old Potawatomi mission at St. Marys, in Pottawatomie County. Priests from St. Marys held mass at a small Irish settlement at Chapman Creek, in extreme eastern Dickinson County, as early as 1859. By 1864 Chapman had a church, and the settlement grew rapidly after the railroad was completed in 1867.[114] Chapman's ethnic heritage is obvious even today: the mascots for the local high school and junior high school, respectively, are the Fighting Irish and the Leprechauns.

The church formalized its mission effort along the Kansas Pacific in 1869 with the designation of Solomon, on the border between Dickinson and Saline counties, as headquarters for an elongated parish that extended to Fort Hays. This decision provided an air of permanency for Solomon itself and induced many loyal churchgoers to purchase land in the vicinity. These included over a hundred Irish-born settlers.[115]

None of the four remaining islands of Irish settlement shown on Map 4.15 contained more than fifty people. The group at Vesper, in Lincoln County, were among the first settlers in their section of the Saline valley, coming before Solomon was designated as the center for missionary efforts.[116] Little research exists on the other clusters. The Barton County group is near Olmitz, a German-Moravian Catholic center. Castleton, in Reno County, is adjacent to the large German Catholic settlement that extends westward from St. Mark.

THE CANADIANS AND THE BOHEMIANS

Like immigrants from the British Isles, most of the 7,367 Canadians present on the central Kansas frontier came as individuals rather than in colonies. They tended to spread themselves evenly over the landscape and to assimilate easily. About 80 percent of them came from Ontario. The good farm land there had nearly all been acquired by the early 1860s and, with the Canadian prairie region not open for settlement until the 1870s, the United States had great appeal for a decade or so.[117] Only once did the British-ancestry mainstream of this flow form a cluster of note in Kansas: a group of 130 people in northwestern Dickinson County (see Map 4.16). This concen-

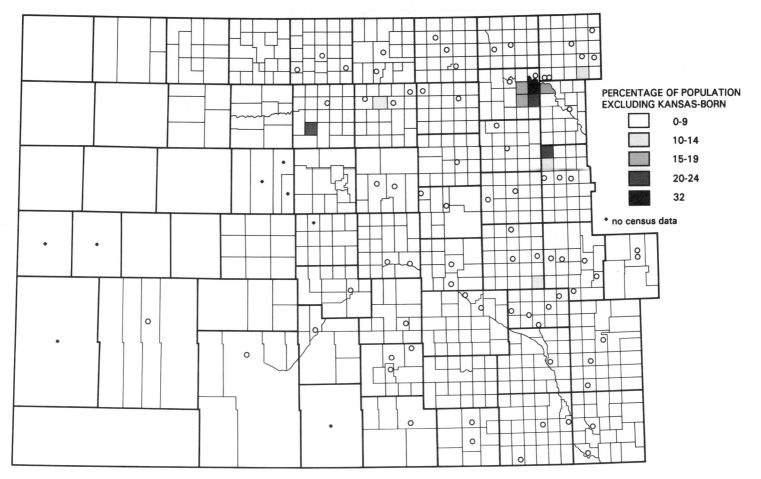

PERCENTAGE OF POPULATION
EXCLUDING KANSAS-BORN

0-9
10-14
15-19
20-24
32

* no census data

MAP 4.16
Natives of British America, 1885 (central and western Kansas). Data from Kansas state census.

tration is located near the English colony at Wakefield, and linkages between the two places are suggested by higher than average concentrations of both English and Canadian settlers in the intervening townships.

People with German and French ancestry, although in the minority of emigrants from British America, formed almost all the significant Canadian agglomerations in Kansas. These groups were not recruited, but most of them had lived elsewhere in the United States before coming to Kansas. They knew how to file homestead entries and most sought out government land north of the railroad belt. Two small German communities came, one to Osborne in 1871 and the other (a Mennonite congregation) to Marion County in 1873, where they founded the town of Canada.[118]

Among the immigrants to frontier Kansas, the presence of some 1,350 French Canadians was perhaps most unexpected. Not only were they ignored by railroad agents, but they also chose Kansas over areas in the Upper Midwest that were more accessible from Quebec and that had a more familiar climate. Four clusters appear on Map 4.16, three of which are interrelated. The exception is in McPherson County, where a few early immigrants from France attracted about fifty Canadians between 1869 and 1871. This settlement never grew and was soon overwhelmed by German and Russian-German peoples. Many of the French joined a local Methodist congregation, and a modern visitor reported that the old names, Belair and La Vie, are now pronounced and written as Blair and Lively.[119]

The most significant French-Canadian settlement in Kansas centers on the small town of St. Joseph, in Cloud County, and by extension, with St. Joseph's parent colony in the marshes of Kankakee County, Illinois. The French presence around Lake Michigan dates to the seventeenth century, and sites there were logical destinations for emigrants when farmland in the St. Lawrence valley became scarce beginning in the 1830s. Bourbonnais, the major Kankakee village, grew rapidly and by 1856 had a population of about six thousand.[120] It then began to assume a new role as a way station for Quebecois who wanted to pioneer farther west. Some went to Nebraska, but Eugene Ouellette and his wife decided to try the Republican valley in Kansas in 1868. Their initial enthusiasm led to a steady stream of migrants over the next decade and to a new community of about twenty-four hundred people.[121]

As lands in the main valley of the Republican had already been claimed, the French located just to the west, near Beaver, Mulberry, and Elm creeks. Their church, first organized in 1873 under the direction of the Reverend Louis Mollier, became the center not only for French culture in the area but for Catholicism as well. Just as mission efforts along the Kansas Pacific and the Santa Fe corridors emanated from Solomon and Wichita, respectively, St. Joseph controlled the Republican valley and the rest of northwestern Kansas. This role was formalized in 1887 when the Diocese of Leavenworth (all of Kansas) was subdivided and new sees were created at Wichita and at Concordia (the urban center closest to St. Joseph).[122]

The percentages shown on Map 4.16 for Cloud County and adjacent areas should at least be doubled to state the French presence properly. Illinois-born people were as numerous in the area as were those born in Quebec, and nearly all of them had French names. Shirley Township, the site of St. Joseph, contained the largest single bloc, but Concordia (the county seat and railroad center) was a close second in total numbers. The principal agencies of the church all eventually located in Concordia, including the Nazareth Academy of the Sisters of St. Joseph and the St. Joseph Hospital. French businessmen were active there, too; their ownership included Bon Marché, the town's leading department store.[123]

The small French cluster in Washington County is closely related to the Cloud County settlement. People moving from Illinois to St. Joseph between 1869 and 1878 usually traveled by train to the railhead of the Union Pacific, Central Branch, at Waterville, just east of Washington County. On their trek overland from Waterville, many of these immigrants saw land they liked and decided to stay. The Washington County settlements thus postdate St. Joseph slightly and served as welcoming posts for later travelers. Neither Palmer nor Clyde, along this route, was founded as a French community, but Clyde especially became an important center. Many families from St. Joseph eventually moved there.[124]

Land costs in Cloud and Washington counties had become expensive enough by the mid-1870s to prompt several of the French families to pioneer once again. The nearest frontier was a hundred miles due west, in Rooks County. Biographical accounts show arrivals there from 1874 until well after the turn of the century, about five hundred in all. Some families came directly from St. Joseph, but most followed the familiar route from Quebec through Kankakee. Early settlement focused on the village of Zurich, but later and more conservative migrants, especially those who came after 1900, tended toward the newer town of Damar, just to the northwest. The Damar group, the "Acadia of Western Kansas," long maintained a reputation for aloofness. A huge church, built between 1912 and 1915, still stands as testimony to their fervor.[125]

Several parallels between the French-Canadian cultural experience and that of Bohemians led to similar settlement patterns for the two groups in Kansas. Both were village-oriented, largely peasant societies, and both had long chafed under the rule of others. Long subjugation to the British Canadians, on the one hand, and to the Austrian Hapsburgs, on the other, produced inward-looking and somewhat clannish peoples. Railroad recruiters largely ignored them and, when they came to the United States, they usually migrated in groups and settled where others of their kind had already established themselves.[126] The 2,334 Bohemians and Moravians in central Kansas in 1885 are thus much more visible on maps of population origin than are, for example, the 4,718 Irish (see Map 4.17).

A movement toward nationalism in Bohemia and Moravia began shortly after 1800 and reached a peak with the revolutionary wars that spread across Europe in 1848. When these uprisings failed, many people lost hope and began an emigration that continued until their nation attained its independence in 1918. The initial waves of Bohemians who came to the United States often traveled first to Chicago and then to settlements in Wisconsin and Iowa. These places, in turn, were large enough by the late 1860s to establish daughter colonies in Nebraska and Kansas. The locations selected often were adjacent to German communities, not a surprising fact considering that Bohemia itself is nearly surrounded by German culture and that most Bohemians knew the language.[127]

The first Kansas Bohemian center developed in Republic County. George McChesney and his Bohemian wife Josephine immigrated in 1866, but growth was delayed two years until the new railroad line from Atchison to Waterville improved local access. Mrs. McChesney, who was from Iowa, recruited groups from Linn County and Marshall County, and another ten families moved from Wisconsin in 1872. They came in search of cheaper land so that they could acquire adequate holdings for growing households. The early families created an all-Bohemian community called New Tabor, but this town gave way in the 1880s to two others on railroad lines: Munden and Cuba.

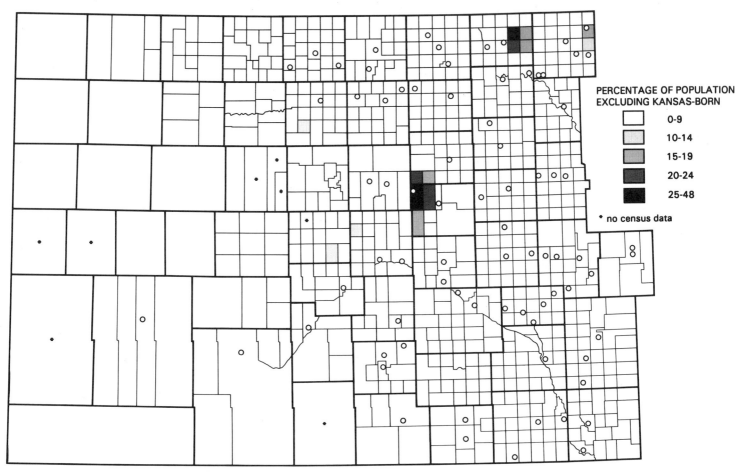

PERCENTAGE OF POPULATION
EXCLUDING KANSAS-BORN

	0-9
	10-14
	15-19
	20-24
	25-48

* no census data

MAP 4.17
*Natives of Bohemia and
Moravia, 1885 (central
and western Kansas).
Data from Kansas state
census.*

By the time immigration slowed in the late 1880s, approximately fifteen hundred Bohemians lived in a block of four townships. In three of the four, they constituted about 75 percent of the populace.[128]

The railroad line to Waterville spurred not only the Republic County Bohemian settlement but also one along the Little Blue River in Washington County. The pioneer, John Pecenka, arrived in 1869, and three hundred or so immigrants joined him from Iowa, Wisconsin, and Michigan as well as from Bohemia itself. Strong connections linked the Republic and Washington communities, but, as a group, the Little Blue people were more religious. Most settlers joined the German-Irish Catholic congregations that had developed around Hanover.[129]

A third Bohemian colony evolved astride the main line of the Kansas Pacific Railroad in western Ellsworth and southwestern Lincoln counties. Although the early settlers appreciated the transportation advantages of this location, they were not recruited to it by railroad agents and they almost never bought their farms from the Kansas Pacific. This community was purely the result of one man's industry. Francis Swehla came to Kansas in 1874 after earlier residences in Iowa and Nebraska. He disliked the people in the Republic County land office and so came south to the Kansas Pacific. Swehla was a moneyed, literate man who decided to write up his region in the Bohemian-American newspapers. As letters came to him, he responded and then helped the new arrivals to find farm properties. By the late 1880s the local Bohemian population had grown nearly as large as the one in Republic County. The Swehla group was more diverse, however, with several Moravian families in Noble Township, and it was more rural at the outset. Later, the towns of Holyrood, Ellsworth, and especially Wilson gradually became known as ethnic centers.[130]

Bohemian and/or Moravian settlers founded six smaller centers in central Kansas, none of which are connected with each other or with the older clusters in Republic and Ellsworth counties. Three were colonies of the Santa Fe, initiated in the 1870s. About twenty-five Catholic families established the town of Pilsen in Marion County and erected there the beautiful St. John Nepomucene church. To the west, in Barton County, is the mixed German-Moravian community at Olmitz as noted in the German discussion. The third group, at Timken in Rush County, was also a mixed colony, with about two hundred Bohemians, Silesians, and Moravians. These people, in contrast with the Pilseners, were rather indifferent to organized religion.[131]

The final three groups have only their isolation in common. Ten families moved to Rooks County between 1878 and 1880; nominally Catholic, they located near the slightly older French-Canadian settlement at Zurich but soon drifted away from the church. A land agent lured a slightly larger group from Wisconsin to extreme southern Kansas in 1876. They were Bohemians but gave their nationality as Austrian to the census interviewer in 1885 and, as a result, they appear on Map 4.11 (near Caldwell in Sumner County) instead of Map 4.17. The last group of note, the Moravian Catholics of north-central Rawlins County, also fails to appear on Map 4.17 because their immigration was just beginning in 1885. Like other pioneers in extreme northwestern Kansas, their path to the area was through Nebraska, and they eventually grew to a community of about two hundred people. A related settlement exists at Jennings, in adjacent Decatur County.[132]

THE YANKEES

New Englanders and other people from the Northern culture states came to central Kansas in only slightly fewer numbers than did Europeans and Upper Southerners; unlike these latter two groups, though, the Yankees spread themselves widely over the landscape. Contemporary accounts note several colonization plans from New York, Wisconsin, and elsewhere, but one has to look carefully to see them amid the general scatter on a map of the scene in 1885 (see Map 4.18). Many townships and a large majority of cities have 10 percent of their immigrant populations from this culture area, but relatively few reach 20 percent, and only two townships and the small city of Barnes achieve the 30 percent level. No New England state by itself provided even 10 percent of

PERCENTAGE OF POPULATION
EXCLUDING KANSAS-BORN

0-9
10-19
20-29
30-32

* no census data

KEY TO STATES
NY   New York

MAP 4.18
*Natives of Northern
states, 1885 (central and
western Kansas). Data
from Kansas state census.
The letter symbol marks a
township in which people
from New York constitute
20 percent of the
immigrant population.
For states included in the
Northern area, see Table
4.1.*

the immigrants to any Kansas township, and New Yorkers were the only Yankees to colonize a
township at the 20 percent level.

Although Yankee immigrants settled everywhere in the state, notably fewer of them went to
the relatively distant lands of the old Osage Reserve in extreme southern Kansas. This was logical
given the assumption that moneyed Yankees would opt for property near the railroads and that
their poorer neighbors would choose to file homestead entries north of the Kansas Pacific grant.
The stereotypic image of Yankees as western urban entrepreneurs, though containing much truth,
has several limitations, and map patterns support it only to a degree.[133] Railroad towns, clearly the
places with the most potential for growth, all had Northern settlers in proportions larger than the
11 percent that defined this group in central Kansas as a whole, but most of the proportions exceeded this mark only moderately. For the larger Santa Fe towns, numbers ranged from 12 percent
at Hutchinson and Dodge City to 16 at Peabody and Great Bend. The figures were similar on the

Kansas Pacific: 13 percent at Abilene and 14 percent at both Salina and Ellsworth (see Table 4.2). Among the smaller railroad cities, only Russell, at 26 percent, stood as exceptional and thus close to the popular Yankee image.

The remarkably consistent percentage of Northern settlers in the various railroad towns is surprising in one sense, for officials of the Kansas Pacific clearly directed more of their recruiting efforts to that region of the country than did their counterparts at the Santa Fe. While Santa Fe agents concentrated in the states of the Old Northwest, Kansas Pacific leaders placed two of their four eastern land offices in New York, along with the headquarters for their National Land Company.[134] The unexpected evenness of the percentages between the towns along the two railroads may be a product of individual entrepreneurs trying to maximize their opportunities. Arguably, a given city would have only so many openings for professionals and business leaders; if Yankees of this bent initially were disproportionately represented in any one place, they might find it advantageous to disperse. This is a difficult assertion to prove, but an examination of the origins of the region's elite population as defined by their appearance in the biographical sketches sections of a massive 1883 state history is instructive (see Table 4.4). In a twelve-county sample, the entrepreneur stereotype is borne out; Yankees appear twice as frequently in the sketches as they do in the census.

A second line of evidence for the entrepreneur hypothesis appears in the settler geography of the northern two tiers of counties. The highest percentages of Northerners occur along two of the most important transportation routes in this region, sites that held maximum promise for urban development. Barnes, the most Yankee city on the map, was the first town on the extension of the Union Pacific Railroad, Central Branch, when it finally was constructed westward from Waterville into Washington County in 1878 (see Map 4.1). Clifton, a little farther along on this route, received 26 percent of its non-Kansas-born population from the Northern states, and Concordia, despite its significant French-Canadian and Scandinavian populations, was still 18 percent Yankee. During the next year, workers extended the track beyond Concordia; at Beloit, the railroad joined and then followed the second of the key regional transportation routes: the broad and fertile valleys of the Solomon River and its South Fork. Beloit recorded a 20 percent Yankee population in 1885, and upstream one finds Cawker City at 27 percent, Alton at 23 percent, and Stockton at 21 percent. The only deviation from expectations is the county-seat town of Osborne at 18 percent, but this dip can be explained by that city's history as a Pennsylvania colony, as will be developed later in this chapter.

Yankee dominance in the railroad cities of the northern counties is greater than in the communities along the lines of the Kansas Pacific and the Santa Fe. Somewhat paradoxically, this circumstance is probably a result of the greater overall attractiveness of railroad towns such as Salina and Hutchinson. These cities were major mixing areas, places so appealing to people of all sorts that it was difficult for any one group to dominate numerically. A related geographical issue in the north concerns the relatively modest Yankee presence along a pair of transportation routes there that

Table 4.4. *Percentage of Settlers from Major Culture Areas Listed in Biographical Sketches and Census Records of Twelve Counties in North-Central Kansas, 1885*

Collection Unit/Culture Area	Cutler Listing of Biog. Sketches[a]	Census Data Excluding Kans.-born[b]
New England (Northern)	29	14
North Midland	52	59
Upper South (South Midland)	5	13
Lower South	1	
Foreign Countries	13	13

Sources: Manuscript Kansas state census, 1885; William G. Cutler, ed., *History of the State of Kansas* (Chicago: A. T. Andreas, 1883).

Note: The twelve counties form a block between the Kansas Pacific Railroad and the Nebraska state line: Decatur, Ellis, Gove, Graham, Norton, Osborne, Phillips, Rooks, Russell, Sheridan, Smith, and Trego.

[a] N = 260

[b] N = 57,756

rivaled the other routes in importance. One is the Republican valley, where town development occurred so soon after the Civil War that most New Yorkers and New Englanders did not arrive in time to participate fully. The other route, the North Fork of the Solomon River, extends from Cawker City due west through southernmost Smith, Phillips, and Norton counties. This valley's fertility and acreage equals that of the South Fork, and it acquired a railroad as well, but towns along this route faced competition for dominance in their counties from more centrally located cities. The entrepreneurial opportunities in the North Fork towns of Kirwin or Lenora were therefore not as great as they were in Stockton or Osborne, where the South Fork offered the advantages of political centrality in addition to those of valley location.

The thesis of Yankee as urban entrepreneur can perhaps also be confirmed by the settlement patterns of the extreme frontier counties of 1885, especially those along the two trans-Kansas railroads. In that year the cities of Ellis and Larned mark the general line between population densities above and below six per square mile (see Map 4.2). Westward of this limit strings of new railroad towns existed but little in the way of agricultural settlement. In these frontier but largely urban counties, Yankee percentages were considerably above the regional norm. The Yankee-urban linkage in this area gains further support from place-names. The county-seat towns of Sharon Springs in Wallace County and Syracuse in Hamilton County are both named after New York communities. Kinsley, another county seat on this section of the Santa Fe, was promoted by a group from

Massachusetts. They not only named the town after a Boston industrialist but also called their main street Massachusetts. In the 1875 census nearly half of the men in the city were born in New England.[135]

The expectation that the Yankee contingent in Kansas would be subdivided into a New England–New York group along the railroads and a poorer group from the newer Northern states of Michigan and Wisconsin in the homestead counties near the Nebraska border is borne out only partially. Five of the six instances in which Wisconsin settlers constituted 10 percent of a township's population were in such predicted locations, but Michigan settlers positioned themselves widely over the state as did New Yorkers (see Map 4.19). The New York pattern suggests that the immigrants to central Kansas from the eastern sections of the Northern culture area were of several distinct types. In addition to the urban-oriented professional and business people, there clearly were many land seekers. Some of this latter group were experienced farmers, but others were poor urban workers sent to the plains by Eastern philanthropists. Whether one conceives of such relocation of the needy in altruistic terms or as a means of getting rid of problem people, New York plutocrats went so far as to appoint a commissioner of emigration and to support the provision of five hundred dollars to aid each family willing to go.[136] Although it is difficult to get an accurate reading on the number of such colonists or on their rates of success in Kansas, the respected scholar John Ise made one suggestive comment about a Connecticut colony in southern Smith County, near his parents' claim: they "represented a particularly motley assortment of talents; and many of these town- and city-bred Yankees were shortly crowded out by the thrifty, hard-working Germans." Another urban group, from Syracuse, New York, went to work in the Kansas Pacific shops at Ellis and had more success.[137]

The seventeen colonies of Northerners in central Kansas large enough to merit discussion in local histories were a varied lot. Besides the group who sought urban employment at Ellis, thirteen of the others formed small, predominantly rural settlements. The three remaining forays were major entrepreneurial efforts: booming the new railroad towns of Kinsley, Peabody, and Russell. The Kinsley effort, in Edwards County, was grandiose. The company leadership from Boston was so confident of immigrants in 1873 that they erected three "colony houses" to provide temporary housing.[138] Their timing was poor, however, as recruitment confronted the realities of the national business panic in 1873 and the grasshopper year in 1874. The town survived, but few New Englanders came and fewer stayed; by 1885 only eleven natives of Massachusetts were left in the city.

The two other urban colonies enjoyed more initial success than Kinsley. Both began a few years earlier, when Kansas was in the midst of a general boom. Peabody was largely the creation of the Wisconsin Kansas Colony Association, a group led by J. E. Cone, who wanted to establish a town just ahead of the westward-building Santa Fe Railroad. In 1870 they claimed a tract of land in Marion County large enough to reduce the odds that the railroad might bypass them. The ploy worked, though barely. The Santa Fe actually built just south of their initial plat, but the Wiscon-

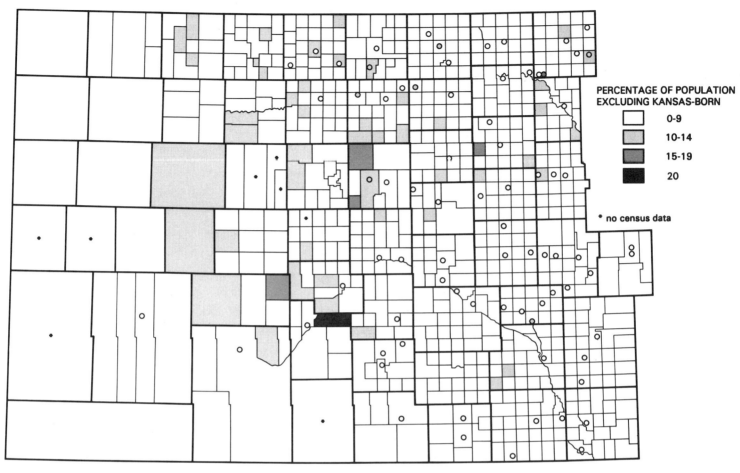

PERCENTAGE OF POPULATION
EXCLUDING KANSAS-BORN

0-9
10-14
15-19
20

* no census data

MAP 4.19
*Natives of New York, 1885
(central and western
Kansas). Data from
Kansas state census.*

sinites quickly merged their Coneburg with a rival town called Peabody. Forty-six Wisconsin natives lived in Peabody in 1885; they were generally prosperous but represented only 4 percent of the
town's immigrant population.[139]

Of the major railroad towns in central Kansas, Russell was the most Yankee because seventy
people from Ripon, Wisconsin, known as the Northwestern Colony, controlled the town from the
outset. This group came to the frontier in 1871 with an initial eye to farm but were offered a quarter-
section of land by the Kansas Pacific if they would establish a city at what was then only a depot
called Fossil Station. The group accepted, living for a while in boxcars provided by the railroad.
The colonists were mostly Congregationalists and had a clause in their charter that demanded
"sober, industrious habits." Their cohesiveness was a factor in Russell's winning the county-seat
election in 1874, and fifty-seven of the group still remained in the city and surrounding township
in 1885. Altogether, 26 percent of the non-Kansas-born population in the town was Yankee.[140]

Very few of the rural or small-town colonies from the Northern culture states are notable on the 1885 map. Some clearly failed outright, as seems to have been the fate of a Brooklyn, New York, party who came to southeastern Ness County in 1878, just ahead of two disastrous cropping years.[141] Other groups apparently had little or no intention of remaining together as a unit in Kansas, the colony being more a means of securing favorable transportation rates and land prices than an effort to maintain cultural ties. An example of the latter phenomenon was in Edwards County, where several families from New York happened to locate in the sand-hill country across the Arkansas River from Kinsley. They did not interact much with one another but by chance constituted 20 percent of the immigrants to sparsely populated Wayne Township (see Map 4.19).[142]

Immigrants established small but self-aware Yankee communities at Hope in Dickinson County, at Bennington in Ottawa County, and at Cawker City in Mitchell County. Michigan people founded both Hope and Bennington in 1872. The Ottawa County group of about one hundred actually located just north of Bennington, while the sixty or so migrants to Dickinson County platted a small town of their own, named after their former residence near Saginaw Bay.[143] Both areas are easily visible as cultural islands on Map 4.18. Cawker City was an urban venture organized by John Huckle of Pennsylvania and E. H. Cawker of Milwaukee, Wisconsin. Although it was not a railroad town when they platted it in 1871, both men knew that their location at the junction of the North and South forks of the Solomon River had potential. They named the principal north-south street Pennsylvania and the east-west one Wisconsin and returned to their respective states to recruit colonists. Twenty-nine Wisconsin natives were in residence in 1885, helping to boost the Yankee total to 27 percent of the immigrant population.[144]

THE NORTH-MIDLAND MAINSTREAM

Immigrants from the North-Midland states form the last of the major culture groups that occupied the central Kansas frontier. To cast them as just another group, however, is to misrepresent their role in the creation of the local society. Not only were they among the earliest arrivals in virtually all the counties in the region, but they also came in numbers that dwarfed those from other places. As was the case in southeastern Kansas, their degree of dominance is difficult to overstate. More people came to the central plains from Illinois, a single North-Midland state, than from the entirety of Europe or from all the Upper Southern or Yankee states (see Table 4.1). Whereas it was rare for a local township to record 40 percent of its immigrant population born in any of the other culture regions, that same 40 percent figure is appropriate only as a starting point for mapping the North-Midland populace. Five cities in the region reported in 1885 that over 70 percent of their residents were North Midlanders: Jewell City, Phillipsburg, Smith Center, Stafford, and Walton; the same was true for an amazing 103 townships (see Map 4.20).

The North-Midland presence in central Kansas was so ubiquitous that it rarely caused comment. Similarly, the easiest (though not the most flattering) way to describe their pattern of occupa-

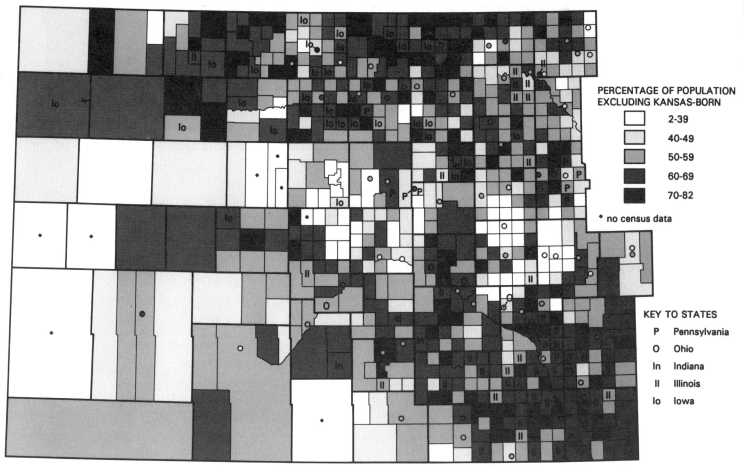

PERCENTAGE OF POPULATION EXCLUDING KANSAS-BORN

- 2-39
- 40-49
- 50-59
- 60-69
- 70-82

* no census data

KEY TO STATES

P Pennsylvania
O Ohio
In Indiana
ll Illinois
lo Iowa

MAP 4.20
Natives of North-Midland states, 1885 (central and western Kansas). Data from Kansas state census. Letter symbols mark cities and townships in which people from a particular North-Midland state constitute 25 percent or more of the immigrant population. For states included in the North-Midland area, see Table 4.1.

tion is as a matrix, the enveloping element in which the other culture groups have been placed. Nearly the only locations with North-Midland percentages under 50 are in the South-Midland strongholds of Barber, Harper, and Graham counties and in the core areas of the various European groups, most obviously the belt of counties from Ellis and Rush eastward to Dickinson and Marion. The difficulty of coming to grips with North-Midland settlers is heightened by their overall moderate behavior. Many of them came in colonies, though not so frequently as did Yankee or European immigrants. Many played important roles as urban entrepreneurs and pioneer stockmen, but not so visibly as did, respectively, Yankees and Upper Southerners.

One way to get beyond the generalization of moderation is to break the North-Midland group into component states. This approach is logical not only because of the sheer numbers involved but also because the immigrants from different sections of the region created distinctive geographies within Kansas. Consider the locations of the state symbols on Map 4.20. Counties with a heavy concentration of Iowans lie north of the Kansas Pacific corridor, Pennsylvanians are clustered within the Kansas Pacific grant, and Illinois and Indiana settlers predominate in south-central Kansas. Such patterns strongly suggest differing motivations within the North-Midland community.

THE PENNSYLVANIANS

Even though twelve hundred miles separate Philadelphia and Salina, nearly thirty-one thousand natives of Pennsylvania lived in central Kansas in 1885. This number so far exceeds predictions based on population and distance that it suggests recruiters were heavily involved in this migration (see Graph 1.3), an assumption largely confirmed by the choice of locations within Kansas. Although Pennsylvanians pioneered in every county of the region, most chose to settle in the vicinity of the Kansas Pacific Railroad (see Map 4.21).

The pattern on the map seems at first to match a stereotype for Yankee settlement: moneyed Easterners who saw the railroad belt as an opportunity to speculate in town development. Certainly some Pennsylvanians fit this mold, but a closer look at map details suggests that most of these immigrants had different goals. Throughout Dickinson, Saline, Ellsworth, and Russell counties (the core of their settlement), they were more apt to live in the country than in cities. The Pennsylvanians in central Kansas, it turns out, are largely of German extraction, descendants of the Lutheran, Brethren, Mennonite, and other groups who came to farm in William Penn's colony in the eighteenth century.[145]

Agents of the Kansas Pacific seem to have decided early on that Pennsylvania Germans were ideal colonists since, like Germans in general, they had reputations as successful farmers. They were experiencing some crowding in Pennsylvania and, as a group, had money enough to purchase the choicest, most expensive tracts within the land grant. Railroad officials tested the recruiting waters first in 1870 with a colony established by Lewis Donmeyer of Johnstown, Pennsylvania, in Saline County, just northeast of Salina. By 1875 a railroad brochure reported that 31,000 acres had been opened for settlement there and a new town called New Cambria begun (named after Donmeyer's home county).[146]

Nearly simultaneously with the Donmeyer effort, a group of German Baptist Brethren (Dunkards) from Cumberland County under the leadership of Samuel Coover decided it was in their financial interest to move to Kansas. Their plan was to exchange expensive Pennsylvania farmland (over a hundred dollars per acre) for what they judged to be equally fertile and accessible, but much less costly, tracts in Kansas (about seven dollars per acre). The difference in price would go toward buying additional property for growing families. Both the Pennsylvania and the Kansas Pacific Railroads cooperated in the move, which was widely reported in the press. About 150 people came in the main immigration of 1872, three coaches plus two baggage cars. They passed over the rough

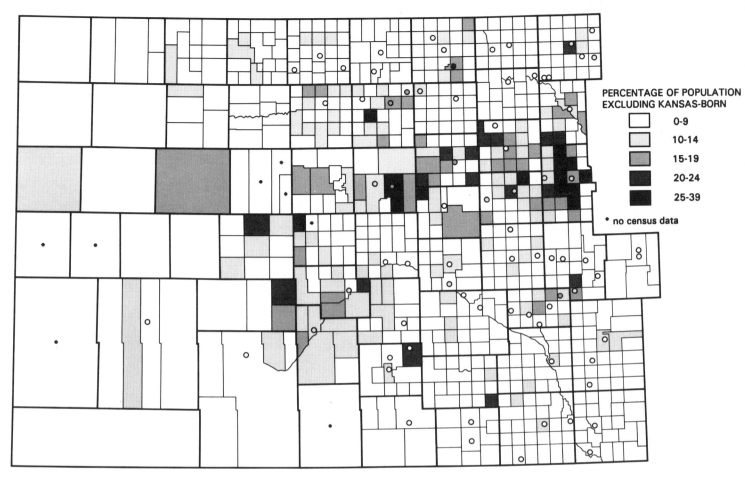

PERCENTAGE OF POPULATION
EXCLUDING KANSAS-BORN

0-9
10-14
15-19
20-24
25-39

* no census data

MAP 4.21
Natives of Pennsylvania, 1885 (central and western Kansas). Data from Kansas state census.

Smoky Hills section of Ellsworth County and settled on the flatlands near the Wilson and Dorrance sidings. A smaller, related group from Adams County pushed on to the next railroad depot at Bunker Hill, and in 1873 yet another small group bought land near Hays.[147]

The promising partnership between Kansas Pacific officials and Pennsylvania-German settlers halted during the economically troubled years of 1873 and 1874, but it revived in 1876, at least partly because of an impressive agricultural exhibit mounted by the state of Kansas at the Centennial Exposition in Philadelphia. By 1878 and 1879 "carloads, almost trainloads" of Germanic peoples were being assembled by railroad agents and church leaders from all over the Susquehanna valley, especially from Cumberland, Dauphin, and York counties. Several thousand came in all, most as members of religious-based colonies from particular townships.[148]

The geography of the migrants of 1878 and 1879 took three main forms. Many of them used the 1872 colony at Wilson for a base and stayed temporarily in a frame building erected there by the railroad while they examined properties for sale. This movement eventually created an important Pennsylvania presence around Sylvan Grove in southwestern Lincoln County, in most of Russell County, and near Walker in eastern Ellis County.[149] Other migrants decided to push another ninety miles or so west, beyond the recent Volga-German settlements, to the raw frontier. Four of these groups stayed within the railroad grant lands: twenty-two Westmoreland Countians and about the same number of Bucks Countians (the Bristol colony) at separate sites south of Buffalo Park (now Park) in Gove County, members of the scandal-ridden Southwestern Agricultural and Migration Company of York in northwestern Rush County, and a small party north of Ellis.[150] Several other entrepreneurs opted for the government land that lay between the two big railroad grants (see Map 3.7), including a group of former steelworkers from Pittsburgh in Ness County and a New York–Pennsylvania combine who were the first to boom Hodgeman County.[151] These frontier groups suffered greatly in the series of drought years that began with their initial settlement year of 1878, and their numbers were much decreased by the time of the 1885 census.

The third segment of the big Pennsylvania immigration of 1878–1879 was one of the best organized and most successful of all the colonies in the state. Several hundred members each from the German Baptist Brethren and the related Brethren in Christ (River Brethren) churches decided to forego western Kansas in favor of the relatively expensive but more humid central section of the state. They selected Dickinson County, where a few of the migrants of 1872 had located, and purchased several thousand acres of privately owned and railroad land north and south of the Kansas Pacific tracks. The Brethren presence actually was even more impressive in the northern section of the county than is shown on Map 4.21; Dunkards from Ohio (the Buckeye colony) joined the larger Pennsylvania contingent there. Ultimately, 2,869 Pennsylvanians called Dickinson County home in 1885.[152]

The congregations of River Brethren in Dickinson County were large enough by 1878 that the general conference of their church decided to dispatch a bishop to Kansas: Jesse Engle of Cumberland County. This in turn led to even more migrants in 1879, a total for the two years of perhaps five hundred, one-third of the entire denominational membership. As they had done at Wilson, Kansas Pacific officials erected a building at Abilene to provide temporary housing. The River Brethren reportedly brought between $300,000 and $500,000 with them to Kansas and immediately established a reputation as a distinctive society of excellent farmers. One of their first ministers was Jacob Eisenhower, grandfather of the thirty-fourth president.[153]

Not all Pennsylvanians in Kansas came to the Kansas Pacific zone. Rival Santa Fe agents advertised among the Mennonites and placed about a hundred settlers near Peabody in Marion County and near Hesston in Harvey County between 1872 and 1875. The appropriately named Pennsylvania Mennonite Church at Hesston is one of their legacies, Hesston College another.[154] Other people formed settlements independent of the railroads. One was headed by John Huckle of Towanda, a cofounder of Cawker City in Mitchell County in 1871; another, more informal assemblage was important in the early history of Jewell City (Jewell County).[155] The biggest and most successful of these enterprises was the Pennsylvania colony of Col. William Bear, who established the city of Osborne. The original group of thirty-five people from Lancaster and Berks counties came by rail to the Union Pacific terminus at Waterville in 1871 and considered several frontier sites before deciding on the Solomon valley. They named their township Penn, laid out their town, and then worked cooperatively to recruit other settlers and to secure the county seat. An unexpected bonus from their efforts was the creation of a Pennsylvania-dominated rural township (Kill Creek) near their urban one. A promotion similar to Osborne, though it occurred later, helped to produce the city of Norwich in southeastern Kingman County.[156]

IOWANS AND NEBRASKANS

Iowans came to central Kansas in numbers comparable to those of Pennsylvanians and shared with those immigrants a distinctive linear pattern of settlement. Whereas the Pennsylvania correlation was with railroad land, though, the Iowans occupied the broad swath of public domain between the Kansas Pacific grant and the Nebraska border (see Map 4.22). The Hawkeyes, one could speculate, came in search of cheap land.

Iowa was itself a recent pioneer area. Initial settlement had taken place during the 1840s and 1850s, but the state still had some public land available for entry after the Civil War. When these facts are considered in the light of earlier American experience, no sizeable number of Iowans could have been expected to move out of the state before about 1885.[157] It is surprising, then, to find nearly forty thousand of them living in central Kansas by that date (see Table 4.1).

The patterns on Map 4.22 suggest that the movement into Kansas became substantial as early as 1870. The lower Republican valley and other places settled in the late 1860s have few Hawkeyes, but Jewell and Mitchell counties, which boomed in 1870, have many. Historians suggest that economic distress underlay most of these moves, a distress that paradoxically had its roots in Western frontier development. As new agricultural lands opened rapidly in the 1850s, the volume of farm products grew more quickly than the market could handle without falling prices. The problem became apparent during the Civil War years and continued throughout the 1870s and beyond. Underfinanced farmers were affected most by the price squeeze, of course, and these people were concentrated on recent frontiers such as Iowa. Many families saw their best hope for survival in selling their partially developed lands for, say, ten dollars per acre, and starting over with a free government homestead. Nebraska attracted most of the Iowa migrants, but northern Kansas was close enough to be appealing as well.[158]

Whether because of poverty, proximity, or perceived cultural similarity, Iowans who came to

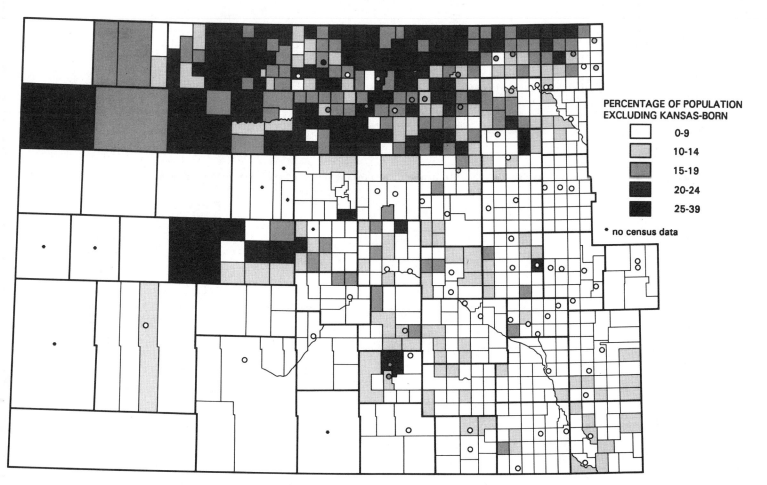

MAP 4.22
*Natives of Iowa, 1885
(central and western
Kansas). Data from
Kansas state census.*

PERCENTAGE OF POPULATION
EXCLUDING KANSAS-BORN

- 0-9
- 10-14
- 15-19
- 20-24
- 25-39

* no census data

Kansas rarely traveled together as large, formal colonies. For the northern counties, the standard sources list only one small group in Mitchell County and another in Graham. Most people apparently traveled overland in small family units, early migrants regularly crossing the Missouri River at Nebraska City and entering Kansas by way of Fairbury, Nebraska. Later, the homes of Iowans living in Jewell and Mitchell counties became halfway houses for people bound for Sheridan County or some other western locale.[159]

Once in Kansas, Iowans seemed to find one another and often settled together. Iowa townships exist in Rooks and Sherman counties, and in Osborne one is called Hawkeye. Early Ness County featured the communities of Clarinda, Sidney, and Iowa in a single township, and both Smith and Washington counties have Iowa Creeks. The most complete case study is for the community of Hawkeye in southwestern Decatur County. Eighteen men, most unknown to one another, left different parts of Iowa in 1879; they met at the federal land office in Kirwin and ended up filing

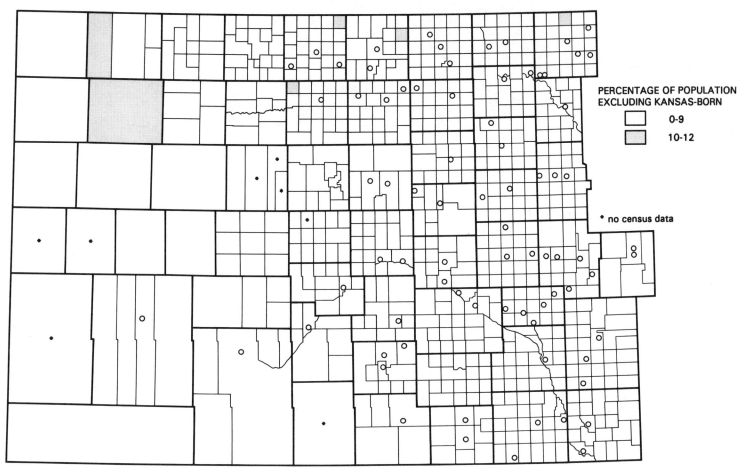

PERCENTAGE OF POPULATION
EXCLUDING KANSAS-BORN

☐ 0-9
▨ 10-12

* no census data

MAP 4.23
*Natives of Nebraska, 1885
(central and western
Kansas). Data from
Kansas state census.*

claims within an area twelve miles square. When their wives and children arrived later that year, a
post office, a cemetery, and a store were built, and the obvious community name selected.[160]

Iowa people systematically worked their way across the northern Kansas frontier throughout
the 1870s, joined eventually by a few Nebraskans (see Map 4.23). About 1877 some of them also
decided to try their chances a little farther south, on the next big section of public land in Ness
and Lane counties, between the two railroad grants (see Map 3.7). By 1877, too, a few Iowans even
had money enough to indulge in modest urban speculation. The most impressive of these efforts,
somewhat unexpectedly, occurred in extreme southern Kansas, creating two interrelated islands of
Iowa culture.

Development prospects in and near the Osage Reserve looked intriguing enough to a group of
investors in Bloomfield, Iowa, that they sent several men to investigate early in 1877. The report
came back positive about a site in Pratt County and another in Harper County. The Pratt location,
on the line between the reserve and the public domain in the northern part of the county, attracted

over a hundred families from the Bloomfield area. Led by a Presbyterian minister, Andrew Axline, they created Iuka, "an Iowa town out and out, only located in Kansas." By 1885 over five hundred Iowans lived in Pratt County, but by then their focus was somewhat diffuse. Many had abandoned Iuka to help found an even newer place, Pratt Center (now Pratt), which had better prospects for railroads and politics. The recommendation for Harper County attracted fewer Iowans, possibly because of the higher land costs on the reserve. J. B. Glenn led twelve families to the site and laid out the city of Harper. Later that year, the Reverend Mr. Axline was brought in to preach the first sermon in town, and relations between the two settlements remained close for several years. Harper could count 216 Iowans as residents in 1885, but with the cattle trade and other business successes, the town had grown so rapidly that by then it had lost much of its early cultural distinctiveness (see Table 4.2).[161]

THE ILLINI

So great was the influx of Illinois people into central Kansas that easy generalization about them is impossible. Individual goals and prospects varied tremendously, and immigrants had their choice of several transportation paths and methods. To complicate matters further, Illinois itself was far from a homogeneous society.[162] The immigrants in Sheridan County who named their new town Chicago probably did not have that much in common with those in Pratt County who founded the village of Cairo. Still, when one steps back and assesses the overall geography of the Illinois settlers, a distinctive pattern emerges (see Map 4.24). Their concentration in the south-central counties clearly sets them apart from the Pennsylvanians and the Iowans.

Several facets of the distribution begin to make sense when one recalls the earlier Illinois residences of several of the major European and Canadian groups to settle in Kansas. Some of the early Mennonites came from Illinois, including those immediately south of Sterling in Reno County and those astraddle the Harvey-McPherson border near Moundridge.[163] The high percentage of Illini in Green Garden Township in southern Ellsworth County is from the German Baptist colony that set out from Will County, near Chicago. Most evident is the practice of French Canadians to live for a while near Kankakee, Illinois, before coming to Kansas; their settlement in Cloud County shows up on the maps as an Illinois phenomenon as much as it does a Canadian one.

Like the Iowans, some Illinois migrants moved to the Kansas frontier by wagon. Most such treks were in the 1860s, before the major railroad promotions, and most settlers went to the closer lands in southeastern Kansas rather than to the central plains. Some families, though, decided to ascend the Kaw. A caravan of fifteen wagons came to the lower Solomon valley in 1866, where they joined with some Ohio people to create the community of Niles in southeastern Ottawa County. By 1885 the Illinois contingent there, in aptly named Lincoln Township, had grown to 109. A second sizeable colony followed the Republican River to the frontier in 1879 and founded Jewell

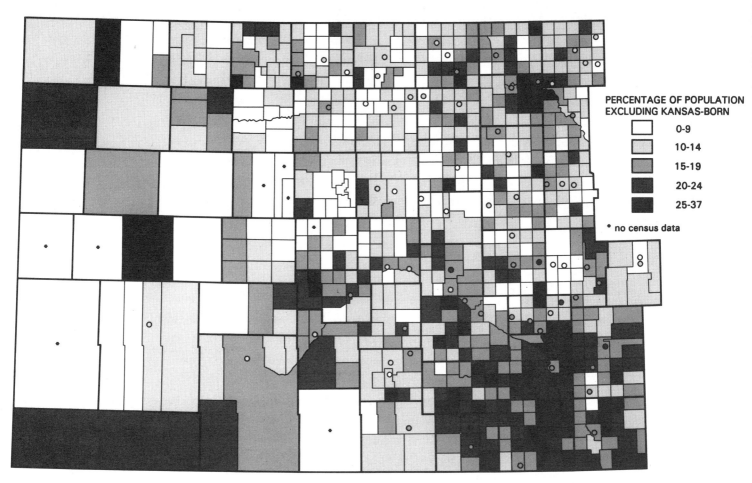

PERCENTAGE OF POPULATION
EXCLUDING KANSAS-BORN

☐	0-9
	10-14
	15-19
	20-24
	25-37

* no census data

MAP 4.24
*Natives of Illinois, 1885
(central and western
Kansas). Data from
Kansas state census.*

City (Jewell County). Eleven families came originally, but their letters soon attracted about two hundred neighbors from home; about half settled in town, half on nearby farmsteads.[164]

Railroads replaced wagons for most of the Illinois migrants by about 1870, but usage varied tremendously from route to route. The Union Pacific, Central Branch, brought many of the Illinois French to Cloud County (or at least as far as Waterville), but no other large, organized groups apparently came this way. Movements on the Kansas Pacific were only a little more spirited; company officials concentrated promotional activity in Pennsylvania and England, but five Illinois colonies did emanate from their Chicago office. Three groups came in 1870–1871. The Reverend W. B. Christopher and his congregation of fifty created the Illinois Prohibition Colony and founded the town of Cheever in northern Dickinson County; some seventy-five Henry Countians located adjacent to the large Swedish group near Falun in Saline County; and two hundred Chicagoans organized a veterans' colony twenty miles north of Ellsworth in southern Lincoln County. None of these sites served as foci for further immigration, and no additional colonization from Illinois took place on the grant until 1878. In that year, however, not only did a sizeable German Baptist group come to southern Ellsworth County, but a mammoth 340,000-acre scheme also arose in Trego County. James F. Keeney, a Chicago real estate developer, and his partner, Albert Warren, combined their skills to create what one scholar has called "the most unequivocal success" of all the colonies in central Kansas. Although the details are not on Map 4.24 because of missing census data, their namesake town of Wakeeney grew from zero to thirty-five hundred in its first year, with Illini prominent among the residents. Drought then took its toll, and Wakeeney was down to 423 people by 1885.[165]

Although it would be patently wrong to call the Illinois presence in and north of the Kansas Pacific corridor insignificant, the numbers of settlers there do pale when compared with those on the lands of the Santa Fe and of the old Osage Reserve. Such a large concentration in south-central Kansas seems puzzling at first, until one remembers the power of railroad advertising. The huge extent by which the number of Illinois immigrants exceeded expectations based on population and distance (see Graph 1.3) and the south-central location both point to a singular causal force: the Santa Fe Railroad.

Illinois farmers in the 1870s were caught in the same price squeeze as Iowans. Whereas Iowa people had a new frontier open to them in nearby Nebraska and northern Kansas, however, the distances were much greater for Illini. Santa Fe officials realized this factor when they began to advertise in earnest after the grasshopper year of 1874. Over half of their sixty land agencies outside Kansas were in either Illinois or Iowa by 1875, and a similar concentration was evident in the home-towns of newspaper editors who came that year on a heavily promoted tour of Santa Fe lands (see Map 4.3). The company sharpened its advertising focus even more over the next several years. In 1876 a railroad excursion party of over two hundred people came principally from Illinois, and in 1877 a trip was arranged exclusively for Illinois editors. The editorial trips, of course, were financed partly to attract those people too poor to be able to explore Kansas on their own.[166]

The Illini who responded en masse to the Santa Fe siren beginning in the summer of 1875 found that most of the company lands in Chase, Marion, McPherson, and northern Harvey counties had already been sold. They were directed farther west and south to one of three locations. Acreage still existed near the main track in Reno and Rice counties, sandwiched between the Mennonite colonies to the east and Barton County's Germania to the west. The alternative was to follow one of the company's two spur lines. The first of these extended south from Florence, in Marion County, to El Dorado, the seat of Butler County; the second ran south from Newton to the raw but rapidly growing city of Wichita (see Map 4.1).

The new settlers apparently chose each of the three alternatives in about equal numbers. Early arrivals homesteaded the government tracts within the railroad grant rather than pay the company five or six dollars per acre; later comers typically ventured a little farther south to buy Osage Reserve land in southern Butler and Sedgwick counties for a dollar and twenty-five cents. Although not free, these Osage holdings were still inexpensive when compared with Illinois prices. When this low cost of land was coupled with the deep discounts on transportation rates provided by the Santa Fe, settlement in Butler or Sedgwick county made a great deal of sense.[167]

The surge of Illini and other settlers along the two railroad spurs initiated a series of private developments in townsites and railroads. Most of these were regionally based and modest in scope, such as the founding of Kingman by people from Hutchinson and of Anthony by a group from Wichita. The cumulative effect was great, however, and by 1884 railroads extended outward from El Dorado and Wichita in a web that encompassed Cowley, Sumner, Harper, and Kingman counties. This network coincided neatly with the zone of dense Illini settlement. Somewhat surprisingly, I can find only two instances of formal Illinois colonies in the entire region: a small group from Shelby County at Pawnee Rock (Barton County) and one from Woodford County southeast of Anthony (Harper County). Illinois people apparently regarded the Santa Fe agents as adequate facilitators for their migration plans.[168]

INDIANANS AND OHIOANS

Of the North-Midland peoples, Pennsylvanians, Iowans, and Illini settled in the most distinctive spatial patterns. The clusterings of migrants from Indiana and Ohio, in contrast, may be interpreted as combinations or hybrids of the ones already seen. This observation should come as no surprise since these two states are intermediate among the other three not only in location but also in age and accumulated wealth. The geography of Hoosiers in 1885 Kansas most resembles that of the Illini, but Ohioans appear to share important elements from all the patterns previously discussed (see Maps 4.25, 4.26).

The similarity between the Illinois and the Indiana migrations echoes other parallels in the early history of the two states. Illinois entered the union in 1818, only two years after Indiana, and migrants to both places had come from the same source areas.[169] Moreover, since both states were largely rural in 1870 and faced similar agricultural problems, Santa Fe officials saw them as nearly comparable recruiting areas. Illinois received more attention and produced more total immigrants only because it had a larger population; on a per capita basis Indianans came to Kansas at a nearly equal rate (see Graph 1.3). Hoosier Township in Kingman County symbolically marks the center of their settlement pattern.

The rural background of Indianans, as compared with most other North Midlanders, is apparent when one looks at the minor role of these peoples in the emerging cities of Kansas. Of the twenty-six largest towns in the region, Hoosiers were present in percentages notably higher than

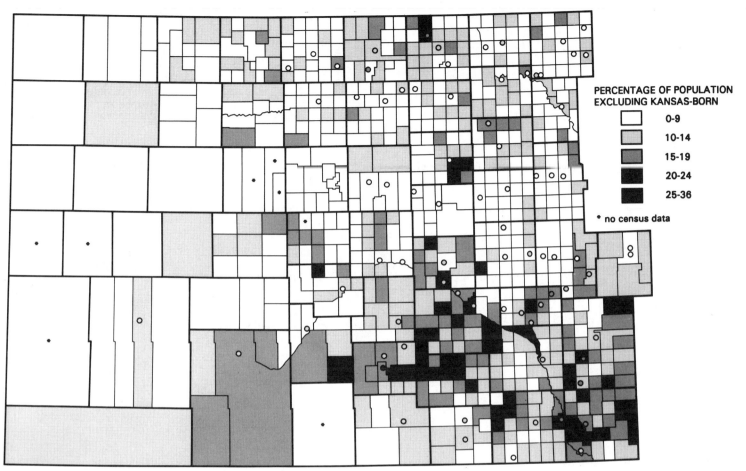

PERCENTAGE OF POPULATION
EXCLUDING KANSAS-BORN

	0-9
	10-14
	15-19
	20-24
	25-36

* no census data

their overall figure in only three: Harper, Wichita, and Winfield (see Table 4.2), compared with eight cities for Ohioans, seven for Pennsylvanians, four for Illini, and one for Iowans. In contrast, Iowans were underrepresented in sixteen cities, Hoosiers in ten, Pennsylvanians in five, Illini in four, and Ohioans in only one. In their efforts to seek out and settle on inexpensive farmland, Hoosiers had more in common with Iowans than with their Illinois or Ohio neighbors.

I can find documentary evidence for six formal colonies from Indiana, and map evidence clearly points to the existence of a seventh. The six were all religiously based: a Dunkard group in northern Jewell County, a United Brethren congregation in northern Smith County, and four Quaker settlements. All but one began in the early 1870s, and none was inspired by railroad agents. The Dunkards, an extension from a community at Guide Rock, Nebraska, just across the border, came to the Burr Oak area in 1870; they numbered about two hundred in 1885, about twice the size of the United Brethren group one county to the west.[170]

MAP 4.25
Natives of Indiana, 1885 (central and western Kansas). Data from Kansas state census.

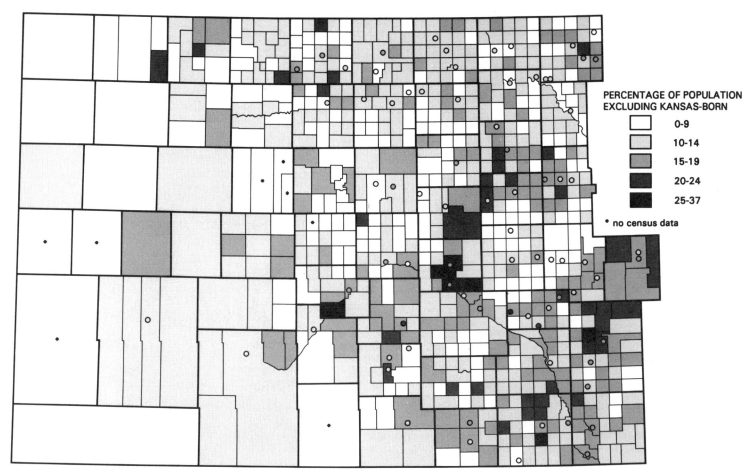

PERCENTAGE OF POPULATION
EXCLUDING KANSAS-BORN

0-9
10-14
15-19
20-24
25-37

• no census data

MAP 4.26
*Natives of Ohio, 1885
(central and western
Kansas). Data from
Kansas state census.*

Most of the Quaker colonists emigrated from Richmond, a major denominational center and home of Earlham College. Richmond people had settled at two sites in eastern Kansas during the territorial period, and favorable reports attracted others to the state as land prices rose in Indiana. A group of two hundred came to North Branch, just north of the Dunkards in Jewell County. Three hundred people founded the Rose Hill community in southwestern Butler County, and 250 others homesteaded near Sterling, in Rice County. The Sterling group came before the Santa Fe tracks had been laid and were well positioned for growth. Subsumption within a larger immigration from adjacent areas of southwestern Ohio (as will be discussed below) cost them much of their identity, however. The seventh and most obvious concentration of Hoosiers is in three townships of Lincoln County (see Map 4.25). These 355 people named a township after their home state and constituted nearly one-third of the local immigrant population, but local historians have ignored their distinctiveness.[171]

The Ohioans who came to Kansas fitted the definition of typical migrants better than did people from any other state. Ohio had enough poor farmers to attract the same advertising that Santa Fe agents were using in Illinois and Indiana; it also contained a large cadre of well-capitalized farmers who, if they chose to migrate, could do so with an ease approaching that of the Pennsylvanians. Ohio was home to large colonies of German Americans as well, and to several major cities, each with full quotas of rich speculators and unemployed laborers. It is easy to imagine Buckeyes as part of almost every opportunity available in frontier Kansas, and the diversity of their locations (see Map 4.26) suggests that this promise was fulfilled.

Three of the eleven major Ohio colonies were established by German Americans in a manner similar to that of their Pennsylvania kinsmen. All were in the Kansas Pacific grant. The oldest and largest of these was by a 200-member Dunkard group who named their Dickinson County township Buckeye in 1870. The next year a Lutheran colony from Berea, led by J. B. Corbett, founded Bunker Hill in Russell County. Finally, in 1876, four Robbens brothers and several other families located south of Walker in Ellis County.[172]

Three other Ohio colonies had their origin in the old Western Reserve of northeastern Ohio. Since the reserve was an area of New England settlement, these communities were all decidedly Yankee in tone. Although they were well organized, none had the success envisioned by their founders. The oldest and most rural of the three was promoted just west of Salina by D. E. Fuller and T. J. Thorpe in 1871. Despite having two hundred members, this group does not show up well on Map 4.26, even in their Ohio Township, because other settlers platted the local town of Bavaria.[173] The second Yankee settlement, Garfield (Pawnee County), was slightly more urban. Leaders for this Volunteer Free Homestead Colony scouted two states in 1873 before selecting a site on the main line of the Santa Fe. Thirty people came originally, mostly from Geneva, and they named their town for their local congressman (and future U.S. president), James A. Garfield; in return, Garfield sent a bell for their Congregational church.[174] By far the most ambitious and speculative of the Ohio groups was the Ashtabula colony in McPherson County. In 1871 Dr. E. L. King carefully selected a central location with an eye to securing the county seat. No sooner had the first forty people arrived and platted King City, however, than they learned that the county's southern tier of townships had been severed to help create a new county (Harvey) focused on the Santa Fe town of Newton. King and his followers realized that they could not fight the power of the railroad, and most of them moved north a few miles to the new center of the county, a place called McPherson.[175]

People from the North-Midland mainstream, neither Dunkards nor transplanted Yankees, made up the bulk of the 51,957 Ohioans who came to Kansas. These migrants tended not to create formal colonies, but, like the Iowans, they often ended up in clusters large enough to generate place-names. Four counties in central Kansas have Ohio townships (Ness, Saline, Sedgwick, and opposite

MAP 4.27
*Generalized nativity
regions, 1885 (central and
western Kansas). Data
from Kansas state census.
Areas left blank are
generally those in which
people from North-
Midland states form the
dominant immigrant
group.*

Stafford), and three others have ones named Buckeye (Dickinson, Ellis, Ottawa). Darkly shaded townships on Map 4.26 bear (or once bore) such transferred city names as Oberlin (Decatur County), Chillicothe (Phillips County), Delphos (Ottawa County), Marietta (Reno and Saline counties), Canton (McPherson County), Toledo (Chase County), Danville (Harper County), and Akron (Cowley County).

The most prominent Ohio grouping is in Rice County; it began in 1871, before the arrival of the Santa Fe Railroad, with a Cincinnati-based group called the Union Emigration Society. The initial people came forty miles overland from Ellsworth, on the Kansas Pacific, and founded the community of New Cincinnati just southeast of present-day Lyons. As was the case at King City, this community originally was a central location in the county before boundaries were switched so as to position Hutchinson better within adjacent Reno County. The Ohioans dispersed after this change, some going north to help found Lyons, and some going south to join the Hoosier settlement on the Arkansas River at Sterling.[176] Over fifteen hundred Ohioans lived in Rice County in 1885, 17 percent of the immigrant population. Their presence must have frustrated C. B. Schmidt a little, for they interrupted his otherwise continuous string of German colonies along the Santa Fe tracks.

CULTURE REGIONS

Contemporary accounts and later histories of the central Kansas frontier emphasize its rapid settlement and its dominance by poor Union veterans. Most of the accounts also stress that the immigrants came from many places. In a typical chronicle, Alfred Bradshaw wrote that migrants to southwestern Reno County "came from as far north as Wisconsin, as far east as Pennsylvania, and from the nearer states like Missouri, Iowa, Illinois, Indiana, and Ohio. There were a few families of Germans just over from the old country."[177]

Although Bradshaw's statement reflects the experience of many places in the state, the collective force of his and many similar claims has overemphasized the heterogeneity of individual townships and counties. Immigrants from a given place tended to locate near one another when they created their new homes, and the generalized nativity patterns in central Kansas for 1885 were every bit as lumpy as those for earlier frontiers in the northeastern and southeastern sections of the state (cf. Maps 2.21, 3.16, 4.27). Europeans and Upper Southerners held dominant or near-dominant positions over considerable territory; Yankees, Pennsylvania Germans, and even Lower Southerners also had their concentrations. As with the earlier summaries, readers should note that most North-Midland peoples are not charted directly on Map 4.27. Their dominance is clearly implied over all the unshaded areas, however, including the entirety of Chase, Jewell, Kingman, Ottawa, Pawnee, Sedgwick, and Smith counties plus others on the far-western frontier. North Midlanders also

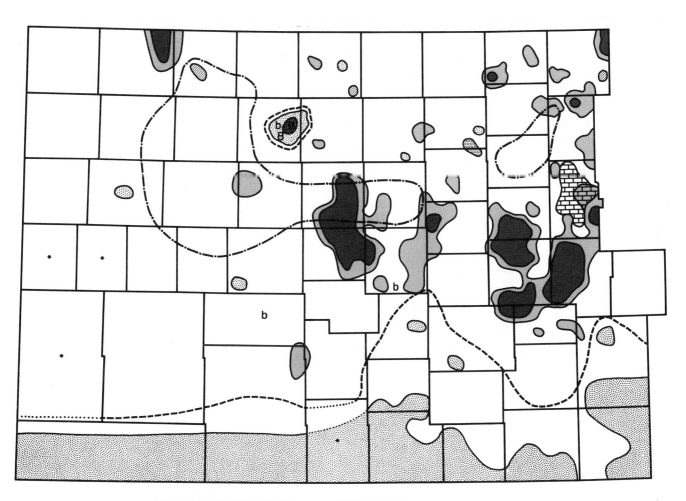

PERCENTAGE OF POPULATION
EXCLUDING KANSAS-BORN

European, 30-49

European, >50

Pennsylvania-born
Germans, 30-49

Northern, 30-49

South Midland, 30-49

South Midland, >50

South Midland plus
Lower Southern, 30-49

KEY TO LINES

--- ratio of Northerners to
South Midlanders and Lower
Southerners is 0.5 to 1

—.— ratio of Northerners to
South Midlanders and Lower
Southerners is 1.5 to 1

KEY TO LETTERS

b   blacks, 15-29% of total population

B   blacks, 30-91% of total population

*   no census data

assumed the same intriguing buffer role in central Kansas that they played in the eastern part of the state: separating peoples with divergent cultural values.

The influence of differing land policies between the railroad belt and its two flanking zones was most pronounced for Upper Southerners. A line marking the ratio of two Southern immigrants for every person from a Northern culture state closely approximates the southern limit of the Santa Fe land grant. South of that line, where Yankees perceived few major opportunities for city growth, Southerners saw a good place to pursue the cattle trade and to avoid taunts by virulent Unionists. Wichita and surrounding Sedgwick County, however, stood as a major exception to this generalization. Early trading opportunities at the junction of the Arkansas and Little Arkansas rivers attracted a group of unusually gifted boosters to this area. Against steep odds, they somehow financed an extension of the railroad from Newton and by 1885 had created a city of sixteen thousand, which was three times the size of either Newton or Hutchinson, its seemingly better-located rivals. More Southerners actually lived in Sedgwick than in neighboring Butler or Reno counties, but in Wichita, Yankees nearly matched their numbers.[178]

The route of the Santa Fe tracks was clearly marked in Marion and Harvey counties by two dense concentrations of Mennonite settlement. Beyond a gap in Rice and Reno counties, where North-Midland people dominated, the linearity continued with the Germania of Barton County and the small, pioneer colonies in Ford County. The Kansas Pacific corridor also could be identified by a string of European communities, especially if one were to count the concentration of Pennsylvania Germans in Dickinson County as part of the pattern. An eastern assemblage of the English at Wakefield, the Dunkards and River Brethren in Dickinson County, and the Swedes around Lindsborg was separated from a western grouping of Bohemians near Wilson and Volga Germans in Ellis and Rush counties by a sizeable break in Ellsworth County. This opening is the heart of the Smoky Hills, a rough sandstone area that the European groups passed over in favor of arable lands. The smaller gap between the Wilson and the Volga Germans was occupied principally by the Wisconsin colonists at Russell and by several Pennsylvania-German groups.

A definite Yankee flavor also was present in the Kansas Pacific corridor. Yankees outnumbered Southerners by a ratio of three to two from Russell County westward through Gove County and then northward into the Sheridan County frontier. Their correlation with urban development was highest in this area as well, on the edge of the agricultural frontier where urban people came close to outnumbering rural ones. Yankees were not able to assert as much dominance over Southern settlers in the more eastern cities along the Kansas Pacific line, probably because of the early influence of the cattle trade in Abilene and Ellsworth.

North of the Kansas Pacific, the North-Midland hegemony was interrupted only sporadically. Yankees were important in a few places thought to be favorable for urban growth, and clusters of Bohemians, Scandinavians, French Canadians, and even Georgians dominated certain easterly locations that had been settled before Iowans began to arrive en masse. Clearly the most distinctive grouping, though, was the black colony at Nicodemus, defined by Kentucky heritage as well as by race.

It is tempting to view the Kansas settlement frontier as complete by 1885 and to turn directly to speculation on the social ramifications of, say, the Nicodemus island in its North-Midland sea or on the continuous presence of South-Midland culture across the whole of southern Kansas. Such musing would be premature for extreme western Kansas, however. That region still had few people in 1885, and settlers there faced severe stress because drought had been a nearly constant presence since 1879. It seems wise to resurvey population origins on this final frontier after it was more fully occupied.

5

The West, 1905 and 1925

Five years of drought between 1879 and 1883 ended the period of tremendous population growth and frontier expansion that had characterized Kansas since the end of the Civil War. People in the newly occupied western section of the state felt the stress of these years particularly hard. Though abandonments were common and many individual lives were devastated, such tragedies caused the nation to lose its appetite for drylands speculation only temporarily. The rains returned in 1884, and with them came railroad companies and land seekers, all convinced that the drought had been an aberration. Growth rates over the next three years, in fact, matched those of the earlier boom. Railroad crews laid 176 miles of new track during the year that ended in June 1885, 607 more in the following season, and an amazing 1,998 during the year of 1886–1887. Three new transregional lines operated on the Kansas High Plains by 1888. Concurrent with the railroad construction, legislators organized twenty-five new counties over the same period, and people moved in by the thousands. Sherman County, in the north, grew from a few scattered residents in 1885 to 5,115 in 1888; Seward, in the south, from zero to 2,250.[1]

Frank Sullivan, an early settler, wrote that Meade County history "reads almost like a fairy tale." His words could have applied to the whole of western Kansas; nearly every piece of railroad and government land had been claimed by the end of 1887, and the country quickly took on "the appearance of an old-established community."[2] An observer in 1888 might easily have reasoned that the frontier period of the state was over. Life in western Kansas has never been simple, though. Five years later the region was largely abandoned.

The collapse of the boom of 1885–1887 is usually blamed on drought although falling agricultural prices and a gradual loss of confidence by creditors also played important roles. Western counties typically lost about two thousand people apiece in 1888, a severe but not fatal blow. When the searing conditions repeated themselves over the next several years, however, even determined settlers decided to leave. Few of them had much in the way of capital reserves, and aid from the outside was effectively ended by a national business depression in 1893.[3] The opening that year of the Cherokee Outlet in the new Oklahoma Territory was a godsend for many: a place to escape from big mortgages and bad memories. Every county history in the region makes note of this melancholy exodus.

The drought that began in 1888 lasted (with the exception of two years) until 1901, a climatic tribulation that has yet to be equaled. Its human impact can perhaps best be described through the experiences of two county-seat towns: Ulysses (Grant County) and Johnson City (Stanton County). Emigration left Ulysses with only about sixty-five people by 1894. These few tried to improve their lot through a series of bond issues, but when conditions stayed bleak, the city became delinquent on payment. In a move reflecting both inspiration and desperation, the remaining people "deeded their lots and property back to the townsite, put their buildings on wheels, and moved to a hill northwest of the old townsite." By founding a New Ulysses, three miles from the old, they escaped complete ruin. The situation in Stanton County was equally as severe. By 1897 the population countywide had dipped to under three hundred, and "not a solitary person lived within the city limits of Johnson City." Wags from outside the area called it the smallest county seat in the world, but the reality was not at all funny. The town had recovered only to sixty-two people by 1913, and they held no local elections between 1895 and 1923.[4]

William Allen White, in an 1895 editorial, worried that the troubles in western Kansas could ruin the good image of the state. He urged citizens to spread the word that Kansas, like Gaul, was divided into three parts. "Eastern Kansas has proven herself good for agriculture; central Kansas is proving herself worthy; western Kansas is a dead failure in everything except the herd."[5] This characterization still applied to much of western Kansas in 1905. Although rains had returned beginning in 1901, potential farmers and business people were much more cautious toward immigration than they had been in earlier years. No county in the region had a population density greater than five people per square mile, and most had fewer than three. The numbers were highest in the relatively cool north, in Kiowa County, and in county-seat towns that happened to be on railroad

MAP 5.1

Reference map for western Kansas, 1905 and 1925.

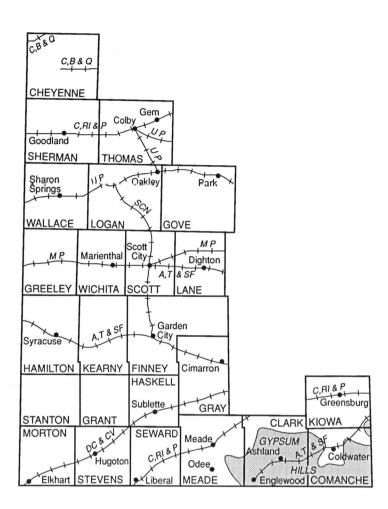

lines (see Maps 5.1, 5.2). Six counties had over twenty-five hundred people; Thomas County led with 4,506. The lowest densities were in the extreme southwest, where five counties lacked railroads; none of these places could claim a thousand citizens, and Morton County had only 211.

The economic immaturity of western Kansas was apparent in its urban populations. Only two places were big enough to be called cities, both of which had names that testified to the earlier, optimistic spirit. Goodland, the seat of Sherman County, had been made a division point on the Rock Island Railroad, one of the new transregional lines built during the late 1880s. It was home to 1,410 people. Along the Santa Fe tracks, many of Garden City's 1,267 citizens hoped that enough water would again flow in the Arkansas River to fill the several hundred miles of irrigation ditches that had been dug in the 1880s. Sugar beets, a new crop, excited many townspeople, and plans were under way to erect a sugar factory.[6]

POPULATION PER SQUARE MILE

☐	0-1
▨	2-5
▨	6-15
■	21
■	42

△ denotes fewer than 100 people

SETTLERS AND STRATEGIES

The simple tripartite model that helped to explain the settlement of central Kansas, based on a midstate railroad belt, cannot readily be applied to western Kansas. Although the main lines of the Union Pacific (as the Kansas Pacific was renamed in 1880) and the Santa Fe still passed through the region and the acreage within the two land grants did sell originally for considerably more than the homesteader's entry fee, newer factors complicated the scene. The extended drought of the 1890s had forced many, probably most, of the original buyers of railroad land off their tracts. In Wallace, Sherman, and Logan counties, for example, 468 of the 837 entries made on the Union Pacific grant between January and October of 1887 were canceled before 1890 because of abandonment; only 205 of the buyers completed payments over the ten-year agreement of sale.[7] Conditions probably were equally bad on the Santa Fe grant. Given the realities of the 1888–1900 period, it is foolish to place undue emphasis on transportation accessibility and the costs of land as determined by the railroads in the 1880s; such factors applied only marginally to the geography of settlers for 1905. The price differential between homestead land and properties on the Osage Reserve is also largely moot for this time and place. The issue of wholesale abandonment applies again, and the reserve itself extended only as far west as the 100th meridian (see Map 3.7); in the counties under discussion for 1905, only Clark, Comanche, and Kiowa were part of it.

The location and sources of the new railroads built in the late 1880s are perhaps the most important single factor in the assessment of settler strategies at the turn of the century. Three lines constructed by two companies were especially significant. The Missouri Pacific Railroad, financed by Jay Gould, neatly bisected the area between the two older tracks on its way to Pueblo. The Chicago, Rock Island and Pacific system filled in the two remaining interstices: one track between the Union Pacific and the Nebraska border and a second between the Santa Fe and Oklahoma Territory (see Map 5.1). The Santa Fe responded to these intrusions by building two major new lines itself. One paralleled the Missouri Pacific; the other extended westward from Wichita into the cattle country of the Gypsum Hills. Finally, the Burlington system penetrated into extreme northwestern Kansas. Officials dropped feeder lines from their Republican valley route to Oberlin, in Decatur County, and later to St. Francis, in Cheyenne County. Competition among these lines was fierce, and their promoters have been called "the most effective immigration agents western Kansas ever had."[8]

The courting of settlers for western Kansas after 1900 differed significantly from that of earlier decades. Although modern communications made more people aware of the region than ever before, these same information sources also ensured that potential migrants would hear about winter blizzards and other liabilities along with the usual positive promotional material. For some reason, fewer people traveled to this frontier in formal colonies than had done so in previous decades. Decisions to migrate apparently were being made less by charismatic religious or other community leaders and more by individuals and small family units. The standard compilations list only five organized expeditions from eastern states, and these took place in the 1870s before the onset of the first major drought. The migrants to western Kansas were also probably even poorer than their recent predecessors. Inspection of the hometowns of officers for major townsite companies, for example, reveals a principal concentration in central Kansas rather than farther east. Kansas entrepreneurs could compete this well only if richer, Eastern financiers were choosing to make their investments in places other than a droughty agricultural frontier.[9]

My reading of the contemporary literature suggests that the settlers who came to western Kansas selected their exact destinations largely on the basis of their intended use of the land and of the relative accessibility of their home states to the several railroad lines that served the region. Ranchers looked for environments different from those farmers looked for; Iowans could reach

Cheyenne County more easily and cheaply than could Tennesseans. This transportation argument applies not only to Iowa, Tennessee, and other states but also within Kansas. By 1905 the Topeka and Kansas City region had been settled for fifty years and parts of central Kansas for thirty-five. Just as many French Canadians from St. Joseph, in Cloud County, migrated to a daughter colony in Rooks County in the 1880s, so it was not unusual in 1905 to find a farmer in Meade County who had been born in Indiana and who had lived for several decades in Reno County before deciding to pioneer once again.

Two sections of the High Plains frontier were positioned to attract well-defined groups of settlers: the area north of the old Kansas Pacific grant and that south of the Santa Fe. Since 1880 the most direct access to the far northwest of Kansas had been from Iowa and Nebraska by way of the Burlington Railroad system. Workers that year had laid track up the Republican valley as far as McCook, Nebraska (just north of Decatur County). The accessibility was improved in 1885 with a feeder line from Republican City across the border to Norton and Oberlin. Oberlin, the terminus, served as a principal gathering place for land seekers in northwestern Kansas during the boom of 1885–1887. Two additional railroads in the late 1880s solidified the Iowa-Nebraska pathway into the region. In 1887 Burlington laborers constructed a second feeder for the Republican valley line up Beaver Creek; it originally terminated near Atwood but two years later was extended to Cheyenne County. Rock Island officials brought the Nebraska connection directly to the second tier of Kansas counties in 1888. Their crews built from Jansen, Nebraska, into Belleville, Kansas, extended the line directly west to Norton, and then angled southwest to Colby, Goodland, and beyond (see Map 5.1). Iowans and Nebraskans thus were the obvious pioneers for Cheyenne, Sherman, and Thomas counties, not only throughout the initial colonization of 1885–1887 but also during the reoccupation of abandoned homesteads after 1900. These people also were well positioned to secure forfeited properties just to the south, on the old Kansas Pacific grant. The only serious challenge to their influence would have come from central Kansans and others who traveled on the Union Pacific; spurs from its main line had been constructed into Colby from the south and southeast in 1887 and 1888 (see Map 5.1).[10]

South of the Arkansas valley route of the Santa Fe, the regional topography is not nearly so uniform as in northwestern Kansas. Crooked Creek, Bluff Creek, Mule Creek, the Medicine Lodge River, and other north-bank tributaries of the Cimarron River and the Salt Fork of the Arkansas have deeply eroded the edge of the High Plains. The result is the Gypsum Hills, a land of mesas, incised valleys, and escarpments in Comanche, Clark, and Meade counties. Rolling, grass-covered sand dunes occupy another sizeable area in southwestern Kansas, which form an elongated belt five to twenty miles wide that extends from Hamilton County eastward through Gray County along the south side of the Arkansas River. Early observers judged both of these broken landscapes as unsuitable places for plow agriculture.

Accessibility to and within southwestern Kansas was also more variable than in the north.

Although two parallel railroads served the Gypsum Hills portion of the area after 1888, residents of extreme southwestern Kansas in 1905 still found themselves without either the cachet of progress or the hard construction dollars that a railroad track would have brought to their struggling frontier economy. People in Haskell, Stevens, and Morton counties had to wait until 1913 before the Dodge City and Cimarron Valley route was pushed through; Grant and Stanton counties did not get rail service until 1923 (see Map 5.1).[11] Poor transportation clearly was a factor in the slow rate of population growth in far southwestern Kansas between 1900 and 1905, especially as people paired this isolation with that area's growing reputation as the hottest and driest section of the state. These counties did possess the physical asset of good surface water, however. The Cimarron River arches from southwestern Morton County northwest into Grant County and then diagonally back across Seward County.

The particular combination of physical conditions, railroad orientation, and localized isolation found in southwestern Kansas was well suited to a ranching economy. Since a similar way of life had developed under parallel conditions a generation earlier in south-central Kansas, this section would seem to be an obvious source for new settlers. Upper Southerners, Illini, and Hoosiers, the core of the population in Medicine Lodge, Wichita, and other cities in the old Osage Reserve, had known about the grazing potential of the far southwest since the early 1870s. Settlers ventured up the Sun City Trail into Comanche County as early as 1873, Dodge City became the primary destination for cattle drives from Texas and Indian Territory in 1875, and by 1879 J. W. Beaty and J. W. McLain had established the famous Point-of-Rocks Ranch on the Cimarron River, adjacent to the Colorado border. Although the homesteader wave of 1885–1887 temporarily overwhelmed the ranchers, they soon dominated again; the cattle business, in fact, was the principal lure for the two railroads built into the region in the late 1880s. Both lines came from cities near the older ranching area (the Rock Island from Hutchinson, the Santa Fe from Wichita), and both terminated near the southern border of the state where they would be convenient for cattle not only from southwestern Kansas but also from the ranches in Indian Territory, Texas, and the unclaimed but well-grassed strip known as No Man's Land.[12]

Potential settlers for the central belt of western Kansas are harder to predict than for either the northwestern or the southwestern corners. An extensive area of broken terrain, such as might attract ranchers, occurs in only one place, along the Smoky Hill River in central and southern Gove and Logan counties. This area is rather removed from places where the traditional ranchers of the state (South-Midland people) had settled, but it was located near the tracks of the Missouri Pacific Railroad. Cattlemen from the long-standing herding area in the Missouri valley between Boonville and Lexington would have had easy access along this direct rail connection.[13]

The North-Midland states, especially Illinois and Indiana, would seem to be the most likely sources of immigrants for the central belt. The three major railroads in this section provided good connections to these states, and fierce competition among the old and new lines had prompted the continuation of 1870s-style recruiting efforts and low fares far into the drought decade of the 1890s.[14] The assumption of greater immigration from Illinois and Indiana at the expense of Ohio and Pennsylvania is based partly on the rapid industrialization of the eastern section of the country at the turn of the century and the resultant abundance of urban jobs there for nearby rural people. Farmland in western Kansas not only was distant from Pennsylvania, but it had also been revealed as a hazardous venture by the events of the 1890s. Illinois farmers, closer to Kansas and farther from eastern cities, would seem more apt to take a chance on the High Plains in 1905.

The logic that predicts a decline in the number of Ohioans and Pennsylvanians on the twentieth-century western frontier also applies to Yankees and to most Europeans. New Englanders knew that Boston and New York financiers had lost millions of dollars on Kansas investments during the recent past. If good jobs could be had in Hartford, Buffalo, or Detroit, why venture farther west? A decision by Santa Fe officials to end their active recruitment program in Europe at this time and to sell their remaining western lands to speculators in large blocks was probably a result of such reasoning.[15] Still, it is easy to imagine exceptions to this line of thinking, especially among certain European groups who were committed to rural life and who already had established colonies in central Kansas. Three such peoples were well positioned to promote new western settlements. The Swedes at Lindsborg had direct access to the Missouri Pacific tracks, the Volga Germans were served by both the Missouri Pacific and the Union Pacific, and the Russian-German Mennonites could move west easily using either the main line of the Santa Fe or its branch that extended west from Great Bend to Scott City. Personal knowledge of the High Plains by young men from these colonies who had worked for the various railroads increased the likelihood for new settlements.[16]

THE SOUTHWEST BETWEEN 1905 AND 1925

A decade of moist years between 1901 and 1911 initiated the reoccupation of western Kansas. People immigrated slowly at first and generally spread across the western landscape from northeast to southwest. By the time of the 1905 census, the eight counties in the southwestern corner had several hundred new residents, but their total population was still only 5,459. Beyond Syracuse (670 people), Liberal (530 people), and several other small railroad communities, only a thin scattering of ranchers occupied the prairies; township densities rarely exceeded one person per square mile (see Map 5.2).

If dry years had alternated with moist ones in some fashion during the first twenty years of this century, it is possible that the ranching economy in southwestern Kansas would have maintained itself in perpetuity. One good growing season followed another nearly without interruption into the mid-1920s, however, and the crops received record prices. This combination proved irresistible even to most ranchers, and anyone who argued for caution was shown new literature on "scientific" dry farming. Proponents of this concept, which began to be touted about 1906, held that lands much more droughty than those in Kansas could be farmed easily through a combination of fallowing, deep plowing, and a frequent working of the top layers of soil to retard evaporation.[17]

As farmers returned to the region, so did railroad promoters. Officials behind the first local venture, the Dodge City and Cimarron Valley Railroad (a subsidiary of the Santa Fe), hoped to profit equally from crops and cattle. They built their line from 1911 to 1913, parallel to the older Rock Island tracks but positioned one county farther to the west (see Map 5.1). The terminus, Elkhart, in Morton County, was a near duplicate of Liberal. When income from this investment proved substantial, Santa Fe officials decided to build a second spur from Satanta (on the Cimarron Valley route in Haskell County) westward through Grant and Stanton counties. This venture in 1922 and 1923 filled the last conspicuous gap in the rail net of the region.[18]

The 1925 census revealed a sizeable increase in local population. The eight counties had grown more than fourfold since 1905 to a total of 22,917. Liberal and Syracuse continued to be important urban places, with 3,372 and 969 people, respectively. Elkhart, with 1,138 residents, was a new center. The two counties with the lowest population totals, Greeley and Stanton, each had over fourteen hundred inhabitants, and local editors there voiced pleasure with the progress. Population densities over most of the rural areas were in the range of two to five people per square mile, figures thought to be well suited to the capabilities of the land (see Map 5.3). Natural gas, a resource that would soon bring prosperity to much of this region, was a year or two from discovery; Black Sunday, the day that would mark the onset of the big dust storms, was a decade away.

Although many new people came to southwestern Kansas between 1905 and 1925, there is no reason to suspect that their origins would differ much from those forecast for 1905. South-central Kansans still knew this area better than anyone else because of their previous experience in the local cattle business. The new railroads linked directly to Wichita and were elaborations of the existing Santa Fe system that had been so influential in the settlement of that earlier Kansas frontier. More Missourians might come than in earlier years, now that Civil War memories were two generations old. Some Oklahomans should be present, too, families, perhaps, of former Kansans who had tried their luck on the Cherokee Outlet during the 1890s and who later decided to move back north to participate in the new prosperity.

MISSOURIANS, BLACKS, AND OTHER SOUTHERNERS

South-Midland people made up 25 percent of the non-Kansas-born residents in the twenty-four counties surveyed for 1905, a figure that far exceeded the 15 percent they recorded in central Kansas for 1885 (compare Tables 4.1 and 5.1). Although some of this increase may be attributed to the preponderance of counties from the southern half of the state included in the 1905 survey, there is little question that Southerners were relatively more active on this western frontier than they had

POPULATION PER SQUARE MILE

☐ 0-1

▨ 2-5

▨ 6 15

■ 20-27

△ denotes fewer than 100 people

been in Kansas since the 1850s. They constituted one-third of the immigrant population in Lane and Scott counties (locations farther north than they had ventured en masse in the central part of the state) and created sizeable enclaves in Sherman and Thomas counties (see Map 5.4). Their activity was even greater over the next twenty years, at least in the southwestern counties (see Table 5.2). Morton, Seward, and Stanton counties each received about half of their immigrants from these states in 1925, up from 35–40 percent in 1905, and the other counties surveyed showed similar gains (see Map 5.5). In both 1905 and 1925, Missourians made up about half of this total.

Given the close historical tie between South-Midland culture and the ranching industry in south-central Kansas and elsewhere, it seems initially puzzling to observe that areas well suited physically for the grazing of cattle, such as the Gypsum Hills and the broad swath of grassed dunes south of the Arkansas River, are not clearly defined on Map 5.4. In 1905 approximately 30 percent of the immigrant population in the townships of the Gypsum Hills and the Sand Hills was born

Table 5.1. *Place of Birth of Western Kansans, 1905*

Collection Unit/Culture Area	No.	(%)	Excluding (by %) Kans.-born	Kans. & Foreign-born
New England (Northern)				
Connecticut	27	(0.1)	0.1	0.1
Maine	45	(0.1)	0.2	0.2
Massachusetts	65	(0.2)	0.3	0.3
Michigan	305	(0.7)	1.2	1.4
Minnesota	101	(0.2)	0.4	0.5
New Hampshire	19	(0.1)	0.1	0.1
New York	598	(1.4)	2.4	2.7
North Dakota	40	(0.1)	0.2	0.2
Rhode Island	7	(0.1)		
South Dakota	24	(0.1)	0.1	0.1
Vermont	56	(0.1)	0.2	0.3
Wisconsin	328	(0.8)	1.3	1.5
Subtotal	1,615	(3.8)	6.5	7.3
North Midland				
Delaware	7	(0.1)		
Illinois	3,725	(8.7)	15.1	16.9
Indiana	2,576	(6.0)	10.4	11.7
Iowa	2,797	(6.5)	11.3	12.7
Nebraska	1,322	(3.1)	5.4	6.0
New Jersey	65	(0.2)	0.3	0.3
Ohio	2,268	(5.3)	9.2	10.3
Pennsylvania	989	(2.3)	4.0	4.5
Subtotal	13,749	(32.2)	55.7	62.2
Upper South (South Midland)				
Arkansas	145	(0.3)	0.6	0.7
Dist. of Columbia	3			
Indian Territory	41	(0.1)	0.2	0.2
Kentucky	944	(2.2)	3.8	4.3
Maryland	65	(0.2)	0.3	0.3
Missouri	3,569	(8.3)	14.5	16.1
North Carolina	95	(0.1)	0.4	0.4

Table 5.1. *Continued*

Collection Unit/Culture Area	No.	(%)	Excluding (by %) Kans.-born	Excluding (by %) Kans. & Foreign-born
Oklahoma	269	(0.6)	1.1	1.2
Tennessee	473	(1.1)	1.9	2.1
Virginia	345	(0.8)	1.4	1.6
West Virginia	288	(0.7)	1.2	1.3
Subtotal	6,237	(14.6)	25.3	28.2
Lower South				
Alabama	20		0.1	0.1
Florida	5			
Georgia	29	(0.1)	0.1	0.1
Louisiana	19	(0.1)	0.1	0.1
Mississippi	55	(0.1)	0.2	0.2
South Carolina	9	(0.1)		
Texas	161	(0.4)	0.7	0.7
Subtotal	298	(0.7)	1.2	1.3
The West				
Arizona	6			
California	62	(0.1)	0.3	0.3
Colorado	300	(0.7)	1.2	1.4
Idaho	20		0.1	0.1
Montana	10			
Nevada	5			
New Mexico	41	(0.1)	0.2	0.2
Oregon	19	(0.1)	0.1	0.1
Utah	5			
Washington	18		0.1	0.1
Wyoming	15		0.1	0.1
Subtotal	501	(1.2)	2.0	2.3
Kansas	18,062	(42.3)		
Foreign Countries				
Belgium	3			
Bohemia	14		0.1	

Table 5.1. *Continued*

Collection Unit/Culture Area	No.	(%)	Excluding (by %)	
			Kans.-born	Kans. & Foreign-born
British America	151	(0.4)	0.6	
Denmark	76	(0.2)	0.3	
England	260	(0.6)	1.1	
France	23	(0.1)	0.1	
German States	856	(2.0)	3.5	
Ireland	160	(0.4)	0.6	
Netherlands	4			
Norway	37	(0.1)	0.1	
Russia	457	(1.1)	1.9	
Scotland	61	(0.1)	0.2	
Sweden	409	(1.0)	1.7	
Switzerland	14	(0.1)	0.1	
Wales	20	(0.1)	0.1	
Other Countries	27	(0.1)	0.1	
Subtotal	2,572	(6.0)	10.5	
Total	42,736[a]	(100.0)	100.0	100.0

Source: Manuscript Kansas state census, 1905.

Note: The region of western Kansas includes Cheyenne, Clark, Comanche, Finney, Gove, Grant, Gray, Greeley, Hamilton, Haskell, Kearney, Kiowa, Lane, Logan, Meade, Morton, Scott, Seward, Sherman, Stanton, Stevens, Thomas, Wallace, and Wichita counties.

[a]This total does not include 1,285 residents for whom no place of birth was recorded. Percentages may not total exactly because of rounding.

in South-Midland states, as was approximately one-quarter of those who lived in the rougher parts of the Smoky Hill valley in Gove and Logan counties. Although this 30 percent figure is higher than the percentage that Southerners reached in western Kansas as a whole, it is comparable with their proportions in the rural, flatland townships of the southwestern counties and also in the larger local towns. South-Midland people, it seems, though still active in the ranching areas in 1905, were no longer defined by or restricted to those areas.

Research by C. Robert Haywood provides a convincing explanation for the general distribu-

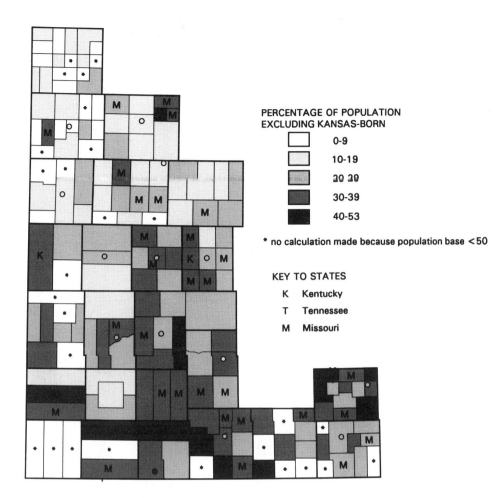

MAP 5.4
Natives of South-Midland states, 1905 (western Kansas). Data from Kansas state census. Letter symbols mark townships in which people from a particular South-Midland state constitute 20 percent or more of the immigrant population. For states included in the South-Midland area, see Table 5.1.

PERCENTAGE OF POPULATION
EXCLUDING KANSAS-BORN

☐	0-9
☐	10-19
☐	20-29
☐	30-39
■	40-53

* no calculation made because population base < 50

KEY TO STATES

K   Kentucky
T   Tennessee
M   Missouri

tions shown on Maps 5.4 and 5.5. "When the open range was abandoned," he wrote, "most of the cowboys did not, in fact, just fade away like old soldiers but stayed on to run small farms or retail stores in the newly established towns."[19] Clearly, no nativity evidence exists that they remained clustered along the routes of the two old wagon roads that once stretched south from Dodge City, neither the Jones and Plummer Trail through Meade County, nor the Fort Supply Trail through Clark County. The only possible legacy of the western branch of the Chisholm Trail into Dodge City was one small group of Texans and other Lower Southern immigrants who constituted 10 percent of the population in Avilla Township on the Oklahoma border in Comanche County. The three trails were relics by 1905, and most people had moved on to new ventures.[20]

The railroad terminals at Englewood, Liberal, and (after 1913) Elkhart exhibited the most enduring linkage between Upper Southern culture and the cattle industry. These towns were designed as livestock-marketing centers, and they became important suppliers not only for the stockyards in Wichita and Kansas City but also for summer pastures in the Flint Hills. Freighting operations to

Table 5.2. *Place of Birth of Southwestern Kansans, 1925*

Collection Unit/Culture Area	No.	(%)	Excluding (by %) Kans.-born	Kans. & Foreign-born
New England (Northern)				
Connecticut	3			
Maine	4			
Massachusetts	12	(0.1)	0.1	0.1
Michigan	93	(0.4)	0.9	1.0
Minnesota	39	(0.2)	0.4	0.4
New Hampshire	4			
New York	89	(0.4)	0.9	0.9
North Dakota	29	(0.1)	0.3	0.3
Rhode Island	1			
South Dakota	28	(0.1)	0.3	0.3
Vermont	11		0.1	0.1
Wisconsin	94	(0.4)	0.9	1.0
Total	407	(1.8)	4.1	4.2
North Midland				
Delaware	1			
Illinois	1,217	(5.5)	12.2	12.7
Indiana	714	(3.2)	7.2	7.4
Iowa	745	(3.4)	7.5	7.8
Nebraska	375	(1.7)	3.8	3.9
New Jersey	13	(0.1)	0.1	0.1
Ohio	391	(1.8)	3.9	4.1
Pennsylvania	175	(0.8)	1.8	1.8
Subtotal	3,631	(16.4)	36.4	37.9
Upper South (South Midland)				
Arkansas	240	(1.1)	2.4	2.5
Kentucky	309	(1.4)	3.1	3.2
Maryland	13	(0.1)	0.1	0.1
Missouri	2,117	(9.5)	21.2	22.1
North Carolina	24	(0.1)	0.2	0.3
Oklahoma	1,388	(6.3)	13.9	14.5
Tennessee	278	(1.3)	2.8	2.9

Table 5.2. *Continued*

Collection Unit/Culture Area	No.	(%)	Excluding (by %)	
			Kans.-born	Kans. & Foreign-born
Virginia	82	(0.4)	0.8	0.9
West Virginia	77	(0.3)	0.8	0.8
Subtotal	4,528	(20.4)	45.4	47.2
Lower South				
Alabama	35	(0.2)	0.4	0.4
Florida	4			
Georgia	26	(0.1)	0.3	0.3
Louisiana	13	(0.1)	0.1	0.1
Mississippi	15	(0.1)	0.2	0.2
South Carolina	5		0.1	0.1
Texas	367	(1.7)	3.7	3.8
Subtotal	465	(2.1)	4.7	4.8
The West				
Arizona	2			
California	36	(0.2)	0.4	0.4
Colorado	378	(1.7)	3.8	3.9
Idaho	10		0.1	0.1
Montana	8			0.1
Nevada	1			
New Mexico	71	(0.3)	0.7	0.7
Oregon	15	(0.1)	0.2	0.2
Utah	3			
Washington	19	(0.1)	0.2	0.2
Wyoming	14	(0.1)	0.1	0.1
Subtotal	557	(2.5)	5.6	5.8
Kansas	12,206	(55.0)		
Foreign Countries				
Austria	10			
Canada	69	(0.3)	0.7	
Denmark	7	(0.1)	0.1	
England	33	(0.1)	0.3	

Table 5.2. *Continued*

Collection Unit/Culture Area	No.	(%)	Excluding (by %)	
			Kans.-born	Kans. & Foreign-born
France	3			
Germany	81	(0.4)	0.8	
Ireland	10		0.1	
Mexico	32	(0.1)	0.3	
Netherlands	2			
Norway	5		0.1	
Russia	67	(0.3)	0.7	
Scotland	13	(0.1)	0.1	
Sweden	38	(0.2)	0.4	
Switzerland	2			
Other Countries	18	(0.1)	0.2	
Subtotal	390	(1.8)	3.9	
Total	22,184[a]	(100.0)	100.0	100.0

Source: Manuscript Kansas state census, 1925.

Note: The region of southwestern Kansas includes Grant, Greeley, Hamilton, Haskell, Morton, Seward, Stanton, and Stevens counties.

[a]This total does not include 773 residents for whom no place of birth was recorded. Percentages may not total exactly because of rounding.

serve the isolated ranches in parts of Texas, Oklahoma, Colorado, and New Mexico provided additional job opportunities for entrepreneurs who knew the cattle business.[21] In 1905 an impressive 40 percent of the immigrant population to Englewood Township in Clark County came from South-Midland states and another 1 percent from Texas; the corresponding figures at Liberal were 41 and 5. These numbers rose even higher in 1925: 52 and 8 percent at Liberal, 53 and 9 percent at Elkhart. Two smaller cattle-marketing centers in the area, Wellsford in northeastern Kiowa County on the Rock Island, and Belvidere in southeastern Kiowa County on the Santa Fe, also had comparable percentages of Southern settlers.

Evidence that many ranchers had moved into new businesses by 1905 can be seen in local urban developments. The platting of Wilmore in Comanche County by cattleman C. C. Pepperd has been well documented, and Upper Southern people founded at least three county seats. Ashland

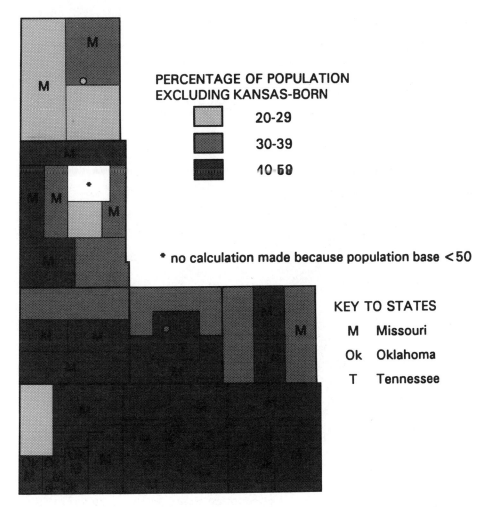

MAP 5.5
Natives of South-Midland states, 1925 (southwest Kansas). Data from Kansas state census. Letter symbols mark townships in which people from a particular South-Midland state constitute 20 percent or more of the immigrant population. For states included in the South-Midland area, see Table 5.2.

PERCENTAGE OF POPULATION
EXCLUDING KANSAS-BORN

20-29

30-39

40-59

* no calculation made because population base < 50

KEY TO STATES

M Missouri

Ok Oklahoma

T Tennessee

(Clark County) and Springfield (Seward County) were named after Kentucky and Missouri settlements, respectively, and Greensburg (Kiowa County) honors Kentuckian and pioneer stagecoach owner D. R. "Cannonball" Green. Lexington (Clark County), West Plains (Meade County), Roanoke (Stanton County), and Rolla (Morton County) are other names transferred from the Upper Southern states. In these communities, as well as in most other towns south from the Missouri Pacific Railroad track, Southerners were present in percentages comparable to the numbers they constituted in the surrounding rural areas.[22]

A comparison of the general distributions of Missourians, Kentuckians, and Tennesseans reveals the texture of South-Midland settlement (see Maps 5.6, 5.7, 5.8, 5.9). By migrating along general lines of latitude, these people collectively reproduced in western Kansas the north-south geographical positioning of their home states. Tennesseans came principally by way of Wichita and

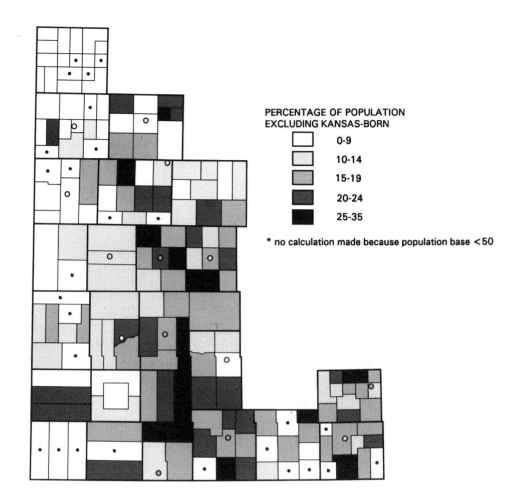

PERCENTAGE OF POPULATION
EXCLUDING KANSAS-BORN

- 0-9
- 10-14
- 15-19
- 20-24
- 25-35

* no calculation made because population base <50

Winfield to the southern two tiers of counties; Kentuckians ventured farther north into Greeley, Lane, and Wichita counties; and Missourians settled nearly to the Nebraska border. These patterns suggest that advertisements by the Missouri Pacific Railroad may have been an important determinant of the settler mix in the northern half of western Kansas. This line tapped the St. Louis–to–Kansas City corridor of Missouri, an area that traditionally had maintained strong connections with Kentucky but only marginal ones with Tennessee.[23] By 1925, 1,388 Oklahomans had also become an important presence in the southwestern counties (see Map 5.10). They were short-distance movers and rarely settled north of the Arkansas River; nearly half lived in Liberal (423) and Elkhart (90).

Concentrations of Upper Southerners were so common throughout most of western Kansas that only a few were seen as distinctive enough to merit attention in local histories and reminiscences. The 155 Missouri colonists in northwestern Thomas County in and near the town of Gem were one of these exceptions, standing out clearly from the general blend of Iowans and Nebras-

PERCENTAGE OF POPULATION
EXCLUDING KANSAS-BORN

0-9
10-14
15
22
25

* no calculation made because population base < 50

kans. Sanford Durrell, Rufus Munkre, and others in this group had come in a train of fourteen wagons from Andrew County, just north of St. Joseph, in 1886. German heritage distinguished another Missouri colony: Lutherans from Cole Camp, in the Ozarks, who moved to Odee in south-central Meade County in 1884 and 1885. They came at the urging of John, Christian, and Elizabeth Schmoker, a pioneer German-Swiss family, who had written about the good land in the valley of Crooked Creek.[24]

Although individual Kentuckians were active in several town companies in the southwestern counties, only two groups came to colonize, and neither of these stayed together through the long dry years. Six families and five single men from Owen County founded the community of Sweet Owen ten miles north of Lakin in the mid-1880s. In 1887, William Allen and C. D. Ellis from Smith's Grove, Kentucky, platted the town of Dermot in northwestern Stevens County. Dermot maintained a post office until 1929, but by 1905 only fifteen Kentucky natives were left in the township. Most Tennesseans in the region were late migrants to Kiowa County who came in small

MAP 5.8
*Natives of Tennessee, 1905
(western Kansas). Data
from Kansas state census.*

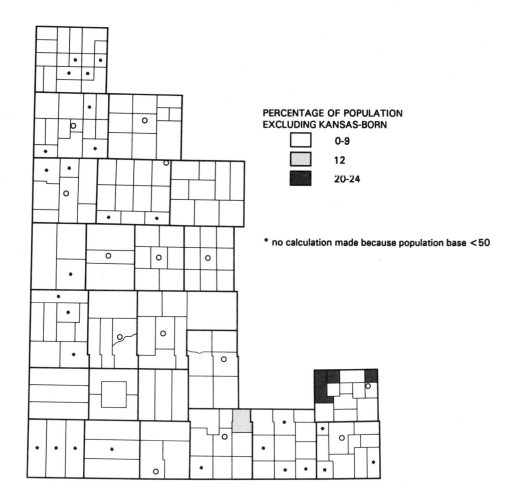

PERCENTAGE OF POPULATION
EXCLUDING KANSAS-BORN

☐   0-9

▨   12

■   20-24

* no calculation made because population base <50

family units from the region north and east of Knoxville and often found work on the Kane Ranch and other cattle operations. One cowboy, Richard Hill, later recalled that he came west to avoid the labor of the tobacco fields. Wellsford, a nearby railroad town, served as a weekend focus for the ranch workers; with two race tracks and a reputation for drinking and gambling, the place fit many of the stereotypes of traditional Appalachian (and cowboy) behavior.[25]

Black migrants, important bearers of Southern culture to both eastern and central Kansas, came to the western counties of the state only in small numbers. Two hundred forty-three lived in the twenty-four counties surveyed for 1905, 137 in the southwestern group for 1925. In both instances, their numbers represented less than 1 percent of the total regional population. Those few who decided to come generally ranged as widely over the landscape as did their white counterparts; they lived equally often in rural and urban settings. One colony existed, an informal affair at Lo-

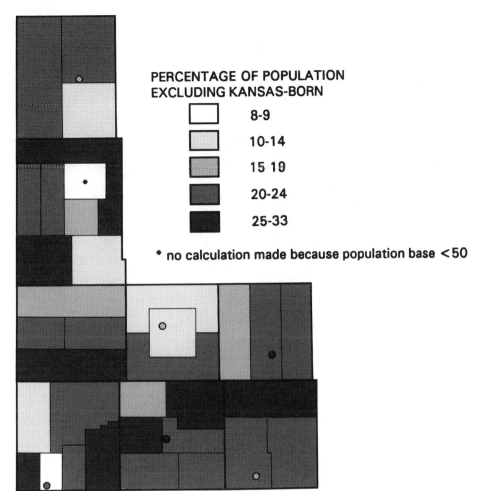

PERCENTAGE OF POPULATION
EXCLUDING KANSAS-BORN

☐	8-9
☐	10-14
☐	15-19
☐	20-24
■	25-33

* no calculation made because population base < 50

gansport Township in Logan County, produced by slow immigration between 1885 and 1905 (see Map 5.11). Nicodemus supplied most of the settlers there, and others came from Ellis, Phillips, and Rooks counties; in all, thirty-four blacks lived in the township in 1905, most of whom had roots in Kentucky or Missouri. No real town ever developed, but a post office existed from 1887 to 1888 and again from 1912 to 1915, the latter time during the brief life of the only north-south railroad in western Kansas, the underfinanced Scott City Northern (see Map 5.1).[26]

EUROPEANS AND MEXICANS

European settlers, who had participated actively in the central Kansas frontier during the 1870s and 1880s, came in far fewer numbers to the western counties. The census reports for 1905 show

MAP 5.10
Natives of Oklahoma,
1925 (southwest Kansas).
Data from Kansas state
census.

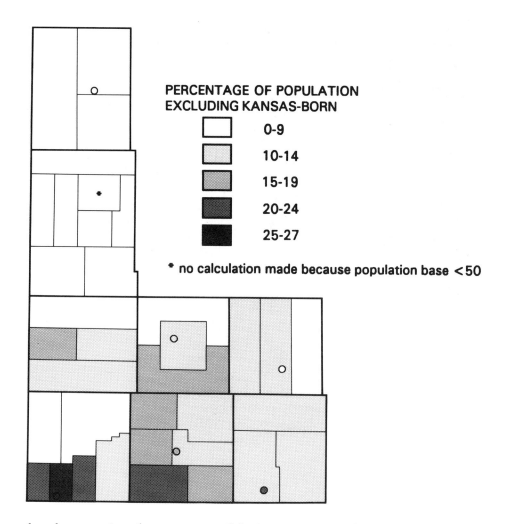

PERCENTAGE OF POPULATION
EXCLUDING KANSAS-BORN

	0-9
	10-14
	15-19
	20-24
	25-27

* no calculation made because population base <50

that they constituted 10.5 percent of the immigrant population, but this figure masked a change in attitude that occurred about 1887 (see Table 5.1). Nearly all the Europeans present in 1905 had come to western Kansas twenty years earlier, during the first wave of occupation. Their absence from the mix of later settlers is apparent in the southwestern counties, the state's last agricultural frontier. Less than 4 percent of the non-Kansas-born residents there in 1925 were from abroad (see Table 5.2).

One could argue that European immigrants were emotionally less attached to dreams of pioneer independence than were Americans of the time and thus were better able to evaluate the difficulties of trying to farm in a semiarid region. Whatever the validity of this thesis, the changing physical conditions of the Kansas frontier were only one of many factors that operated to modify patterns of European emigration greatly between 1870 and 1900. The numbers of people who left England and Germany declined, for example, as industrial growth in those countries provided

164 : Peopling the Plains

PERCENTAGE OF TOTAL POPULATION

☐	0-4
▨	5-9
■	33

△ denotes fewer than 100 people

more jobs than before. Similar decline in numbers from the Hapsburg Empire was related to a lessening of political tensions there after 1871. More generally, newspapers in several countries tried to limit emigration through campaigns that stressed high unemployment rates, prejudice, violence, and other darker aspects of American life.[27] Perhaps sensing such changes in attitude, officials of the Santa Fe Railroad radically altered their policy for land disposal in the early 1880s. They sold the remaining grant acreage in the state to individual speculators in large blocks and, by the end of 1886, were essentially finished with the land business.[28] Their decision, more than any other single factor, limited the ethnic variety present in southwestern Kansas before 1925.

Maps of the European presence show a dispersed pattern in the northern and central sections of the region but only minimal representations on the old Santa Fe grant and in the other southern counties (see Maps 5.12, 5.13). Colonies existed in the corridor of the Union Pacific but no more so than in the homestead lands to its north and south. Although Europeans constituted more than

MAP 5.12

Natives of European and other foreign countries, 1905 (western Kansas). Data from Kansas state census. Letter symbols mark townships in which people from a particular foreign country constitute 20 percent or more of the immigrant population.

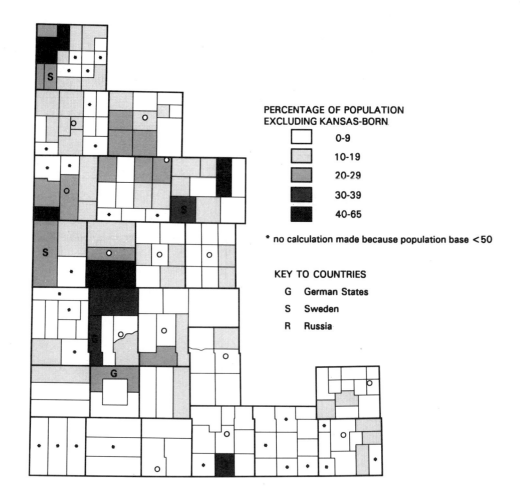

PERCENTAGE OF POPULATION
EXCLUDING KANSAS-BORN

- 0-9
- 10-19
- 20-29
- 30-39
- 40-65

* no calculation made because population base < 50

KEY TO COUNTRIES
G German States
S Sweden
R Russia

40 percent of the immigrant population in six western townships in 1905 and more than 50 percent in three, nowhere were they really numerous. Payne Township, in Gove County, was the leader with seventy-six of its people born in Russia and thirty elsewhere abroad. The city of Goodland, in Sherman County, was second, with forty Germans, twenty-four Scandinavians, and twenty-eight others born overseas. In general, towns recorded slightly lower percentages of Europeans than did the surrounding townships.

The 856 Germans in the western counties in 1905 displayed settlement characteristics similar to those for Europeans as a whole. They came in small groups to scattered locations but generally avoided the more expensive tracts along the Union Pacific. Besides the forty who lived in Goodland, the largest concentrations were in Cheyenne County's Porter Township (25) and at Odee (24) in Meade County (see Map 5.14). Most of the settlements were able to maintain an ethnic identity despite their small size because of shared religious belief. All were Protestant; most were Lutheran.

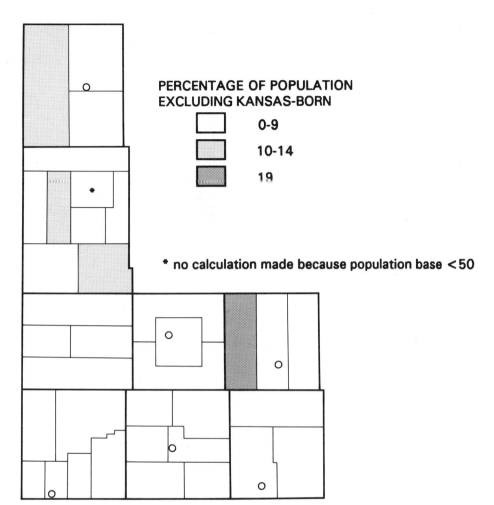

MAP 5.13
*Natives of European and
other foreign countries,
1925 (southwest Kansas).
Data from Kansas state
census.*

PERCENTAGE OF POPULATION
EXCLUDING KANSAS-BORN

0-9

10-14

19

* no calculation made because population base < 50

Germans were the initial settlers in the majority of their communities. A group of Ohio Synod Lutherans settled near Bird City in northeastern Cheyenne County in 1881, followed three years later by the Missouri Synod colonists to Meade County. German Methodists, many from Nebraska, came to two townships in southern Cheyenne County during the big land rush of 1885–1887, as did several families to Kiowa County. A Lutheran group from Worden, Illinois, occupied an isolated area in southern Wichita County.[29] The twenty-three, eighteen, and sixteen Germans who are responsible for the shaded townships in Finney, Grant, and Kearny counties, respectively, were apparently transient settlers, since they do not appear in later censuses.

Although only about half as many Russian-Germans and Swedes came to western Kansas as did Germans, they typically settled in larger individual communities. Most of these places began as formal colonies, with roots in the older ethnic towns of central Kansas. Promoters at Victoria, Lindsborg, and elsewhere hoped to provide needed homes for their kinspeople and to make a profit

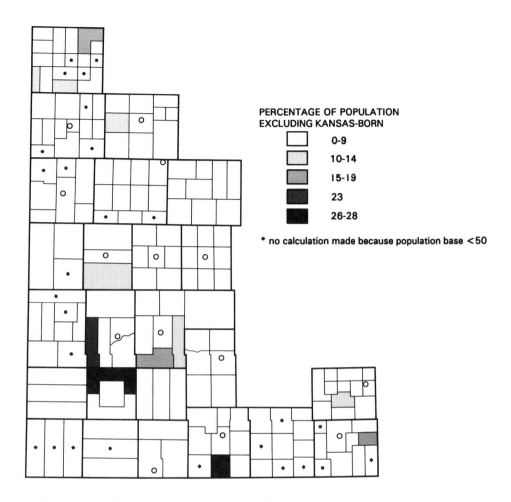

MAP 5.14

Natives of German states, 1905 (western Kansas). Data from Kansas state census.

PERCENTAGE OF POPULATION
EXCLUDING KANSAS-BORN

	0-9
	10-14
	15-19
	23
	26-28

* no calculation made because population base < 50

in the process. They usually selected sites directly west of their hometowns, near one of the trunk railroads; the colonies thus could be easily peopled and supplied.

The oldest and largest of the Russian-German concentrations, in northwest Cheyenne County, was one of the few that lacked a connection to central Kansas (see Map 5.15). Its founders came from five Lutheran villages along the lower Dniester River, near the Black Sea, and had heard about Kansas through three local German pioneers, Jacob Buck and George and J. G. Benkelman. The first colonists arrived in 1885, but migration continued until 1914, with a total of about four hundred people. Each of the five villages maintained its distinctiveness in Kansas. Their peoples formed five separate churches and never cooperated enough to create a town; some were American Lutheran, others Missouri Synod.[30]

A continuing stream of land seekers into Ellis County prompted the Catholic communities there to sponsor three daughter colonies in the west during the 1890s. The first, Marienthal, was initiated in 1892 by twenty-six families on abandoned homestead land in southeastern Wichita

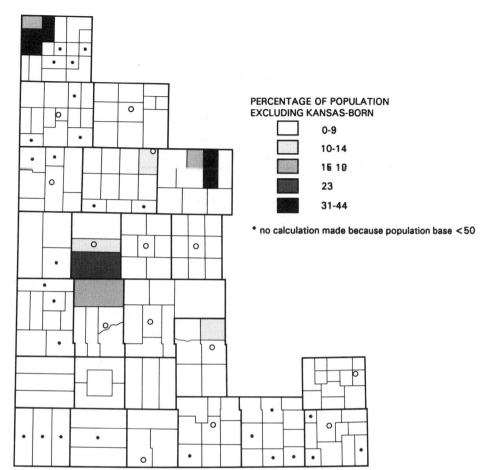

PERCENTAGE OF POPULATION
EXCLUDING KANSAS-BORN

	0-9
	10-14
	16 10
	23
	31-44

* no calculation made because population base <50

County. The support of kinspeople helped them to establish a church and town the next year, despite the droughty conditions. With a good location along the track of the Missouri Pacific, Marienthal eventually grew to about two hundred residents, who were prosperous enough by 1910 to build a new and larger church.[31]

Ellis Countians located their other two colonies near the main line of the Union Pacific, at Park, in Gove County, and thirty miles farther west, near Oakley. Peter Schamber, who had moved to the siding at Park to work as a section foreman, promoted the Gove County venture. He organized the first Catholic church in the town, placed advertisements in ethnic newspapers that promised good land for five to six dollars per acre, and helped new arrivals to find property. Over a hundred colonists had come by 1905, and the parish continued to grow rapidly for several decades to a peak membership of 1,044 in 1938. Most of the emigrants were from the Black Sea area. The Oakley settlement was largely an overflow from the Park colony; thirteen Russian families lived there in 1905, along with several German ones.[32]

Although emigration from Russia ended in 1914, population growth in central Kansas resulted in the founding of new Russian-German communities on the western plains into the 1940s. Some three hundred people went into the Garden City area shortly after 1905 to work in the new sugar beet fields. Lydia, a small community in extreme southern Wichita County, was colonized by Methodists from Rush and Russell counties between 1903 and 1907; their holdings abutted those of the Marienthal Catholics. The 1925 census showed five Mennonite families in southeastern Hamilton County, but the group never grew large enough to construct a church building (see Map 5.13). A larger Mennonite congregation of about fifty moved from Canada to Haskell County sometime just before 1925 but did not stay (see Map 5.13). Other ventures were more successful, including a mixed group of three hundred Kleine Gemeinde and Mennonite Brethren in Meade County beginning in 1906, a Holdeman colony in southern Gray and northeastern Haskell counties in 1912, some Mennonite Brethren in northern Gray County in 1922, and another Holdeman group in northern Scott County in 1943. This last-named colony, from McPherson County, formed Heartland Mills, one of the nation's major producers of organic grains.[33]

Nearly as many Swedes (409) as Russian-Germans (457) lived on the western plains in 1905, some of whom had immigrated because of military conscription laws passed by the Swedish government in 1885, 1887, and 1892.[34] Small clusters emerged in Cheyenne, Sherman, and Thomas counties in 1885 and 1886, but they never dominated the population in their townships and were quickly assimilated (see Map 5.16). In contrast, some one hundred or so immigrants to Lewis Township in Gove County had this hilly country largely to themselves; they built a church and store but soon grew dissatisfied with the quality of the land. By 1905 only thirty Swedes remained in the area, and they abandoned their church in 1916.[35]

Lindsborg served as an entrepot for most of the new Swedish immigrants. Local pastors supplied the Gove County pulpit and, in 1886 and 1887, townspeople organized two major colonization companies. The first, the Southwestern Swedish Townsite Company, was a joint venture with fellow Swedes from Page County, Iowa, and Fillmore County, Nebraska. C. J. Falk and other leaders targeted land near the Union Pacific siding of Boaz, in Logan County. They sent in two hundred new homesteaders between 1886 and 1889, who promptly voted to change the name of the station to honor one of their home counties. The Page settlement survived the hard decade of the 1890s but at the cost of approximately half of the original settlers.[36]

The second, and larger, Lindsborg promotion took place at two sites in Wallace and northern Greeley counties in 1887. Swan Ferlin (or Ferlen) and J. M. Ericson joined with a group of Chicago ministers who wanted to establish a Lutheran community "away from the noise of the city." Their Swedish Colonization Company selected two sites: an isolated area in southwestern Wallace County and adjacent Greeley County where they could set up their own township (called Stockholm) and a promising urban setting on the Union Pacific called Eagle Tail (a name they changed to Sharon Springs). Since the Chicago ministers favored the rural site, Stockholm Township at-

**PERCENTAGE OF POPULATION
EXCLUDING KANSAS-BORN**

☐	0-9
▨	10-14
▧	15-19
■	20-24
■	34-65

* no calculation made because population base < 50

tracted three hundred Swedes and Sharon Springs only one hundred. Several families each came from Gowrie and Burlington, Iowa, from Altoona, Illinois, and from Lindsborg.[37]

The Swedes at Stockholm built a church, two schools, and a blacksmith shop, and J. M. Ericson established a lumberyard and became mayor at Sharon Springs. Both groups survived the 1890s with only minor defections, but the incipient town at Stockholm failed when a rumored railroad never materialized. The Lutheran congregations at the two settlements cooperated with each other and with the Page group from the beginning. They established a joint pastorate in 1892, an arrangement that continues today with two ministers serving four churches.[38]

As fewer and fewer European settlers came to western Kansas after 1887, one would expect the foreign-born percentage to drop in the region. It did fall until 1925, but at that point an increase in immigration from a new source, Mexico, outpaced the European decline. The beginnings of the change can be seen in a single township on Map 5.13, where 10 percent of the non-Kansas-born population at Medway, in Hamilton County, came from Mexico. This group was part of a movement that began when officials of the Santa Fe Railroad sought a source for unskilled labor on their section gangs. The construction of a sugar mill at Garden City in 1906 created an additional demand for low-paid workers, especially in the irrigated beet fields along the Arkansas River that supplied the mill. Most Mexicans immigrated originally for railroad jobs, but many switched to field work once they learned that growers would employ women and children. The pay was extremely low, but the company did provide minimal housing. From 71 natives of Mexico in Kansas in 1900, the number increased to 8,429 in 1910 and to 13,770 in 1920. Statewide, about 75 percent of the males worked for the Santa Fe and the Rock Island railroads, but employment in the beet industry remained high in the southwestern counties. The Mexican-born population in Finney County went from zero in 1905 to 268 in 1925. Upstream on the Arkansas ditches, 128 Mexicans lived in Kearny County in 1925 and 18 in Hamilton County.[39]

YANKEES AND NORTH-MIDLAND PEOPLES

The Yankee component to Kansas settlement, which had been strong since the days of the New England Emigrant Aid Company, essentially disappeared after the mid-1880s. The disastrous winters of 1884–1885 and 1885–1886 ended the local range-cattle industry and with it the careers of many Northeastern financiers who had "thrown these herds upon the ranges as so many pawns in the game that was being played in the brokerage offices in Chicago and New York."[40] Investors who had put their money into Kansas towns rather than into cattle suffered similar losses after 1888 as drought nearly shut down the western third of the state. The physical relocation of Ulysses to escape New York creditors was an extreme example of this tragedy (see p. 143).

Only 6 percent of the immigrant population in the western counties surveyed in 1905 came from states in the Northern culture area, most of them from New York, Michigan, and Wisconsin (see Table 5.1). As in earlier years, the few settlers who came spread themselves widely over the landscape, with slightly higher densities in the northern counties. They reached a concentration of 9 percent in Sherman County, but only two townships (Eureka in Cheyenne County and Llanos in Sherman County) were as much as 15 percent Yankee (see Map 5.17).

I found no evidence of any organized colonies from Northern states except for the early and short-lived Syracuse group in Hamilton County. Of the original fifteen to twenty families who came in 1873 to found the county-seat town, only three people were left by 1885 and only one by 1905.[41] The township names of Itasca (near the center of Sherman County) and Michigan (in northeastern Scott County) suggest the existence of shared identity, but no Minnesotans lived in the former place in 1905 and only eight Michiganders in the latter. The correlation between Yankees and urban settlement continued in 1905, though to a lesser degree than in 1885, but was absent in 1925. Goodland, the largest city in the region, also had the highest concentration of Northern settlers with 12 percent.

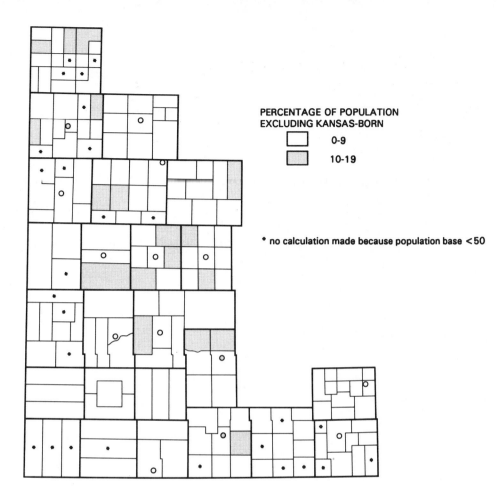

MAP 5.17
Natives of Northern states, 1905 (western Kansas). Data from Kansas state census. For states included in the Northern area, see Table 5.1.

PERCENTAGE OF POPULATION
EXCLUDING KANSAS-BORN

☐ 0-9

▨ 10-19

* no calculation made because population base <50

The host of economic, political, and social changes that produced declines in the participation of European and Yankee settlers on the Kansas frontier in the early twentieth century did not immediately affect migration from the North-Midland states. Their proportion of the population mix in 1905 was nearly identical to what it had been in 1885, a dominating 56 percent (see Table 5.1). This identity masked predictable shifts within the North-Midland group, however, whereby a decrease in settlers from the more industrialized eastern section (New Jersey, Pennsylvania, and Ohio) was offset by increases from the west (Iowa and Nebraska). This east-to-west shift accelerated over the next two decades. Illinois and Indiana joined the group of states with waning percentages by 1925, and, with only Iowa and Nebraska left to send new settlers in quantity, drops of about 15 percentage points in the North-Midland share of immigrants to southwestern counties were typical (see Maps 5.18, 5.19).

As of 1905 North Midlanders dominated not only the region as a whole but also twenty-one of its twenty-four component counties. The highest total, 61 percent, was in Thomas County, but

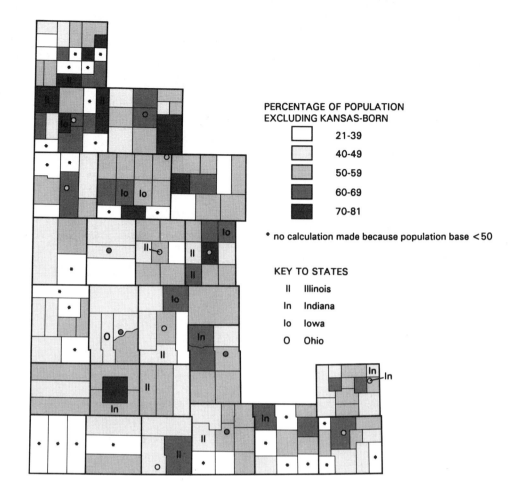

MAP 5.18
Natives of North-Midland states, 1905 (western Kansas). Data from Kansas state census. Letter symbols mark cities and townships in which people from a particular North-Midland state constitute 25 percent or more of the immigrant population. For states included in the North-Midland area, see Table 5.1.

PERCENTAGE OF POPULATION EXCLUDING KANSAS-BORN

	21-39
	40-49
	50-59
	60-69
	70-81

* no calculation made because population base <50

KEY TO STATES

Il   Illinois

In   Indiana

Io   Iowa

O   Ohio

even the two lowest percentages, 45 in Seward County and 47 in Wichita County, were impressive; they were higher in both cases than any competing culture group could muster. At a more detailed level, North-Midland people constituted 70 percent or more of the immigrants to twelve townships, most of them concentrated near the Nebraska border. The places of marginal presence coincide with islands of European settlement: Russian-Germans in northwestern Cheyenne, northeastern Gove, and southern Wichita counties; Swedes in southwestern Gove and southwestern Wallace counties; and Germans in southern Meade County. No predilection toward urban or rural residence is obvious for the group as a whole. Goodland and Garden City, the largest cities, recorded percentages of 53 and 56, respectively. For smaller places, the range was from 41 percent at Liberal to 67 at Colby.

Pennsylvanians and Ohioans made little cultural impact on individual counties of western

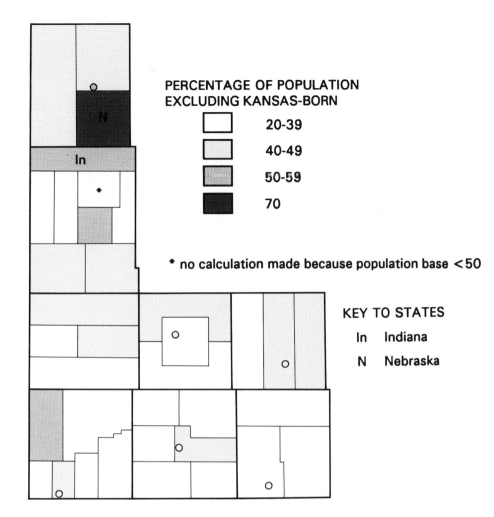

MAP 5.19
Natives of North-
Midland states, 1925
(southwest Kansas). Data
from Kansas state census.
Letter symbols mark
townships in which people
from a particular North-
Midland state constitute
25 percent or more of the
immigrant population.
For states included in the
North-Midland area, see
Table 5.2.

PERCENTAGE OF POPULATION
EXCLUDING KANSAS-BORN

20-39

40-49

50-59

70

* no calculation made because population base < 50

KEY TO STATES

In   Indiana

N   Nebraska

Kansas because most of them migrated as individuals and found opportunities in widely scattered locations. Such dispersion had been a hallmark of Ohio settlers in central Kansas, so its continuation was not surprising. It was a sharp departure for Pennsylvanians, however; well-organized Germanic groups had dominated a sizeable Pennsylvania contingency in central Kansas, peoples who bought land together and favored sites along the Union Pacific Railroad. One small portion of this 1870s migration came to western Kansas, about forty-five farmers from Bucks and Westmoreland counties who settled in northeastern Gove County, near Park. Thirty-six Dunkards still resided there in 1905, but no new Pennsylvanians came from the east once the region proved droughty in 1879 and 1880 (see Map 5.20). A Soldiers and Sailors Colony organized in Philadelphia in 1879 by C. P. Charlton was another victim of this drought. Meade County was its destination, but only twenty-nine Pennsylvania natives lived there in 1905, no more than four in any one township.

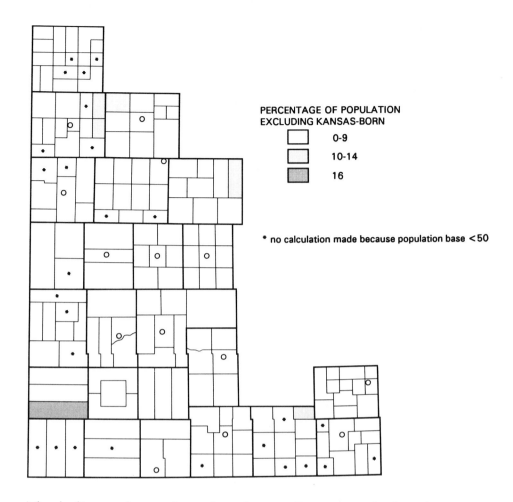

PERCENTAGE OF POPULATION
EXCLUDING KANSAS-BORN

☐ 0-9

☐ 10-14

▨ 16

* no calculation made because population base < 50

The shading on the map in southern Stanton County is misleading, for it represents only eleven Pennsylvania settlers.[42]

Twice as many Ohioans lived in western Kansas in 1905 as did Pennsylvanians (2,268 versus 989), but they were no more clustered (see Map 5.21). The three townships with percentages above 20 were all sparsely populated places where only sixteen or seventeen Ohioans resided. A slight concentration exists within the old Santa Fe land grant, probably the result of sales by agents for the big speculators who had purchased most of this land from the railroad. One such person is known to have attracted "a number of families" from Ohio to Hamilton County during the mid-1880s.[43] Ohio and New Jersey people also owned the Western Irrigation and Land Company, which operated an irrigation ditch on the south side of the Arkansas River between Lakin and Garden City.[44] A mineral springs resort in southern Logan County was easily the most publicized Ohio venture in the region. George A. Hay and a group of investors from Coshocton bought 280 acres on Hackberry Creek in 1887, erected a series of commercial buildings, and alternately named the

PERCENTAGE OF POPULATION
EXCLUDING KANSAS-BORN

☐	0-9
☐	10-14
▨	15-19
▨	20-24
■	29

* no calculation made because population base < 50

place St. Augustine and Augustine Springs. Augustine remains as a township name, but the project did not survive the dry 1890s. The post office closed in 1895, and only sixteen Ohioans lived in the area in 1905.[45]

Iowans and Nebraskans became major contributors to the new Kansas population just as most young Pennsylvanians and Ohioans decided that other economic opportunities were preferable to a long migration to a dryland farm. Mortgage indebtedness was high in the western Middle West, and, as farm prices fell throughout the 1880s and 1890s, many people there decided to seek new land. Northwestern Kansas was an obvious choice: close at hand, with good soil, and easily reached by rail. The Burlington system traversed the heart of Iowa and Nebraska from east to west, and by 1885 one could travel on it directly to Kansas. Oberlin, the terminus, was home to a federal land office and adjacent to the nearly unoccupied counties of Cheyenne, Thomas, and Sherman (see Map 4.2).[46]

The pattern of settlement could be easily predicted. In 1905 over half of the Iowa natives in

MAP 5.22

*Natives of Iowa, 1905
(western Kansas). Data
from Kansas state census.*

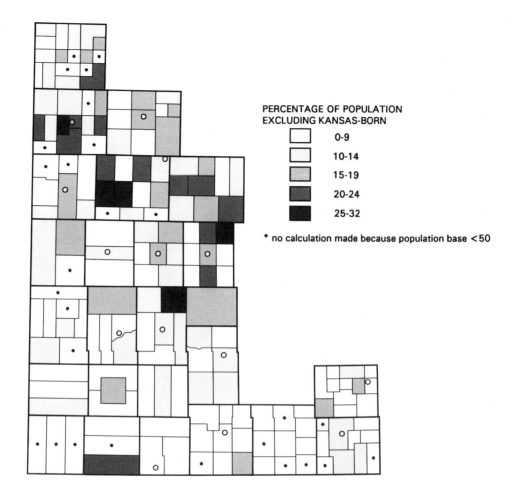

PERCENTAGE OF POPULATION
EXCLUDING KANSAS-BORN

0-9
10-14
15-19
20-24
25-32

* no calculation made because population base <50

western Kansas lived in the northern three tiers of counties, as did 80 percent of the Nebraskans (see Maps 5.22, 5.23). Later, once this northwestern frontier had passed, people spread over a larger area, helping to resettle abandoned lands in the Union Pacific corridor and then places farther to the south. By 1925 the two states had even supplied 12 percent of the immigrants to southwestern Kansas (see Maps 5.24, 5.25).

Iowans achieved their greatest density in Sherman County, where they made up 17 percent of the non-Kansas-born settlers in 1905. Their impact was a little less in neighboring Cheyenne and Thomas counties, the former because of early and significant European settlement and the latter because spurs of the Union Pacific opened access to this area from many sources. In these three counties, as well as those farther to the south, Iowans favored rural locations over urban ones, a probable reflection of their common backgrounds in poverty and in agriculture.

Cyrenus Emmons led the first organized colony of Iowans into western Kansas in 1879, a Quaker congregation that settled White Rock Township in northeastern Lane County. This loca-

PERCENTAGE OF POPULATION
EXCLUDING KANSAS-BORN

	0-9
	10-14
	15 19
	20-24

* no calculation made because population base < 50

tion seems unlikely until one recalls the map of Iowa immigration for 1885 and remembers that this settlement was part of a pattern of bypassing expensive railroad land in favor of homestead sites beyond. Most of the other group settlements occurred during the boom years of the 1880s. Iowa was a source area for the Swedish colonies in Logan and Wallace counties, and Nebraskans also contributed to the former group. Several Welsh settlers from Ottumwa moved to Harrison Township in southeastern Wallace County, and Germans from Warren County founded the St. Theresa community in northern Wichita County. Dodge County, Nebraska, was the previous home for a Dunkard community of about 125 people who settled Quinter, in Gove County. The symbolic core for rural Iowa on the Kansas plains, though, was created by twelve Mennonite families from Pulaski, under the leadership of Fred Funks; they moved to the isolated southeastern corner of Sherman County in 1887 and named it Iowa Township.[47]

Some Iowans and Nebraskans had money enough to participate in urban speculation. Iowan A. M. Nixon cooperated with two Kansans from Barton County to plat Scott City in 1879, a site

MAP 5.24
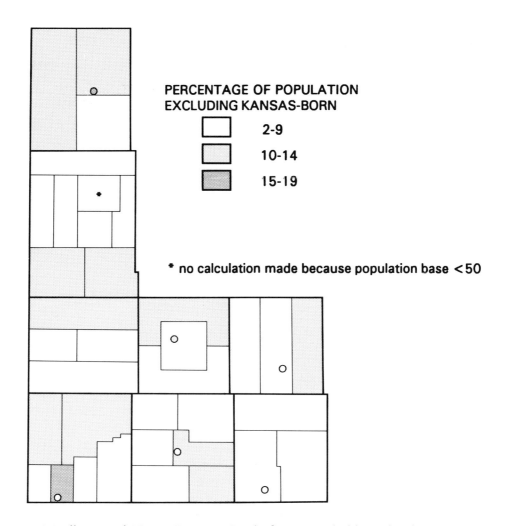

PERCENTAGE OF POPULATION
EXCLUDING KANSAS-BORN

☐ 2-9

☐ 10-14

☐ 15-19

* no calculation made because population base <50

originally named Nixon. Dr. J. L. Gandy from Humboldt, Nebraska, was an important political operative in early Sherman County; he founded the initial town in the county (near present-day Goodland) but became unpopular because of questionable business practices. The most involved speculation occurred in Gove County, where E. A. Benson of Davenport, Iowa, bought 250 sections of land from the Union Pacific in 1885. Benson, his brother H. H., and three other Davenport investors platted Gove City, built the Benson House hotel there, and then lobbied successfully to have the town named the county seat. The general promotion was lucrative enough to interest even the sitting governor of the state, William Larrabee, who became a stockholder in a bank at Grainfield in the north-central section of the county and had a local township named in his honor.[48]

After 1905 Iowans and Nebraskans migrated to Kansas largely in piecemeal fashion; nearly two thousand of them lived in the southwestern counties by 1925 but concentrations were rare. The

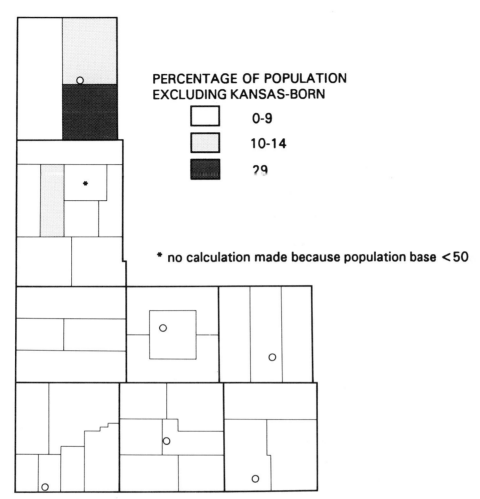

PERCENTAGE OF POPULATION
EXCLUDING KANSAS-BORN

0-9

10-14

29

* no calculation made because population base <50

exception was in Greeley County, where one of the pioneers in large-scale western agriculture, Simon Fishman, decided to invest in 1920. Fishman came from Sidney, Nebraska, "where he had developed thousands of acres of farm ground." He brought in fifteen modern tractors and a following of people from his former home. Essentially, he took over Harrison Township, an event local people have called "the greatest change in Greeley County history" (see Map 5.25).[49]

Illinois and Indiana supplied almost as many people to western Kansas as the other North-Midland states combined, one-quarter of the total immigrants (see Table 5.1). As was the case on earlier Kansas frontiers, however, these people rarely evoked commentary from contemporary observers or from later historians. Their settlements were neither as clustered as those of Iowans or Nebraskans nor as culturally distinctive as those of Missourians or Europeans. Some Indianans escaped anonymity through migration in religious-based colonies, but the Illini were nearly invisible.

MAP 5.26
*Natives of Illinois, 1905
(western Kansas). Data
from Kansas state census.*

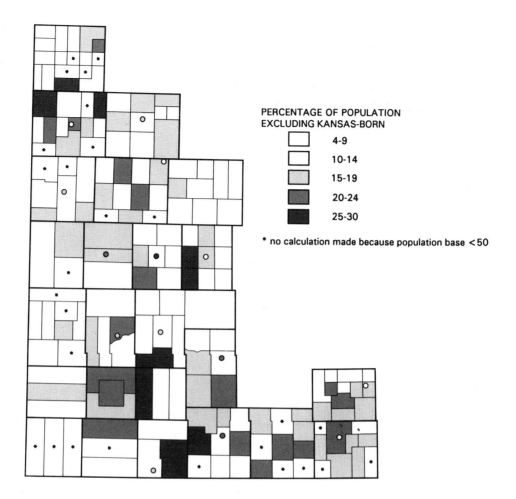

PERCENTAGE OF POPULATION
EXCLUDING KANSAS-BORN

	4-9
	10-14
	15-19
	20-24
	25-30

* no calculation made because population base <50

Illinois immigrants spread themselves widely across western Kansas, an expected pattern since connections were easily made between the two states on all the local railroads (see Maps 5.26, 5.27). The Burlington and the Rock Island lines passed through northern Illinois on their way out of Chicago; the Santa Fe and the Union Pacific took a more southerly route from the same city. Most of the migrants were farmers, often tenants who had found that rising land prices in Illinois gave them little hope of owning land unless they ventured west. A Chicago newspaper estimated that three thousand such people would leave central Illinois in 1892.[50] The Illini in western Kansas resist easy generalization, however. Several of the European groups in the area had Illinois roots, and many of the Illinois natives who had followed Santa Fe advertising to central Kansas in the 1870s later moved west as ranchers, town speculators, and government officials. The rural areas and the towns in the new counties drew them in similar proportions.

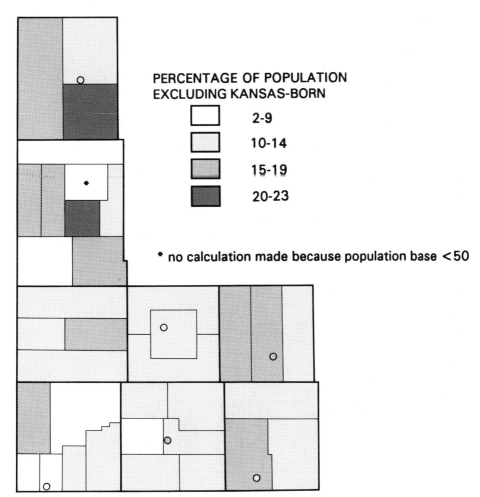

MAP 5.27
*Natives of Illinois, 1925
(southwest Kansas). Data
from Kansas state census.*

**PERCENTAGE OF POPULATION
EXCLUDING KANSAS-BORN**

2-9

10-14

15-19

20-23

* no calculation made because population base < 50

   Illinois-born Swedes can be seen in Gove and Wallace counties (compare Maps 5.16 and 5.26), and Illinois German peoples came to Lydia (on the Kearny-Wichita county line) and to northeastern Gove County. George Foidel led thirty Presbyterian families from Monmouth to western Greeley County in 1887, where they provided the impetus for the name Colony Township. Town-founding efforts included Belvidere (Kiowa County), Englewood (Clark County), and Streator (Sherman County), all name transfers, and Mullinville, in Kiowa County, founded by Alfred Mullin of Chicago.[51] Two railroad routes, however, provide the clearest indication of Illini entrepreneurship. The Illinois share of township populations was high from central Kiowa County to Liberal, along the tracks of the Rock Island, and from southeastern Kiowa County to Englewood on the Santa Fe. Since both of these railroads built westward from the core of earlier Illinois settlement in south-central Kansas, this correspondence seems logical. Twenty-three percent of the immi-

MAP 5.28

Natives of Indiana, 1905 (western Kansas). Data from Kansas state census.

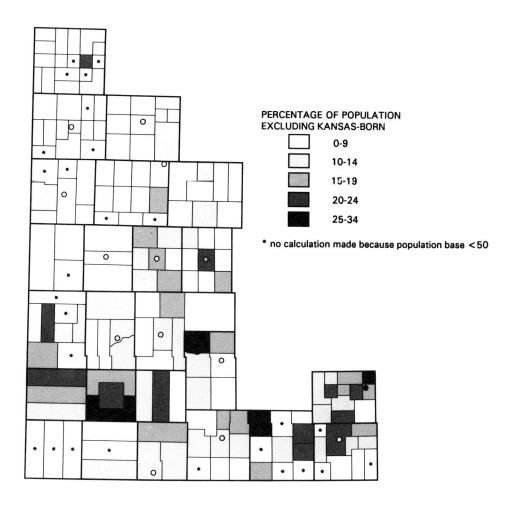

PERCENTAGE OF POPULATION
EXCLUDING KANSAS-BORN

☐	0-9
☐	10-14
☐	15-19
☐	20-24
☐	25-34

* no calculation made because population base <50

grants to Meade Center (now Meade), where railroad and county-seat functions were combined, were Illinois natives. Liberal, which lacked the county-seat designation until 1892, had a more modest 16 percent.

Indianans mirrored their pattern of 1885 in both 1905 and 1925—a distinct clustering in the southern section of the state (see Maps 5.28, 5.29). This orientation derived originally from strong recruiting efforts by agents of the Santa Fe Railroad, and, to a degree, this process continued west of Wichita. Townships along the Santa Fe spur through Comanche and Clark counties were marked by high percentages of Hoosiers. A large secondary movement westward from south-central Kansas was an even more important source of settlers. Hoosiers were among the Kingman people who founded Greensburg and the Harper people who settled Coldwater. They joined other Winfield entrepreneurs to plat Protection (Comanche County), Ashland (Clark County), Veteran (Morton County), and Johnson City (Stanton County). Place-name transfers from Indiana were

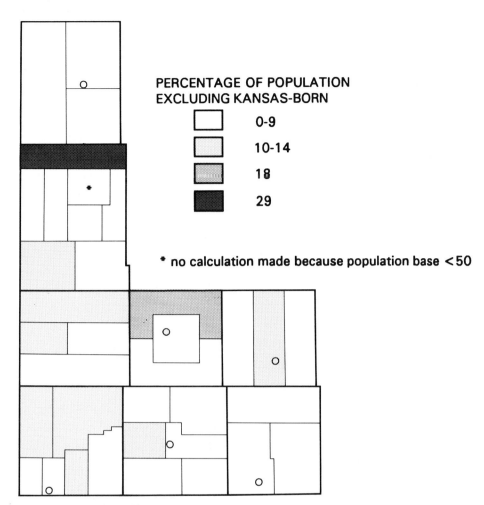

PERCENTAGE OF POPULATION
EXCLUDING KANSAS-BORN

0-9

10-14

18

29

* no calculation made because population base < 50

all in the southern counties as well: Avilla and Evansville in Comanche County, Elkhart in Morton, Lafayette and Valparaiso in Stevens, and Wabash in Gray.[52]

The largest single concentration of Indianans occurred in northeastern Kiowa County in the small town of Haviland, a Quaker settlement begun in 1884 when Benjamin Albertson and three other men judged the area to have good farming possibilities. Twenty-five families immigrated the next year, and in 1886 they platted a town along the new Santa Fe grade. The name chosen honored Laura Haviland, a fellow Quaker famous for her humanitarian work with fugitive slaves. Albertson's advertisements in the *Christian Worker Magazine* brought more Hoosiers to the area, and the community was large enough by 1892 to build an academy. This school evolved into Friends Bible College by 1930 and operates today as Barclay College. The census agent recorded 147 Indiana natives living in the immediate vicinity of Haviland in 1905; they constituted 34 percent of the town's immigrant population.[53]

The success of Haviland led to several other colonies of Indiana Quakers in southwestern Kansas. A group from Bloomington, led by Hiram and Ruth Newlin, settled north of Coldwater in 1885. Lafayette, in Stevens County, began in 1887 with the migration of two Haviland families: Norton and Anna Hockett, and Thomas and Ellen Hockett. In turn, the Lafayette community produced small outposts in Grant and Stevens counties. Nixon Rich and Isaiah Kershner promoted another settlement near Fowler in northeastern Meade County; this group was large enough by 1906 to start an academy.[54]

CULTURE REGIONS

The tableau of settlement had a simpler design in western Kansas than elsewhere in the state. Whether because of local climatic extremes, new economic opportunities in cities, or other factors, many groups who had been important contributors to life in central Kansas chose not to migrate farther west in large numbers. The English, the Irish, the Bohemians, and the French Canadians were notable in this regard as were New Yorkers and others from Northern culture states, Pennsylvania Germans, and black Americans. The stage was left to be occupied principally by people from the North-Midland states west of Pennsylvania and, increasingly, by Missourians and other Upper Southerners. The two groups together constituted 80 percent of the immigration to the counties surveyed in 1905 and the same again in 1925.

The generalized nativity regions represented on Map 5.30 reflect data for 1905 in the northern and eastern sections of the region and for 1925 in eight southwestern counties. Overall, the pattern is simpler than those of earlier decades but just as sharply regionalized. Its most striking feature is a large area dominated by South-Midland immigrants, the first time since the Civil War period that this group had been so influential over so large an area. In 1905 their percentages along the southern tier of counties from Clark through Morton were comparable to those recorded in 1885 farther east along this tier, in the range of 33 to 40 percent. The numbers in counties farther to the north, however, were higher than in similar locations in central Kansas. Motivations that underlie this South-Midland surge are unclear but probably involve the lateness of industrialization in the Upper South compared with the North-Midland and Northern states; Southern people pursued traditional agricultural frontiers longer. This change in migration rates increased after 1905, at least for the southwestern counties. An influx of Missourians and Oklahomans over the next twenty years made South-Midland people a majority over the entirety of three counties and parts of five others.

The corridor of the Santa Fe Railroad, a distinctive nativity region throughout central Kansas because of European recruitments and Yankee urban entrepreneurs, is not visible on Map 5.30. In the absence of Germanic and New York settlers, an amalgam of South Midlanders, Illini, and Hoosiers expanded into the grant; farther east, this group had been largely restricted to the Osage

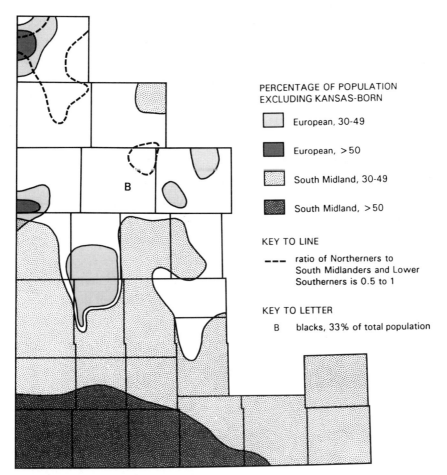

MAP 5.30
*Generalized nativity
regions, 1905/1925 (western
Kansas). Data from
Kansas state census. Areas
left blank are generally
those in which people
from North-Midland
states form the dominant
immigrant group.*

PERCENTAGE OF POPULATION
EXCLUDING KANSAS-BORN

European, 30-49

European, >50

South Midland, 30-49

South Midland, >50

KEY TO LINE

--- ratio of Northerners to
South Midlanders and Lower
Southerners is 0.5 to 1

KEY TO LETTER

B   blacks, 33% of total population

Reserve. A new cultural transition zone occurs near the Missouri Pacific Railroad, midway between the Santa Fe and Union Pacific lines. Missourians came to this area in sufficient numbers to provide Southern flavor, but enough Europeans and others also ventured south from the Union Pacific settlements to establish significant linkages to the larger mix of people that traditionally characterized northern Kansas.

The northern half of western Kansas in 1905 could be described as an appliqued quilt wherein blocks of relatively exotic cultures are laid on a base fabric of North-Midland peoples. A typical county would have a slight majority of its population from North-Midland states, with another third from a secondary group, variously composed of Swedes, Russian-Germans, blacks, and even white Upper Southerners. Yankee percentages never reached this high of a level, but their small clusterings added texture to the overall design. Europeans were more numerous within the old Union Pacific corridor than outside of it, a reflection not only of their continuing desire to purchase land in blocks but also of good rail connections to parent ethnic colonies in central Kansas.

Pioneer settlement was a much longer and more traumatic process in western Kansas than elsewhere in the state. The economy switched from ranching to farming within the 1880s, back to ranching in the 1890s, and then again to farming at the turn of the century. People came and went by the thousands, but, even though some changes occurred in the migration patterns, the general source areas for the various subregions were remarkably constant. The economy established in northwestern Kansas by 1905 or so has remained largely a farming one based on wheat. Life in the southwestern counties, however, would change again and again. Large reserves of natural gas under Stevens County and its neighbors, discovered in the late 1920s, brought a prosperity that was temporarily dashed by the Dust Bowl experience of the 1930s. More recently, center-pivot irrigation using the Ogallala Aquifer has created an economic chain reaction. Local farmers now commonly grow corn and alfalfa even on the sand hills, and the corn, in turn, has brought cattle-feeding and meatpacking industries to Liberal, Garden City, and other places. This roller coaster of activity has necessarily been accompanied by population shifts. Increases in Mexican immigration (Hispanics now constitute one-quarter of the population in Garden City) and the recruitment of Vietnamese workers for the packing plants in the 1980s have been well documented.[55] Southwestern Kansas, like the coal communities of Crawford County and the larger cities of eastern Kansas, has changed much since its initial settlement.

6

Population Origins in Perspective

Distinctions among cultural groups in Kansas have never been so pronounced as they were during the territorial period of the late 1850s. Kentuckians of that era came from a different world than did Massachusetts people. When the politics of slavery and state-making were added to long-standing differences in speech, religion, and other ways of life, it is little wonder that Northerners and Southerners founded rival towns and that Kansas bled for a decade. By 1885, 1905, and 1925, however, not only had the issues of the Civil War faded but so too had some of the cultural distinctiveness. North still differed from South, but significant mixing of peoples had occurred in Illinois, Indiana, and Ohio, the states that contributed most heavily to the postwar settlement of Kansas. New Englanders, North Midlanders, and Upper Southerners arrayed themselves in discernible bands across the rural counties of these three states. In major cities such as Chicago and Cincinnati, these groups were joined by Europeans and others.[1]

The degree to which cultural attitudes had blended in Kansas and other Midwestern states by the late nineteenth century is debated, but the nativity maps shown throughout the previous chapters demonstrate that people from each of the older culture areas continued to cluster with their own kind across the Kansas plains. Similar discussion over the relative strengths of forces promoting homogeneity and heterogeneity extends to present-day America as well.[2] The issue is fascinating, but it can hardly be resolved in the conclusion to a study of population origins. If one chooses to emphasize the homogeneity of modern Kansas culture, time-honored traditions of Republican dominance and centrist Methodist theology provide persuasive arguments. I happen to be more interested in diversity, however, including its persistence in the face of modern communications and transportation, and it is this issue that I concentrate on here.

Having mapped patterns of religious, political, and educational diversity for northeastern Kansas in 1865 in chapter three, I will demonstrate similar heterogeneity statewide for 1885 in this chapter and then discuss the modern scene. Several ongoing cultural mechanisms have created new regions in the state, but manifestations of the old nativity patterns endure as well. The maps in this chapter are intended only as examples. Just as I have enjoyed consulting Neale Carman's atlas of European enclaves in Kansas as I wonder about such patterns as the vote for Ross Perot in 1992 or the location of ethnic restaurants, I hope that readers will use the nativity maps presented here in a spirit of similar adventure.[3]

HISTORICAL PATTERNS

Let us begin with some representative distributions from the late nineteenth century. Clearly one legacy of nativity was place-names. Major European examples have been noted in earlier chapters. Direct transfers of town and township names from the eastern states, such as Newton in Harvey County (Massachusetts), Dubuque in Russell County (Iowa), and Ashland in Clark County (Kentucky), coincide nicely with the various degrees of clustering noted for the peoples themselves (see Maps 6.1, 6.2, 6.3). Southern names are bunched, for example, and Yankee ones dispersed (cf. Map 6.4). The relative frequency of the transferred names from each area also reflects the tendencies of the various culture groups toward urban life. The sixty-two names from Northern culture states represent 30 percent of the total transfers known to have been made from the Eastern states, a number several times greater than the percentage of actual Yankee settlers in Kansas. Such overrepresentation in town names is what one would expect from urban entrepreneurs (see Tables 3.1, 4.1, 5.1, 5.2). The nineteen Southern names, in contrast, represent 9 percent of the transfer stock, a figure that is far lower than the actual Southern presence in Kansas. Name transfers from the North-Midland states, predictably, fall between the two extremes. Both the pattern and the percentage reflect the actual experience of these settlers.[4]

One could argue that place-name selection is only a one-time exercise in nostalgia and therefore not reflective of continuing cultural behavior on the Kansas frontier. Agricultural practices should offer more convincing evidence. One linkage has already been described, that between Upper Southern peoples and the early development of cattle ranching in the state. The major grain crops, in contrast, were grown by most immigrants although Russian-Germans and other Europeans

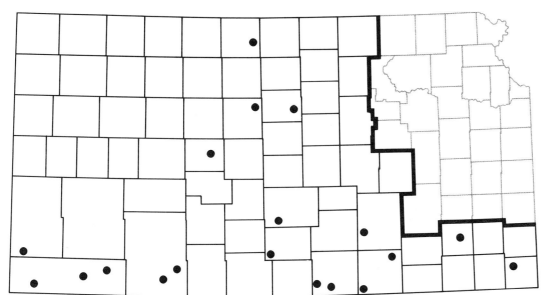

MAP 6.1
*Town and township
names transferred from
South-Midland and
Lower Southern states.
Data from John Rydjord,*
Kansas Place-Names
*(Norman: University of
Oklahoma Press, 1972);
Sondra Van Meter McCoy
and Jan Hults,* 1001
Kansas Place Names
*(Lawrence: University
Press of Kansas, 1989);
and other sources.*

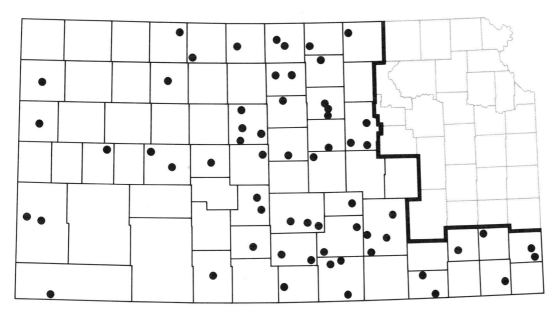

MAP 6.2
*Town and township
names transferred from
Northern states. Data
from John Rydjord,*
Kansas Place-Names
*(Norman: University of
Oklahoma Press, 1972);
Sondra Van Meter McCoy
and Jan Hults,* 1001
Kansas Place Names
*(Lawrence: University
Press of Kansas, 1989);
and other sources.*

MAP 6.3

Town and township names transferred from North-Midland states. Data from John Rydjord, Kansas Place-Names *(Norman: University of Oklahoma Press, 1972);* Sondra Van Meter McCoy *and Jan Hults,* 1001 Kansas Place Names *(Lawrence: University Press of Kansas, 1989); and other sources.*

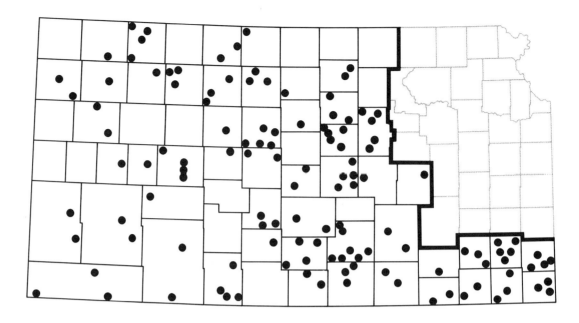

had little to do with corn initially. Winter wheat became important for all groups after 1874, a year in which this crop alone survived grasshoppers and drought. Mennonites, particularly Bernhard Warkentin in the mid-1880s, led the way in the transition from soft to hard varieties of wheat, but despite many folk stories to the contrary, the Russian-Germans were not solely responsible for the varieties that gradually came to dominate the Kansas scene.[5]

A classic distinction between rural Northerners and rural Southerners was their choice of draft animals. Both groups used oxen for the initial breaking of the sod, but thereafter many Southerners preferred mules over horses for routine field work. The tendency was strongest in the Lower South, where horses outnumbered mules only by 2 to 1. The ratio in favor of horses rose to between 7 and 10 to 1 in the Upper South and was higher still in North-Midland states.[6] In Kansas, the horse-mule ratio for 1885 defines the areas of South-Midland influence almost perfectly (see Map 6.5). The lowest ratio (2.3 to 1) was in Doniphan County, heart of the old Missouri migration during the 1850s. Other places lower than 4 to 1 included Cherokee County in the southeastern corner and several counties in or near the Gypsum Hills. Settlers from Missouri and Kentucky in the north-central counties of Graham, Osborne, and Rooks also brought their mules along with them. Throughout southern Kansas the ratios actually are biased more toward mules than one would expect from the nativity data. The numbers provide a strong argument, in fact, that most of the Illinois and Indiana settlers who were so numerous in this part of Kansas came from counties near the Ohio River and were themselves bearers of Upper Southern culture.

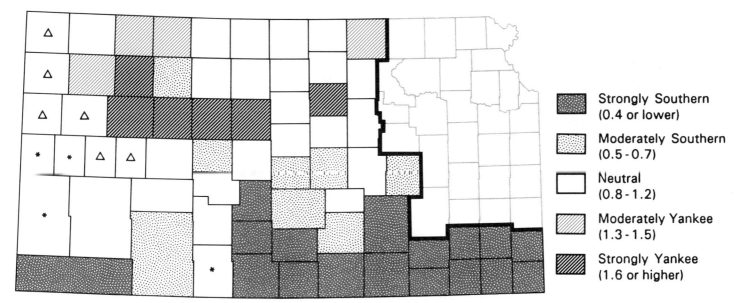

△ no ratio calculated because the total of the two groups was less than 100   * no census data

Legend:
- Strongly Southern (0.4 or lower)
- Moderately Southern (0.5 - 0.7)
- Neutral (0.8 - 1.2)
- Moderately Yankee (1.3 - 1.5)
- Strongly Yankee (1.6 or higher)

MAP 6.4
Ratio of natives of Northern states to natives of South-Midland and Lower Southern states, 1885. Data from Kansas state census.

European immigrants in Kansas were not particularly distinctive with regard to draft animals, but several groups were unique in other agricultural matters. The directors of the First Swedish Agricultural Company, for example, encouraged Lindsborg colonists to try broomcorn, and it quickly emerged as an important cash crop.[7] The 5,523 acres of it reported in McPherson County for 1885 was two thousand acres more than in any other county in the state. Mennonites had mulberry groves (for silkworms) during their early years in Kansas, and nearly every Russian-German settlement featured fields of sunflowers (for seeds), watermelon, and tobacco (see Map 6.6). Watermelons were a commercial crop in Ellis County until the 1950s, but the other two items were grown mainly for personal use; the men were avid cigar smokers, and sunflower seeds are still known locally as "Russian peanuts."[8]

The list of traditional social traits that I used to evaluate the distinctiveness of Yankee and South-Midland settlements in northeastern Kansas (chapter 3) provides several additional cultural measures that should be relevant for the rest of the state. One item, an orientation of Northerners toward cities, has already been shown to have continued into the 1880s (see Tables 3.3, 4.2, 4.4). The issue of university location, important in the state in 1865, had been largely resolved two decades later, but religion and politics were ongoing and easily quantifiable cultural concerns. Attitudes toward alcohol, another trait on the original list and one about which many groups had strong feelings, was put to a statewide vote in 1880.

A preliminary map I prepared of the proportion of the population in each county who be-

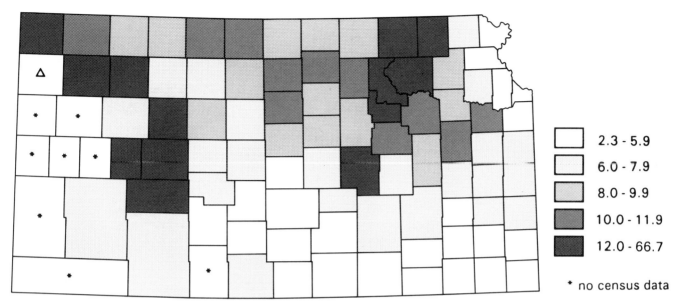

△ no ratio calculated because the total of the two groups was less than 100

MAP 6.5

Ratio of horses to mules and asses, 1885. Data from Kansas state census.

longed to a church organization in 1886 revealed rates across southern Kansas about half those of the old Yankee counties in the Kaw valley. High rates typified many ethnic counties as well. An absence of Mennonite and other groups from the church census, however, made this project statistically suspect overall. An alternative was to compare memberships in denominations clearly associated with Yankee and Southern peoples (see Map 6.7).[9] An influx of Northerners into the cities of northeastern Kansas between 1865 and 1886 modified the religious character of several counties, but settlers by and large retained their traditional religious affiliation after they moved to the state. Nicodemus Baptists rendered Graham County a religious island as well as a racial one, and a small Congregational college made Greenwood County more Northern than its early settlement would have predicted. Large membership in the freethinking Christian church (Disciples of Christ) accounts for the unexpected Southern patterns in Cloud, Mitchell, and Republic counties.

The election for governor in 1884 is a good one to examine for general cultural patterns. A Democrat, George Glick, had won the office in 1882 for the first time in state history and was attempting a second term. Voters from both major parties thus had strong incentives to cast ballots. The issue of regional loyalty to candidates, usually an interpretative problem, also is eliminated for this year because both Glick and his Republican opponent, John Martin, happened to live in Atchison. The chief campaign issue was Prohibition, whether the restrictive law passed in 1880 should be resubmitted to the people for another vote; Democrats said yes, Republicans no.[10]

Martin defeated Glick by a vote of 146,777 to 108,284. Although one can see evidence of tradi-

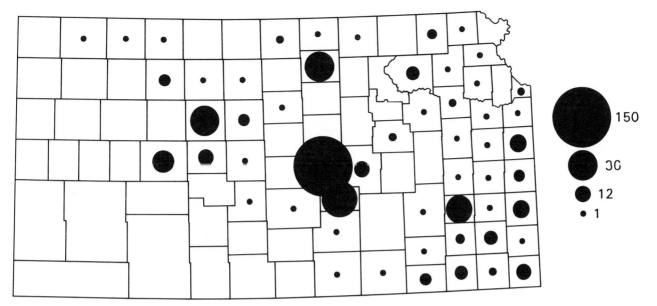

MAP 6.6
Acres of tobacco harvested,
1885. Data from Kansas
state census.

tional Democratic orientation by natives of Missouri and other Upper Southern states, the most striking geographical feature is that party's strength in several ethnic counties (see Map 6.8). This affiliation was new to such groups. The European immigrant communities in Kansas had formed under Republican state administrations, and, since government officials generally had treated them well, they tended to become Republicans themselves. The Swedes in McPherson and Republic counties are classic cases in point, unwavering in their party allegiance throughout the nineteenth century. Once the Republican platform officially adopted a Prohibitionist plank in 1874, however, many of the other European settlers began to listen to political alternatives. Some of these people saw Prohibition as silly, others as hypocrisy, and most felt that the law would curtail further European immigration to the state.[11]

Most Mennonites were not yet active in politics in 1884, and both the Wabaunsee County Germans and the Pennsylvania-German colonists in Dickinson, Osborne, and Russell counties stayed in the Republican camp. French Canadians and Bohemians split on the issue (the Cuba group preferred the Republicans, the Wilson group the Democrats), but most of the other Europeans embraced the Democratic position. Ellis Countians, in fact, recorded the highest Democratic percentage in the state (56), and the German vote was instrumental in the impressive party showings in Barton, Ellsworth, Geary, and Leavenworth counties. Danish Democratic votes helped to counter a larger Republican bloc in Lincoln County as did Irish voters in Dickinson, Nemaha, and Pottawatomie counties.[12]

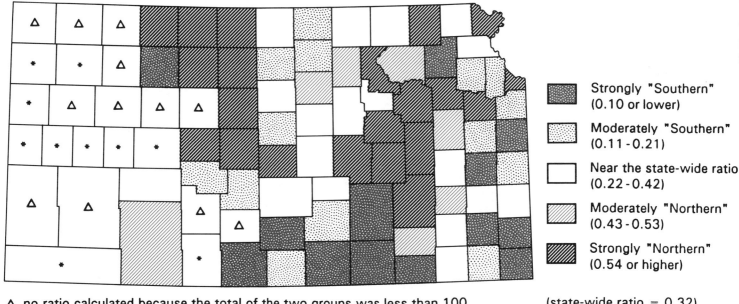

▨	Strongly "Southern" (0.10 or lower)
▨	Moderately "Southern" (0.11 - 0.21)
☐	Near the state-wide ratio (0.22 - 0.42)
▨	Moderately "Northern" (0.43 - 0.53)
▨	Strongly "Northern" (0.54 or higher)

△ no ratio calculated because the total of the two groups was less than 100   (state-wide ratio = 0.32)

* no data, or no membership in these denominations

MAP 6.7
Ratio of membership of Congregational, Unitarian, Universalist, Seventh-Day Adventist, and Wesleyan churches to membership of Christian and Baptist churches, 1886. Data from Fifth Biennial Report of the Kansas State Board of Agriculture, 1885–1886 *(Topeka: Kansas Publishing House, 1887).*

In addition to revealing political independence in many European communities, the 1884 vote also suggests that some South-Midland settlers were in the process of modifying their traditional voting behavior. South Midlanders had become Democrats during the time of Andrew Jackson, when that party stood for Western rights, and most of them remained so when they came to Kansas in the 1850s. Given this heritage and the relatively tolerant attitude this culture traditionally had accorded to alcohol, it is surprising to see that the proportion of Democratic votes in the southern tiers of counties seldom exceeded 40 to 45 percent. To be sure, these figures were 10 percentage points higher than those in the Iowa-influenced, heavily Republican counties of north-central Kansas, and exceptions could be found on the southwestern frontier, but they still were lower than would be predicted by the old South-Midland stereotype.

The possibility that the lukewarm response of southern Kansans to the Democratic candidate in 1884 resulted from an issue other than alcohol is dispelled by a look at the voting pattern on the actual Prohibition referendum four years earlier (see Map 6.9).[13] People in counties such as Butler, Cowley, Elk, and Sumner not only favored Prohibition but they also gave it some of the highest percentages in the state. Perhaps these Kansans had decided that, once the frontier period had ended, it would help their personal and regional prosperity to support the majority Republican party in the state. Perhaps the Christian and other evangelical churches were especially active in the region at this time (as they were in many Southern states). The newer, southwestern counties

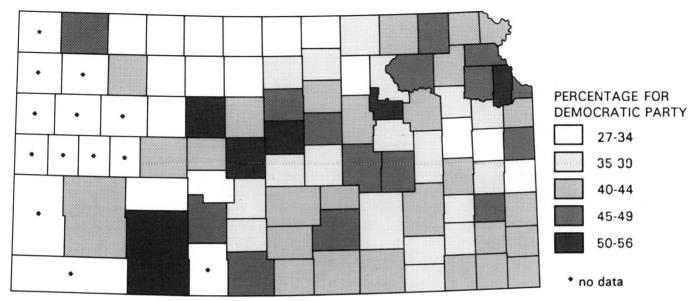

PERCENTAGE FOR
DEMOCRATIC PARTY

☐	27-34
☐	35 39
☐	40-44
☐	45-49
☐	50-56

* no data

MAP 6.8
*The vote for governor,
1884. Data from* Fifth
Biennial Report of the
Secretary of State of
the State of Kansas,
*1885–1886 (Topeka:
Kansas Publishing House,
1886), pp. 66–67.*

of the state exhibited the more expected South-Midland behavior: 53 percent of the voters in Ford County opted for Glick in 1884; only 20 percent of them favored Prohibition.

The correlation between dry and Republican votes is high. Robert Bader calculated a coefficient of .43 using 1880 election data, and one can easily see that the counties shaded heavily on Map 6.8 tend to have light or no shading on Map 6.9.[14] The most interesting exceptions are Graham and Rooks counties; residents of the Nicodemus area there, like most black Americans, embraced the Republican party because of its stand against slavery. As Upper Southern people, though, they saw Prohibition as undesirable. Only 37 percent of Graham County residents voted for the referendum, the lowest figure in north-central Kansas.

BORDER COMPARISONS

Before turning to twentieth-century cultural patterns in the state and how they may relate to the old nativity regions, it would seem useful to attempt a comparison of these nativities across the borders of the state. Studies of Kansas or any other political entity carry with them the unstated assumption that the borders of that unit form a significant human divide. Such an assumption makes sense in many instances, but it certainly should be questioned within the United States. Few barriers to interstate migration have ever existed, and one could argue that the Kansas-Nebraska line would have been nearly meaningless to a settler coming west from, say, Ohio in 1875. Kinship ties, land costs, ease of transportation, and the other factors discussed at length in earlier chapters

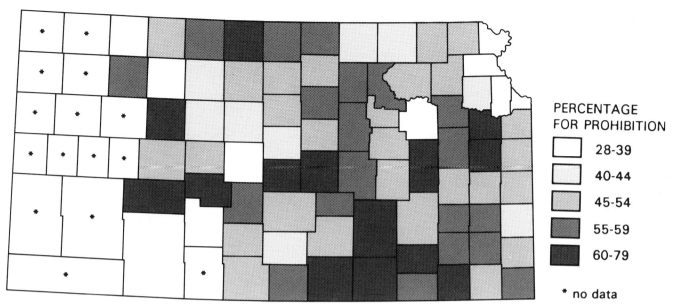

PERCENTAGE
FOR PROHIBITION

☐ 28-39

☐ 40-44

▨ 45-54

▨ 55-59

▨ 60-79

* no data

MAP 6.9
*The vote on the
Prohibition referendum,
1880. Data from Robert
S. Bader,* Prohibition
in Kansas: A History
*(Lawrence: University
Press of Kansas, 1986), pp.
269–70.*

would all loom as more significant concerns in the choice of a homesite. Differences in nativity might be more apparent along the Kansas-Missouri border, of course, where bitterness and strife were common at least through the Civil War years. The differences should be stronger still between Kansas and eastern Oklahoma because Indian Territory remained a political reality until 1907.

The state census data that form the core of this book cannot be used to evaluate cross-border similarities, of course, but potentially useful information was published as part of the federal census of 1880. For each county in a state, counts exist for foreign-born residents as well as for those native to the nine states that contributed the largest numbers to the population of that state.[15] These groupings of source states for Kansas, Missouri, and Nebraska are similar to one another, although not identical, but no data exist for areas adjacent to Kansas in unsettled Colorado and in Indian Territory.

I was able to create four measures for comparative purposes. Three are the same across both the Missouri and the Nebraska lines: New Yorkers as a surrogate for the Northern culture states; Illini, Indianans, Iowans, Ohioans, and Pennsylvanians as a nearly complete reflection of North-Midland immigration, and all foreign-born residents. The South-Midland contingent is represented by Missourians in the Kansas-Nebraska border counties, by the Kentucky-Missouri-Tennessee total in Kansas counties that border Missouri, and by the Kentucky-Tennessee-Virginia total in Missouri counties that border Kansas. In all cases, I calculated percentages based on the total non-native-born population.

The four measures reveal no sharp breaks in the nativity patterns along either border (see Map 6.10). New Yorkers came to both sides of the Kansas-Nebraska line in almost equal numbers, and,

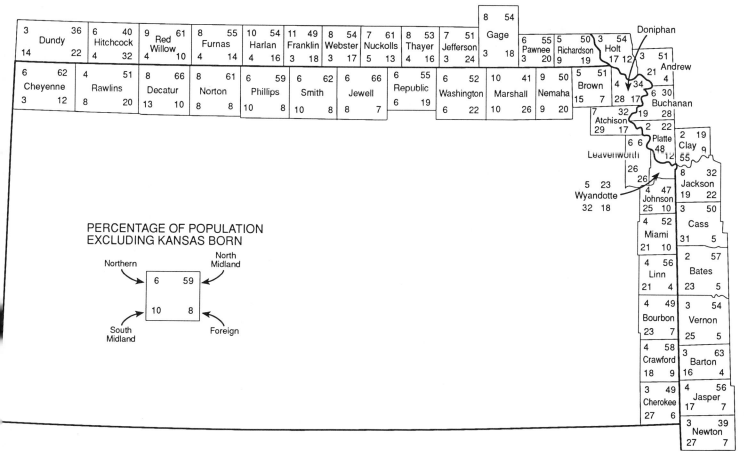

PERCENTAGE OF POPULATION EXCLUDING KANSAS BORN

MAP 6.10
Settlers from major culture areas along the Kansas-Missouri and Kansas-Nebraska borders, 1880. Data from U.S. census. For states used to represent the various culture areas, see text.

as far west as Republic County, the same is true for the other groups. The border counties in western Nebraska have slightly lower percentages of Missourians and North Midlanders than do the ones in adjacent Kansas, however, and a correspondingly higher European contingent. The difference probably was a result of the Burlington Railroad, which passed through southern Nebraska and had superior connections with Chicago, a major distribution point for new immigrants from abroad.

The Kansas-Missouri border was no barrier either; the biggest distinction there was between urban and rural counties. Those counties with large cities—Atchison, Leavenworth, and Wyandotte on the Kansas side, Buchanan (St. Joseph) and Jackson (Kansas City) in Missouri—had much larger foreign percentages than did the others and somewhat higher New York components as well. Such traits characterized most Midwestern cities. Rural counties south of Kansas City were almost identical across the border, but north of that city an extremely high immigration of Ken-

Population Origins in Perspective : 199

tuckians made Clay and Platte counties distinctive. This Kentucky migration, creating the enclave known as Little Dixie in Missouri, followed the north bank of the Missouri River upstream all the way from St. Louis but stopped near St. Joseph.[16] These same people pioneered in Atchison and Leavenworth counties in Kansas, of course, but whereas German and other immigrants after the 1850s modified the nature of these Kansas places, rural Missouri stayed the same. North of St. Joseph, the nativity patterns of Andrew and Holt counties in Missouri have the familiar North-Midland dominance characteristic of most rural counties in Kansas and Nebraska.

THE MODERN CULTURAL SCENE

Students of Kansas geography are confronted with a major inconsistency when they compare the historic nativity patterns shown in this atlas with modern delimitations of American culture regions. Although *Washington Post* reporter Joel Garreau might be said to have followed the argument of North-Midland dominance in the state when he included the entire area as part of the "breadbasket" section of the country, the more usual position has been to divide the state with a north-south line passing near Russell, Great Bend, and Medicine Lodge. The eastern section is usually labeled as part of the Midwest; the High Plains is sometimes said to be a world unto itself or sometimes a subset of either the West or the Midwest.[17] Assuming, for the moment, that this modern east-west division is accurate, how are we to account for the change? Has recent migration into and within the state been large enough to replace the old pattern with an essentially new one? Alternately, is the current east-west division the product of some cultural force other than, or in addition to, nativity? If this latter scenario is correct, the older, nineteenth-century patterns may still remain intact, existing perhaps as subdivisions within the new dichotomy.

Postfrontier immigration would seem a logical way to account for a new pattern of cultural values. For Kansas, though, major growth has been limited to perhaps twenty counties. It is most obvious in and near the metropolitan centers of Kansas City and Wichita, at the army bases in Geary and Leavenworth counties, near the meatpacking plants at Garden City, and at the university communities in Douglas and Riley counties. People from all regions of the country have come into these places during the postfrontier period as have many foreign-born immigrants. By 1930, for example, over five hundred Mexican natives lived in each of eight counties along the main line of the Santa Fe Railroad, led by Wyandotte, Shawnee, and Sedgwick. Some ten thousand Slovenes, Italians, French, Belgians, and other Europeans worked in the coal mines of Crawford and Cherokee counties in 1915, and a similar number of Germans, Irish, Poles, Croatians, and other immigrants labored in the packing houses of Wyandotte County. Much smaller but locally important later immigrant groups included nine hundred Welsh to Lyon County, two thousand Swedes to Osage County, two thousand Irish to Pottawatomie County, and, most recently, between two and three thousand Southeast Asians to the Garden City area. The long-time presence of American

Indians, who had been essentially ignored in the early censuses, was gradually acknowledged in Brown, Jackson, and nearby urban counties.[18]

Besides the influx of new immigrants to the state, at least two other social changes have the potential to alter traditional culture patterns. Rural-to-urban migration, as important a force in Kansas as elsewhere in the country, has been a fact of life for literally thousands of families. The process underlies the stagnant or declining populations found in the majority of Kansas counties, but I suspect it has been relatively unimportant in changing the patterns of regional culture. If, as seems logical, most of the growth for cities such as Concordia, Newton, and Wellington has come at the expense of counties adjacent to them, the character of each section of the state should remain fairly well intact.[19]

A second possible force that might modify cultural geography is what folklorist Suzi Jones has called "regionalization."[20] A group of people who come to a particular place begin to interact with each other and with local environmental conditions; over time, they incorporate the fruits of that interaction into their general cultural outlook. Jones has written about the impact of rainy weather and a lumbering/fishing economy on the folklife of the people in Oregon who live west of the Cascade Mountains. A similar argument easily could be made for the High Plains. Settlers in this area clearly had to modify their traditional agricultural behavior in order to survive. It is only a small jump to imagine that a combination of this new economy, a shared experience of weather extremes, and the gradual accumulation of family and local history would produce new expressions, attitudes, and values. A political secessional movement in southwestern Kansas in 1992 and 1993 would seem to be a recent example of such independent spirit. Other writers have identified distinctive character traits. Some claim optimism is strong on the plains because it is a necessary attribute for survival in a land of irregular rainfall and violent storms. Others point to the development of friendliness and cooperation as responses to a small population.[21]

Paul Phillips tried to evaluate the strength of an east-west cultural division in Kansas during the late 1970s and found several measures that seemed to support the regionalization process. A higher percentage of people belonged to churches in western counties than in eastern ones, for example, perhaps because the social benefits offered by church membership were needed more in an area where low population density made other formal opportunities for socializing rare. The somewhat isolated Westerners also increased their contact with new ideas by subscribing to more magazines per capita. General conservatism for western Kansans was suggested by their selection of more traditional first names for their children, compared with their eastern neighbors.[22]

If one accepts the regionalization argument as valid, and I do, the cultural geography of Kansas in the late twentieth century theoretically should contain new culture areas not only in western Kansas but also in the fast-growing cities of the state where people from varied origins are interacting with a rapidly changing social environment. This ongoing process, though, should in no way preclude a significant legacy from the old settlers. Most counties in Kansas, especially those

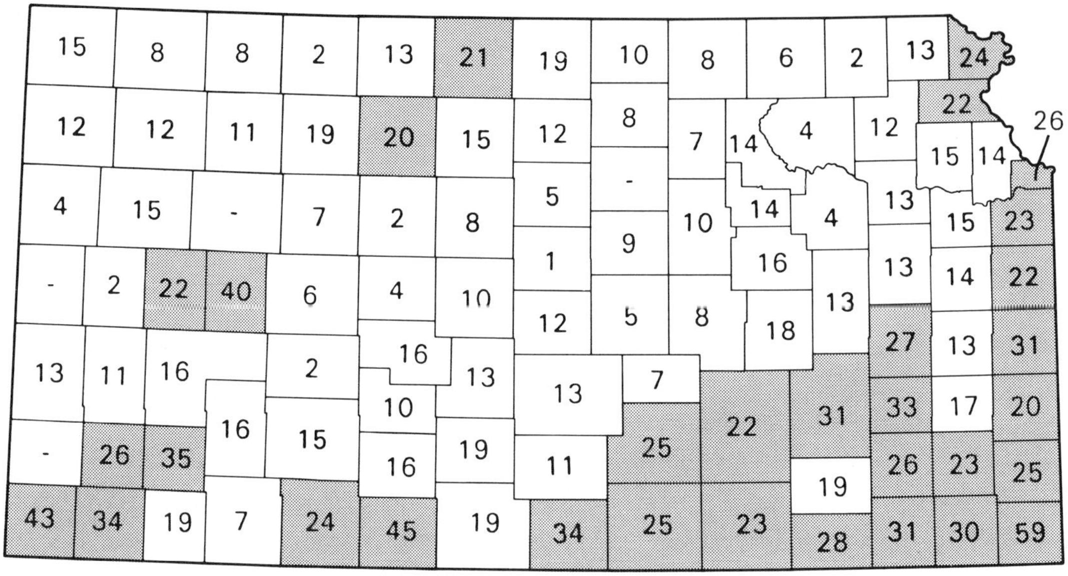

MAP 6.11

Six southern denominations, 1980 (percentage of total adherents): Assemblies of God, Disciples of Christ, Christian Churches and Churches of Christ, Church of God (Cleveland, Tenn.), Presbyterian Church in the United States, Southern Baptist Convention. Data from Bernard Quinn et al., Churches and Church Membership in the United States, 1980 *(Atlanta: Glenmary Research Center, 1982), pp. 111–20.*

beyond the irrigation area in the southwest and the transportation corridors of Interstate 70 and the Arkansas valley, have grown little or not at all since about 1900.[23] Their peoples are largely descendants of nineteenth-century settlers, and their traditional geographical and cultural distinctions remain intact.

The patterns of many cultural traits in the 1980s and 1990s look quite familiar to any reader of this book. In religion, for example, denominations with a heritage in the Southern states reach their greatest strength in eastern and southern Kansas (see Map 6.11). A recent study of dialect shows a nearly identical distribution as does the incidence of barbeque restaurants (see Map 6.12). Affiliations with political parties have a somewhat more complex pattern (see Map 6.13).[24] Kansas continues to be a truly Republican state, but people in the southern and eastern counties are generally less zealous in their support of the Grand Old Party than are those in northern locations. South-Midland heritage explains most of these instances but fails to do so in several counties in southwestern Kansas. These places, more enthusiastically Republican than the nativity data would have predicted, have had some of the highest per capita incomes in the state in recent decades. Royalties from a large dome of natural gas centered beneath Stevens and Grant counties have been supplemented since the 1960s by monies from center-pivot irrigation. Since local incomes now match the Republican stereotype and since that party has always been a strong supporter of the domestic oil and gas industry, political affiliations have gradually changed as well. It is regionalization in action.

Ethnicity remains clearly visible in Kansas, both in people's minds and on the landscape. In politics, unwavering support by Mennonite and Swedish settlers for the Republican party is appar-

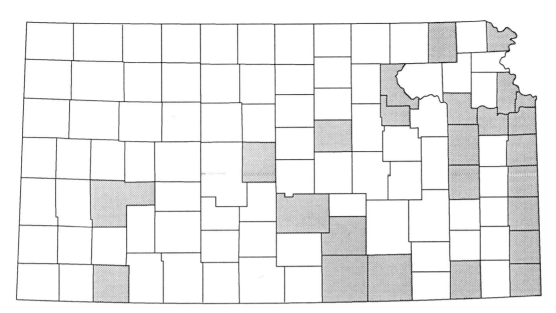

MAP 6.12
Counties with barbeque restaurants, 1993. Data compiled by Laura M. Moley from local telephone directories and the Kansas Business Directory *(Omaha, Nebr.: American Business Directories, 1993).*

ent on Map 6.13. The Democratic orientation of the Volga Germans is even more visible, making Ellis County the sole stronghold of that party west of the Missouri border counties. The only politicians who happened to speak German there in the 1880s were Democrats as were the only local German newspapers. The stance of the party against Prohibition solidified their allegiance. The two other areas of Democratic strength in the state developed where ethnicity and blue-collar, industrial employment coincided: the coal mines of southeastern Kansas and the meatpacking plants of Wyandotte County. Both, of course, were postfrontier developments.[25]

Perhaps the best measure of continued ethnic awareness comes from a question on the federal census forms of 1980 and 1990. People were asked to write in the name of ethnic or national groups with whom they identified closely. The results, for most groups in Kansas, correspond closely to the geographical patterns set down in the nineteenth century (see Maps 6.14, 6.15). German affiliation is extremely strong, ranging from about 10 percent of the population in eastern Kansas to a high of 50 percent in Ellis County. The percentages in Barton, Dickinson, McPherson, and Wabaunsee counties (34 in Barton, 23 in each of the others) are perhaps a little lower than one might expect based on the earlier maps, and those in extreme western Kansas higher. The twentieth-century migration of Russian-German peoples into the High Plains probably accounts for the latter phenomenon. I suspect that their numbers were greater than has yet been documented and that they have stayed in western Kansas in higher percentages than have other settlers.[26]

The French-Canadian, Czech, and Scandinavian affiliations occur in familiar locations. Seven percent of McPherson County residents recorded a Swedish identification, a figure held down by the big Mennonite population in the southern half of that county. Mexican and African-American

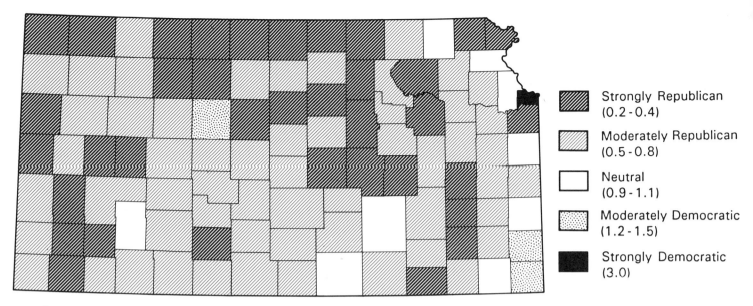

Strongly Republican
(0.2 - 0.4)

Moderately Republican
(0.5 - 0.8)

Neutral
(0.9 - 1.1)

Moderately Democratic
(1.2 - 1.5)

Strongly Democratic
(3.0)

MAP 6.13
*Ratio of Democratic
to Republican voter
registration, 1990. Data
from* Election Statistics,
State of Kansas: 1990
Primary and General
Elections *(Topeka:
Secretary of State Bill
Graves, n.d.), pp. 20–24.*

affiliations show major shifts over the past century, the Mexican one, of course, rising from none
to a substantial presence. Blacks in Kansas have urbanized faster than have other groups. Only 1
percent of the residents of Graham County, the site of Nicodemus, claimed an African-American
heritage, and the old exoduster centers of Labette and Montgomery counties recorded affiliations
of only 4 and 5 percent, respectively. The showing of Geary County (12 percent) is caused by
soldiers at Fort Riley and that of Wyandotte County (20 percent) by the long-standing racial sepa-
ration of the Kansas City population by the line between Johnson and Wyandotte counties.

CODA

Geographers, like most travelers, go into the world in search of diversity. We soon learn that
regional foods, architectures, crops, and religions are as important to the creation of landscape
character as are topography and climate. By seeing how others eat, build, grow, and pray, we stimu-
late our minds and, incidentally, learn about ourselves. In an ideal situation, such variety would be
accompanied by mutual respect for traditions and behavior. Groups would not set out deliberately
to assimilate one another or to create a pecking order of social status. Although no place has yet to
achieve a utopian blend of diversity and understanding, much of Kansas, together with other sections of the United States that have not experienced recent large inflows of new migrants, comes
closer to it today than it has at any time in its past. Ethnic festivals grow in popularity and are
attended by people from many backgrounds. Accents are seen as interesting rather than as status-
marking, and regional foodways form a major focus for new restaurants and cookbooks.[27]

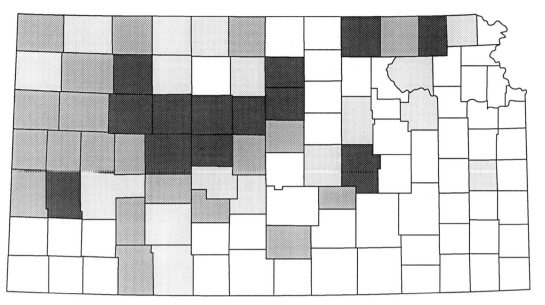

MAP 6.14
*People who claim
identification with
German ancestry, 1980.
Data from U.S. census.*

PERCENTAGE OF POPULATION

	5-19
	20-24
	25-34
	35-50

Although some of the recent praise for diversity may be fueled by a fear that homogeneity looms on the horizon, other observers make a strong case for a continuing, even growing sense of regional identity. Americans yearn to establish roots, they say, to slow down their pace of life and to rediscover the local pleasures of family and community.[28] Ironically, this neoregionalism is also promoted by the same ease of transportation and communication that would seem to be destroying it. As geographer Wilbur Zelinsky has argued, when restless Americans move about, they do so with a purpose. The destinations generally are where individuals expect to find others like themselves. On one level this process has created such distinct cultural communities as college towns and retirement meccas, and on a larger scale, it has fostered much of the regional character now associated with the Colorado mountains, Vermont, and the suburbs of Washington, D.C. Outmigration of discontented souls also leaves rural counties in the Midwest, South, and High Plains as more homogeneous than they were before.[29]

One can see the self-sorting process of social reinforcement operating throughout modern Kansas. Douglas, Johnson, Leavenworth, and Riley counties are growing places, each with strong cultural appeals to certain types of people. Ellsworth and Barber counties retain their Czech and Upper Southern characters, respectively, because few new people come there to live. When this

MAP 6.15

People who claim identification with African-American, Czech, French-Canadian, Mexican, or Scandinavian ancestry, 1980. Data from U.S. census.

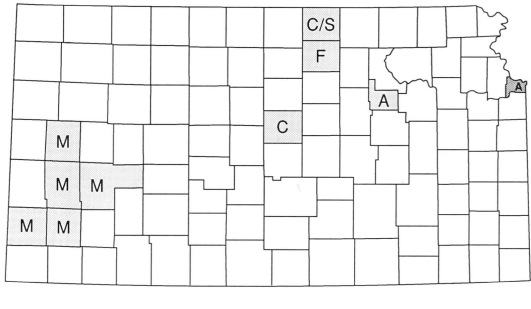

PERCENTAGE OF POPULATION

☐	0-9
▨	10-19
▦	20

KEY TO GROUPS

A African-American
C Czech
F French Canadian
M Mexican
S Scandinavian

sorting idea is seen in conjunction with Suzi Jones's regionalization process, the dynamic is even more interesting. The peoples in Clay and Wallace counties, though of similar historical backgrounds, have evolved attitudes and values somewhat different from one another after a century of coping with disparate climates, economies, and degrees of isolation. It makes for a fascinating, constantly evolving collage, and I urge readers to go and experience the process as it occurs.

In my personal travels and in reading about the state, I am amazed at how much of the old cultural heritage remains yet saddened by many losses. Alma and Hanover still look and feel Germanic, but I find little that seems English in Wakefield. The locations of Kansas State University, the University of Kansas, and Washburn University stand as important legacies of New England influence, but Wabaunsee and many other Yankee towns have nearly faded from the scene. Some messages are obvious, others understated. The magnificence of such churches as St. Fidelis in Victoria, St. Francis in St. Paul, and St. Joseph in Damar puts one in awe of the religious commitment possessed by many new immigrants at a time when money was in extremely short supply. The modest CSPS fraternal lodges and "national" cemeteries found in all major Czech centers throughout the state convey a more subtle message; these structures serve important societal roles often reserved for churches and are continuing testimony to the distrust that many Bohemians felt for organized religion following bouts with the Reformation and Counter-Reformation in their homeland.

Another and perhaps more significant way to examine the legacy of population origins is to look at individuals and groups in the context of the state as a whole. Frank Carlson, arguably the most respected politician in Kansas history, was a product of the Cloud County Swedish community. A rival for that honor, Dwight Eisenhower, came from a River Brethren colony south of Abilene. Noted humanists William Inge and Gordon Parks were from South-Midland stock, with Parks, of course, belonging to the state's black community as well. The Anschutz Science Library and the Anschutz Sports Pavilion on the campus of the University of Kansas honor the name of one of Russell County's pioneer Volga-German Lutheran families. Such a list could be extended easily, but the point is to emphasize another ongoing process. In addition to retaining such regionalisms as foodways and political party affiliation, the various groups in the state consciously and unconsciously have borrowed from one another's values to create the cultural characteristics that encompass the state in its entirety.

Aidan McQuillan, in a recent comparison of the farming practices of French-Canadian, Mennonite, Swedish, and old-stock American settlers in the state, provides an argument for how one important part of the social amalgam called Kansas may have formed. He first found that agricultural adjustments were much more complicated than mere assimilation to the American norm. Influences went more than one way, and the stronger ones may even have gone from Europeans to the old-stock Americans. In particular, Mennonites developed the most successful strategy for farming the central plains, one which their non-Mennonite neighbors gradually adopted. McQuillan concludes his book by wondering if the Mennonite influence did not extend beyond matters of agriculture. The winter-wheat belt in Kansas is conservative in its religious, social, and economic life, a sharp contrast to the liberal, even radical heritage that emerged in the area of spring-wheat production in the Dakotas. Is it more than coincidence that the Kansas social philosophy "is most vividly expressed in a political conservatism and religious fundamentalism that echoes the old Russian Mennonite values?"[30] Whether or not one agrees with McQuillan, his speculation adds to the case for the study of population origins. The legacies endure, sometimes in fascinating and indirect ways.

Notes

PREFACE

1. Gregory S. Rose, "Information Sources for Nineteenth Century Midwestern Migration," *Professional Geographer* 37 (1985): 66–72.

2. William A. Bowen, *The Willamette Valley: Migration and Settlement on the Oregon Frontier* (Seattle: University of Washington Press, 1978); Russel L. Gerlach, *Settlement Patterns in Missouri: A Study of Population Origins, with a Wall Map* (Columbia: University of Missouri Press, 1986); John C. Hudson, "Migration to an American Frontier," *Annals of the Association of American Geographers* 66 (1976): 242–65; Terry G. Jordan, "Population Origins in Texas, 1850," *Geographical Review* 59 (1969): 83–103; idem, "Population Origin Groups in Rural Texas," *Annals of the Association of American Geographers* 60 (1970): 404-5 (with a color map); Douglas K. Meyer, "Illinois Culture Regions at Mid-Nineteenth Century," *Bulletin of the Illinois Geographical Society* 18 (December 1976): 3–13; Michael O. Roark, "Oklahoma Territory: Frontier Development, Migration, and Culture Areas" (Ph.D. dissertation, Department of Geography, Syracuse University, 1979); Gregory S. Rose, "Hoosier Origins: The Nativity of Indiana's United States–Born Population in 1850," *Indiana Magazine of History* 81 (1985): 201–32; William C. Sherman, *Prairie Mosaic: An Ethnic Atlas of Rural North Dakota* (Fargo: North Dakota Institute for Regional Studies, 1983); William C. Sherman and Playford V. Thorson, eds., *Plains Folk: North Dakota's Ethnic History* (Fargo: North Dakota Institute for Regional Studies, 1988); Hubert G. H. Wilhelm, "The Origin and Distribution of Settlement Groups: Ohio: 1850," Department of Geography, Ohio University, 1982, mimeographed. An innovative mapping of population origins for the entire Middle West using biographical information from county histories is John C. Hudson, "North American Origins of Middlewestern Frontier Populations," *Annals of the Association of American Geographers* 78 (1988): 395–413.

3. These issues are reviewed in two studies by John C. Hudson: "Theory and Methodology in Comparative Frontier Studies," in *The Frontier: Comparative Studies,* ed. David H. Miller and Jerome O. Steffen (Norman: University of Oklahoma Press, 1977), pp. 11–31, and "The Study of Western Frontier Populations," in *The American West: New Perspectives, New Dimensions,* ed. Jerome O. Steffen (Norman: University of Oklahoma Press, 1979), pp. 35–60.

CHAPTER I. AN AMBIGUOUS CULTURAL HERITAGE

1. An excellent guide to the literature on regional subcultures is Michael Steiner and Clarence Mondale, *Region and Regionalism in the United States: A Source Book for the Humanities and Social Sciences* (New York: Garland Publishing Company, 1988).

2. John C. Hudson, "North American Origins of Middlewestern Frontier Populations," *Annals of the Association of American Geographers* 78 (1988): 395–413, and Wilbur Zelinsky, *The Cultural Geography of the United States,* rev. ed. (Englewood Cliffs, N.J.: Prentice-Hall, 1992), pp. 97, 118–19.

3. Terry G. Jordan and Matti Kaups, *The American Backwoods Frontier: An Ethnic and Ecological Interpretation* (Baltimore: Johns Hopkins University Press, 1989).

4. Hubert G. H. Wilhelm, "The Origin and Distribution of Settlement Groups: Ohio: 1850," Department of Geography, Ohio University, 1982, mimeographed; Gregory S. Rose, "Hoosier Origins: The Nativity of Indiana's United States–Born Population in 1850," *Indiana Magazine of History* 81 (1985): 201–32; Douglas K. Meyer, "Illinois Culture Regions at Mid-Nineteenth Century," *Bulletin of the Illinois Geographical Society* 18 (December 1976): 3–13; idem, "Native-Born Immigrant Clusters on the Illinois Frontier," *Proceedings of the Association of American Geographers* 8 (1976): 41–44. The possibility of banded cultures in Kansas has been suggested by Albert B. Cook, "Perspectives for a Linguistic Atlas of Kansas," *American Speech* 53 (Fall 1978): 199–209. For the mixing thesis, see John C. Hudson, "The Middle West as a Cultural Hybrid," *Pioneer America Society Transactions* 7 (1984): 35–45.

5. The phrase is that of John J. Ingalls; it was quoted by William Allen White, "Kansas: A Puritan Survival," in *These United States: A Symposium*, ed. Ernest Gruening, 2 vols. (New York: Boni and Liveright, 1923), 1:1.

6. Robert S. Bader, *Hayseeds, Moralizers, and Methodists: The Twentieth-Century Image of Kansas* (Lawrence: University Press of Kansas, 1988), p. 129, and James C. Malin, "Kansas: Some Reflections on Culture Inheritance and Originality," *Journal of the Central Mississippi Valley American Studies Association* 2 (Fall 1961): 3–19. Bader provides a good summary of William Allen White's Kansas imagery.

7. Fred B. Kniffen, "Folk Housing: Key to Diffusion," *Annals of the Association of American Geographers* 55 (1965): 551, and Zelinsky, *Cultural Geography*, p. 13.

8. Suzi Jones, "Regionalization: A Rhetorical Strategy," *Journal of the Folklore Institute* 13 (1976): 105–20.

9. W. A. V. Clark, *Human Migration*, Scientific Geography Series, vol. 7 (Beverly Hills, Calif.: Sage Publications, 1986).

10. C. Robert Haywood, "Pearlette: A Mutual Aid Colony," *Kansas Historical Quarterly* 42 (1976): 263–76; idem, "The Hodgeman County Colony," *Kansas History* 12 (1989): 210–21; John C. Hudson, "Two Dakota Homestead Frontiers," *Annals of the Association of American Geographers* 63 (1973): 442–62; idem, "Migration to an American Frontier," *Annals of the Association of American Geographers* 66 (1976): 242–65; D. Aidan McQuillan, *Prevailing Over Time: Ethnic Adjustment on the Kansas Prairies, 1875–1925* (Lincoln: University of Nebraska Press, 1990); Robert Ostergren, *A Community Transplanted: The Formative Experience of a Swedish Immigrant Community in the Upper Middle West, 1835–1915* (Madison: University of Wisconsin Press, 1988). The complexity of settlement study can be illustrated by the following residence history as reported in John C. Hudson's "Theory and Methodology in Comparative Frontier Studies," in *The Frontier: Comparative Studies,* ed. David H. Miller and Jerome O. Steffen (Norman: University of Oklahoma Press, 1977), p. 21: "Mr. Carroll was born to Irish parents in Oshkosh, Wisconsin in 1863. From 1879 to 1883 he worked in upper Michigan lumber camps; 1883—returned to Oshkosh to do carpentry work; 1884—went to Dakota to look for land; 1885—returned to Oshkosh; 1886—moved to Carrington, North Dakota and did farm work, took a tree claim near Sykeston and did summer work on the Dalrymple 'bonanza' at Casselton; 1877—had an elevator job at Hunter, North Dakota; 1888—returned to Carrington and went into carpentry business, but worked in Wisconsin lumber camps each winter; 1891—returned to Oshkosh and married a Miss Vogel, originally from Milwaukee; 1895—returned to Carrington and established a permanent home."

11. Michel Foucault, *Power/Knowledge: Selected Interviews and Other Writings, 1972–1977,* ed. Colin Gordon (New York: Pantheon Books, 1980), and Anthony Giddens, *The Constitution of Society* (Berkeley: University of California Press, 1984). See also Cole Harris, "Power, Modernity, and Historical Geography," *Annals of the Association of American Geographers* 81 (1991): 671–83.

12. Milton B. Newton, Jr., "Cultural Preadaptation and the Upland South," *Geoscience and Man* 5 (1974): 143–54, and Jordan and Kaups, *American Backwoods*, pp. 32–35.

13. Clark, *Human Migration*, pp. 56–58, and *Standard Highway Mileage Guide* (Chicago: Rand McNally and Company, 1982). Distances were measured from state capitals to Kansas City (in most cases) for 1850 and 1860 and to Salina for 1870, common points of entry to the frontier zone for those years. For states and territories directly north or south of Kansas, points on the nearest Kansas border were substituted. Federal censuses had to be used for the models to ensure consistency across the nation.

14. Elmer L. Craik, "Southern Interest in Territorial Kansas, 1854–1858," *Kansas Historical Collections, 1919–1922* 15 (1923): 360–61.

15. Malin, "Kansas: Some Reflections," pp. 6, 12–13.

16. E. G. Ravenstein, "The Laws of Migration," *Journal of the Royal Statistical Society* 48, pt. 2 (1885): 198.

17. Russel L. Gerlach, *Settlement Patterns in Missouri: A Study of Population Origins, with a Wall Map* (Columbia: University of Missouri Press, 1986), pp. 22–23.

18. Paul W. Gates, *Fifty Million Acres: Conflicts over Kansas Land Policy, 1854–1890* (Ithaca, N.Y.: Cornell University Press, 1954), and David M. Emmons, *Garden in the Grasslands: Boomer Literature of the Central Great Plains* (Lincoln: University of Nebraska Press, 1971).

19. Clark, *Human Migration;* Everett S. Lee, "A Theory of Migration," *Demography* 3 (1966): 47–57; Curtis C. Roseman, "Migration as a Spatial and Temporal Process," *Annals of the Association of American Geographers* 61 (1971): 589–98; William A. Bowen, *The Willamette Valley: Migration and Settlement on the Oregon Frontier* (Seattle: University of Washington Press, 1978); John M. Faragher, *Sugar Creek: Life on the Illinois Prairie* (New Haven, Conn.: Yale University Press, 1986); Haywood, "Pearlette," pp. 263–76; idem, "Hodgeman County," pp. 120–21; Hudson, "Two Dakota," pp. 442–62; idem, "Migration," pp. 242–65; Terry G. Jordan, "Population Origins in Texas, 1850," *Geographical Review* 59 (1969): 83–103; McQuillan, *Prevailing Over Time,* pp. 15–84; Michael J. O'Brien, *Grassland, Forest, and Historical Settlement: An Analysis of Dynamics in Northeast Missouri* (Lincoln: University of Nebraska Press, 1984); Ostergren, *A Community Transplanted.*

CHAPTER 2. THE NORTHEAST, 1865

1. Paul W. Gates, *Fifty Million Acres: Conflicts over Kansas Land Policy, 1854–1890* (Ithaca, N.Y.: Cornell University Press, 1954), p. 4, and Elmer L. Craik, "Southern Interest in Territorial Kansas, 1854–1858," *Kansas Historical Collections, 1919–1922* 15 (1923): 342.

2. H. Craig Miner and William E. Unrau, *The End of Indian Kansas: A Study of Cultural Revolution, 1854–1871* (Lawrence: Regents Press of Kansas, 1978), pp. 3–5.

3. James C. Malin, *The Nebraska Question, 1852–1854* (Lawrence, Kans.: privately printed, 1953); Craik, "Southern Interest," p. 340; Lloyd Lewis, "Propaganda and the Kansas-Missouri War," *Missouri Historical Review* 34 (1939): 9–10.

4. James C. Malin, "The Proslavery Background of the Kansas Struggle," *Mississippi Valley Historical Review* 10 (1923): 285–305. For overviews of the possibilities for slavery in the West, see Charles W. Ramsdell, "The Natural Limits of Slavery Expansion," *Mississippi Valley Historical Review* 16 (1929): 151–71, and Charles D. Hart, "The Natural Limits of Slavery Expansion: Kansas–Nebraska, 1854," *Kansas Historical Quarterly* 34 (1968): 32–50.

5. Craik, "Southern Interest," p. 344; Alice Nichols, *Bleeding Kansas* (New York: Oxford University Press, 1954), p. 29; Gary L. Cheatham, "Divided Loyalties in Civil War Kansas," *Kansas History* 11 (1988): 93. For overviews of the Missouri perspective, see William E. Parrish, *David Rice Atchison of Missouri: Border Politician* (Columbia:

University of Missouri Press, 1961), pp. 161–91, and Michael Fellman, *Inside War: The Guerrilla Conflict in Missouri during the American Civil War* (New York: Oxford University Press, 1989).

6. Craik, "Southern Interest," pp. 437–48.

7. Gates, *Fifty Million*, pp. 56–57.

8. Ibid., p. 55, and Craik, "Southern Interest," p. 350.

9. John N. Holloway, *History of Kansas* (Lafayette, Ind.: James, Emmons and Company, 1868), p. 106.

10. Gates, *Fifty Million*, pp. 109–41.

11. Russel L. Gerlach, *Settlement Patterns in Missouri: A Study of Population Origins, with a Wall Map* (Columbia: University of Missouri Press, 1986), pp. 22–23.

12. Craik, "Southern Interest," pp. 400–401.

13. David Dary, *More True Tales of Old-Time Kansas* (Lawrence: University Press of Kansas, 1987), pp. 17–23.

14. Cheatham, "Divided Loyalties," pp. 93–107.

15. Ibid., p. 103; Craik, "Southern Interest," pp. 443–46; Lewis, "Propaganda," p. 10; Albert Castel, *A Frontier State at War: Kansas 1861–1865* (1958; rept., Lawrence: Kansas Heritage Press, 1992), p. 211.

16. James R. Shortridge, "The Expansion of the Settlement Frontier in Missouri," *Missouri Historical Review* 75 (1980): 82–86.

17. James R. Shortridge, "The Post Office Frontier in Kansas," *Journal of the West* 13 (July 1974): 89–91.

18. Samuel A. Johnson, *The Battle Cry of Freedom: The New England Emigrant Aid Company in the Kansas Crusade* (Lawrence: University of Kansas Press, 1954).

19. About three thousand people actually came, but no more than two-thirds of them are thought to have stayed as permanent residents. See Johnson, *Battle Cry*, p. 296; Louise Barry, "The Emigrant Aid Company Parties of 1854," *Kansas Historical Quarterly* 12 (1943): 115–55, and idem, "The New England Emigrant Aid Company Parties of 1855," *Kansas Historical Quarterly* 12 (1943): 227–68.

20. James C. Malin, "Kansas: Some Reflections on Culture Inheritance and Originality," *Journal of the Central Mississippi Valley American Studies Association* 2 (Fall 1961): 12–13.

21. Johnson, *Battle Cry*, p. 53.

22. Ibid., pp. 79–85.

23. Ibid., pp. 84–86.

24. William E. Connelley, "The Lane Trail," *Kansas Historical Collections, 1913–1914* 13 (1915): 268–79.

25. Johnson, *Battle Cry*, pp. 191–95.

26. Ibid., p. 82.

27. Ibid., pp. 245–46, and Peter Beckman, "The Overland Trade and Atchison's Beginnings," in *Territorial Kansas: Studies Commemorating the Centennial* (Lawrence: University of Kansas Publications, 1954), pp. 148–63.

28. Walter L. Fleming, "The Buford Expedition to Kansas," *American Historical Review* 6 (October 1900): 38–48, and James C. Malin, *John Brown and the Legend of Fifty Six* (Philadelphia: American Philosophical Society, 1942), pp. 122–24.

29. L. Wallace Duncan and Charles F. Scott, eds., *History of Allen and Woodson Counties, Kansas* (Iola, Kans.: Iola Register, 1901), pp. 21–24, 612, and Richard B. Sheridan, "From Slavery in Missouri to Freedom in Kansas: The Influx of Black Fugitives and Contrabands into Kansas, 1854–1865," *Kansas History* 12 (1989): 39.

30. Michael F. Doran, "Population Statistics of Nineteenth Century Indian Territory," *Chronicles of Oklahoma* 53 (1975–1976): 501–6, and Cheatham, "Divided Loyalties," pp. 96–99.

31. Sheridan, "From Slavery," pp. 28–38.

32. Ibid., pp. 37–43.

33. Ibid.

34. J. Neale Carman, "Continental Europeans in Rural Kansas, 1854–1861," in *Territorial Kansas,* p. 172.

35. Ibid., p. 194.

36. Peter Beckman, *The Catholic Church on the Kansas Frontier, 1850–1877* (Washington, D.C.: Catholic University of America Press, 1943), p. 42.

37. Carman, "Continental Europeans," p. 165.

38. J. Neale Carman, "Germans in Kansas," *American-German Review* 27 (April–May 1961): 4; Eleanor L. Turk, "Selling the Heartland: Agents, Agencies, Press, and Policies Promoting German Emigration to Kansas in the Nineteenth Century," *Kansas History* 12 (1989): 155–56; J. Neale Carman and Associates, *Foreign-Language Units of Kansas,* vol. 2, *Account of Settlement and Settlements in Kansas* (Lawrence: University Press of Kansas, 1974), pp. 591–94, 978–80.

39. Beckman, *Catholic Church,* pp. 34, 49.

40. Carman, "Continental Europeans," pp. 184–89, and Carman and Associates, *Account of Settlement,* pp. 1243–46.

41. Carman, "Continental Europeans," pp. 189–95, and Carman and Associates, *Account of Settlement,* pp. 1145, 1550–53.

42. Carman, "Continental Europeans," pp. 176–79.

43. Carman and Associates, *Account of Settlement,* pp. 644–46, 704–7, 1318.

44. No single source deals with the North-Midland peoples in early Kansas, but perhaps the best point of departure is the biography of James Lane by Wendell H. Stephenson, *The Political Career of General James H. Lane,* Publications of the Kansas State Historical Society, vol. 3 (Topeka: Kansas State Printing Plant, 1930). Lane, however, was atypical; he obviously does not fit the "moderate character" representation described here.

45. In addition to the sources cited above, see J. Neale Carman, *Foreign-Language Units of Kansas,* 3 vols. (Lawrence: University Press of Kansas, 1962, 1974), and Nell Irvin Painter, *Exodusters: Black Migration to Kansas after Reconstruction* (New York: Alfred A. Knopf, 1977), pp. 146–59.

46. *Kansas Free State,* Lawrence, February 7, 1855, quoted in William E. Connelley, *An Appeal to the Record* (Topeka: privately printed, 1903), p. 123. See also Lewis, "Propaganda," pp. 3–17, and Bernard A. Weisberger, "The Newspaper Reporter and the Kansas Imbroglio," *Mississippi Valley Historical Review* 36 (1950): 633–56.

47. I thank Sally Hayden for bringing the Marysville geography to my attention.

48. Johnson, *Battle Cry,* pp. 76–78, 287–303; Frank R. Kramer, *Voices in the Valley: Mythmaking and Folk Belief in the Shaping of the Middle West* (Madison: University of Wisconsin Press, 1964), pp. 63–104; Terry G. Jordan and Matti Kaups, *The American Backwoods Frontier: An Ethnic and Ecological Interpretation* (Baltimore: Johns Hopkins University Press, 1989), pp. 1–7, 64–127.

49. Quoted by Carolyn Jones, *The First One Hundred Years: A History of the City of Manhattan, Kansas, 1855–1955* (Manhattan, Kans.: Manhattan Centennial, 1955), p. 40.

50. G. Raymond Gaeddert, *The Birth of Kansas* (Lawrence: University of Kansas Publications, 1940), pp. 34–76.

51. Quoted by Weisberger, "Newspaper Reporter," p. 651.

52. Johnson, *Battle Cry,* pp. 88, 248–50, 298, and Peter McVicar, *A Historical Sketch of Washburn College* (Burlington, Kans.: Republican-Patriot Printers, 1886), p. 2.

1. *Fifth Biennial Report of the Kansas State Board of Agriculture* (Topeka: State Printer, 1887), p. 10.

2. Ibid., map inside back cover.

3. Eugene F. Ware, "The Neutral Lands," *Kansas Historical Collections, 1897–1900* 6 (1900): 151.

4. Paul W. Gates, *Fifty Million Acres: Conflicts over Kansas Land Policy, 1854–1890* (Ithaca, N.Y.: Cornell University Press, 1954), p. 195.

5. Frederick N. Howell, "Pittsburg, Kansas, and Its Industries," (Master's thesis, Department of History, University of Kansas, 1930), p. 3.

6. Gates, *Fifty Million*, p. 174.

7. The best accounts of these land wars are Lula Lemmon Brown, *The Cherokee Neutral Lands Controversy* (Girard, Kans.: Girard Press, 1931), and Gates, *Fifty Million*, pp. 153–229.

8. Listings and discussions of colonies can be found in George Root, "Notes on Kansas Colonies," MSS Division, Kansas State Historical Society, Topeka, n.d., and in Nell B. Waldron, "Colonization in Kansas from 1861 to 1890" (Ph.D. dissertation, Department of History, Northwestern University, 1923). Three black colonies, as opposed to Euro-American ones, were established in southeastern Kansas and are discussed later in this chapter.

9. Quoted in Gates, *Fifty Million*, p. 174.

10. Howell, "Pittsburg," p. 10.

11. Gates, *Fifty Million*, pp. 244–47.

12. V. V. Masterson, *The Katy Railroad and the Last Frontier* (Norman: University of Oklahoma Press, 1952), p. 70.

13. Erasmus Haworth, *Annual Bulletin on Mineral Resources of Kansas for 1897* (Lawrence: University Geological Survey of Kansas, 1898), p. 36.

14. Michael Fellman, *Inside War: The Guerrilla Conflict in Missouri during the American Civil War* (New York: Oxford University Press, 1989).

15. Eugene F. Ware, "History of Sun-Gold Section," in *The Heritage of Kansas: Selected Commentaries on Past Times,* ed. Everett Rich (Lawrence: University of Kansas Press, 1960), pp. 85–86.

16. Fellman, *Inside War,* pp. 231–66, and James R. Shortridge, "The Expansion of the Settlement Frontier in Missouri," *Missouri Historical Review* 75 (1980): 85–87.

17. Howell, "Pittsburg," pp. 30–31.

18. Haworth, *Annual Bulletin,* p. 36, and Thomas R. Walther and Robert K. Ratzlaff, "Industrialization on the Frontier: A Case Study, Crawford County, Kansas, 1870–1914," *Red River Valley Historical Review* 6 (Fall 1981): 19.

19. Angelo Scott, "How Natural Gas Came to Kansas," *Kansas Historical Quarterly* 21 (1954): 233–39.

20. Arrell M. Gibson, *Wilderness Bonanza: The Tri-State District of Missouri, Kansas, and Oklahoma* (Norman: University of Oklahoma Press, 1972), pp. 14–40.

21. Irene G. Stone, "The Lead and Zinc Field of Kansas," *Kansas Historical Collections, 1901–1902* 7 (1902): 245–48.

22. Howell, "Pittsburg," pp. 49–50.

23. Edward King, "The Great South: The New Route to the Gulf," *Scribner's Monthly* 6 (July 1873): 264, 266.

24. The two best general accounts of the border war are Albert Castel, *A Frontier State at War: Kansas 1861–1865* (1958; rept., Lawrence: Kansas Heritage Press, 1992), and Michael Fellman, *Inside War*.

25. Terry G. Jordan, "Population Origins in Texas, 1850," *Geographical Review* 59 (1969): 90–93, and William

A. Bowen, *The Willamette Valley: Migration and Settlement on the Oregon Frontier* (Seattle: University of Washington Press, 1978), pp. 20–25.

26. Fellman, *Inside War,* pp. 231–40.

27. Russel L. Gerlach, *Settlement Patterns in Missouri: A Study of Population Origins, with a Wall Map* (Columbia: University of Missouri Press, 1986), pp. 22–23, and Shortridge, "Expansion of the Settlement Frontier," p. 87.

28. Ware, "Neutral Lands," p. 156.

29. Stone, "Lead and Zinc Fields," pp. 243–60, and Gibson, *Wilderness Bonanza.*

30. F. A. North, *The History of Jasper County, Missouri* (Des Moines, Iowa: Mills and Co., 1883), p. 389.

31. Gerlach, *Settlement Patterns,* pp. 22–23. Some of the Tennessee natives in this section were black, especially in Baxter Springs. They were part of a colony established by Benjamin Singleton and were not closely involved with the lead industry.

32. Frances Revard, "Osage Mission," *St. Paul Journal,* May 7, 1942 (included in a scrapbook of clippings about Coffey and Neosho counties held by the Kansas Collection at the University of Kansas); W. W. Graves, *History of Neosho County* (St. Paul, Kans.: Journal Press, 1949), 1:135; Gary L. Cheatham, "Desperate Characters: The Development and Impact of the Confederate Guerrillas in Kansas," *Kansas History* 14 (1991): 151.

33. J. Neale Carman, *Foreign-Language Units of Kansas,* vol. 1, *Historical Atlas and Statistics* (Lawrence: University of Kansas Press, 1962), pp. 111, 207, 211, 299, 312.

34. J. Neale Carman and Associates, *Foreign-Language Units of Kansas,* vol. 2, *Account of Settlement and Settlements in Kansas* (Lawrence: University Press of Kansas, 1974), p. 1602, and T. F. Rager and John S. Gilmore, *History of Neosho and Wilson Counties, Kansas* (Fort Scott, Kans.: L. Wallace Duncan, 1902), p. 919.

35. Rager and Gilmore, *History of Neosho and Wilson Counties,* and Graves, *History of Neosho.*

36. Charles W. Burgess, "Mining Costs in the Missouri-Kansas District," *Mining and Engineering World* 38 (April 1913): 804, and Walter Williams, *The State of Missouri* (Columbia, Mo.: K. W. Stephens Press, 1904), p. 294.

37. Gibson, *Wilderness Bonanza,* pp. 201–5.

38. William E. Powell, "European Settlement in the Cherokee-Crawford Coal Field of Southeastern Kansas," *Kansas Historical Quarterly* 41 (1975): 150–65.

39. Carman, *Historical Atlas,* p. 111.

40. Nell Irvin Painter, *Exodusters: Black Migration to Kansas after Reconstruction* (New York: Alfred A. Knopf, 1977), pp. 108–17, 146–49, and Robert G. Athearn, *In Search of Canaan: Black Migration to Kansas, 1879–80* (Lawrence: Regents Press of Kansas, 1978), pp. 76–77.

41. Waldron, "Colonization in Kansas," p. 124. Singleton also founded a second colony in Kansas, at Dunlap, in Morris County, also sometimes known as the Singleton Colony.

42. Gibson, *Wilderness Bonanza,* p. 202.

43. Painter, *Exodusters,* pp. 160–83, and Randall B. Woods, "Integration, Exclusion, or Segregation?: The 'Color Line' in Kansas, 1878–1900," *Western Historical Quarterly* 14 (1983): 181.

44. Painter, *Exodusters,* pp. 177–78, 194–95, and Athearn, *In Search of Canaan.*

45. Painter, *Exodusters,* pp. 184–85.

46. Ibid., pp. 200-201, 230–31, and Nelson Case, *History of Labette County, Kansas* (Topeka: Crane and Company, 1893), p. 57. According to Painter, the main source counties in Texas were Burleson, Grimes, Nacogdoches, Walker, Waller, and Washington.

47. Athearn, *In Search of Canaan,* pp. 79, 270. The Little Coney Colony is located in Little Caney Township.

I can find no information on whether the colony name is a corruption of the township label. The second colony of the relief association was in Wabaunsee County.

48. Ibid., p. 262; Charles C. Drake, *Who's Who: A History of Kansas and Montgomery County, Including the Cities of Coffeyville, Independence, Cherryvale, and Caney* (Coffeyville, Kans.: Coffeyville Journal Press, 1943), p. 38; Paul F. Harper, *Surely It Floweth with Milk and Honey: A History of Montgomery County, Kansas, to 1930* (Independence, Kans.: Independence Community College Press, 1988), p. 128.

49. Rager and Gilmore, *History of Neosho and Wilson Counties*, p. 894.

50. Charles W. Thornthwaite and Helen I. Slentz, *Internal Migration in the United States* (Philadelphia: University of Pennsylvania Press, 1934), p. 10, and Fred A. Shannon, *The Farmer's Last Frontier: Agriculture, 1860–1897* (New York: Holt, Rinehart, and Winston, 1945), pp. 35–38.

51. Allan G. Bogue, *From Prairie to Cornbelt: Farming on the Illinois and Iowa Prairies in the Nineteenth Century* (Chicago: University of Chicago Press, 1963), p. 55.

52. Root, "Notes on Kansas Colonies."

53. Richard L. Power, "Wet Lands and the Hoosier Stereotype," *Mississippi Valley Historical Review* 22 (1935): 33–48.

54. Howell, "Pittsburg," p. 47.

55. Powell, "European Settlement"; Daniel C. Fitzgerald, "'We Are All in This Together': Immigrants in the Oil and Mining Towns of Southern Kansas, 1890–1920," *Kansas History* 10 (1987): 17–28.

56. John G. Clark, *Towns and Minerals in Southeastern Kansas: A Study in Regional Industrialization, 1890–1930*, Special Distribution Publication 52 (Lawrence: State Geological Survey of Kansas, 1970).

57. Harper, *Surely It Floweth*, pp. 128–33; Woods, "Integration, Exclusion," pp. 181–98; Arnold Cooper, "'Protection to All, Discrimination to None': The Parsons Weekly Blade, 1892–1900," *Kansas History* 9 (1986): 58–71.

58. Gibson, *Wilderness Bonanza*, pp. 258–59.

59. Terry G. Jordan and Matti Kaups, *The American Backwoods Frontier: An Ethnic and Ecological Interpretation* (Baltimore: Johns Hopkins University Press, 1989), pp. 1–7, 64–127.

CHAPTER 4. THE CENTRAL PLAINS, 1885

1. Paul W. Gates, *Fifty Million Acres: Conflicts over Kansas Land Policy, 1854–1890* (Ithaca, N.Y.: Cornell University Press, 1954), p. 244.

2. *New York Tribune*, February 27, 1880 (quoted in Gates, *Fifty Million*, p. 273).

3. Paul W. Gates, "The Homestead Law in an Incongruous Land System," *American Historical Review* 41 (1936): 652–81.

4. Richard Sheridan, *Economic Development in Southcentral Kansas, Part 1A: An Economic History, 1500–1900* (Lawrence: University of Kansas School of Business, 1956), pp. 89–92, and Gates, *Fifty Million*, pp. 194–229.

5. The best treatment of laws pertaining to the public domain is Paul W. Gates, *History of Public Land Law Development* (Washington, D.C.: Government Printing Office, 1968). A useful companion volume for the plains region is Fred A. Shannon, *The Farmer's Last Frontier: Agriculture, 1860–1897* (New York: Holt, Rinehart, and Winston, 1945).

6. Craig Miner, *West of Wichita: Settling the High Plains of Kansas, 1865–1890* (Lawrence: University Press of Kansas, 1986), p. 32.

7. The maps are scattered throughout the *Fourth Annual Report of the State Board of Agriculture, 1875* (Topeka: George W. Martin, 1876).

8. Roy M. Robbins, *Our Landed Heritage: The Public Domain, 1776–1970,* 2d ed. (Lincoln: University of Nebraska Press, 1976), p. 213; 14 U.S. Statutes, pp. 66–67; 19 U.S. Statutes, p. 73.

9. 16 U.S. Statutes, pp. 320–21.

10. 17 U.S. Statutes, pp. 49–50.

11. Chester M. Destler, "Agricultural Readjustment and Agrarian Unrest in Illinois, 1880–1896," *Agricultural History* 21 (1947): 104–16, and Gates, *Fifty Million,* pp. 244–47.

12. Thelma J. Curl, "Promotional Efforts of the Kansas Pacific and Santa Fe to Settle Kansas" (Master's thesis, Department of History, University of Kansas, 1961), pp. 20–23, and David M. Emmons, *Garden in the Grasslands: Boomer Literature of the Central Great Plains* (Lincoln: University of Nebraska Press, 1971), pp. 57–62.

13. Curl, "Promotional Efforts," pp. 42–43.

14. Ibid., p. 101. The railroad published a pamphlet about the event that contains names and addresses of and quotations from the invited editors: *Kansas in 1875: Strong and Impartial Testimony to the Wonderful Productiveness of the Cottonwood and Arkansas Valleys* (Topeka: Atchison, Topeka and Santa Fe Railroad Company, 1875).

15. L. L. Waters, *Steel Trails to Santa Fe* (Lawrence: University of Kansas Press, 1950), p. 243.

16. Curl, "Promotional Efforts," p. 150.

17. Henry King, "Picturesque Features of Kansas Farming," *Scribner's Monthly* 19 (November 1879): 133.

18. John A. Martin, "The Progress of Kansas," *North American Review* 142 (1886): 355.

19. George Root, "Notes on Kansas Colonies," MSS Division, Kansas State Historical Society, Topeka, n.d., and Nell B. Waldron, "Colonization in Kansas from 1861 to 1890" (Ph.D. dissertation, Department of History, Northwestern University, 1923).

20. Curl, "Promotional Efforts," pp. 44, 49–51, 56–58, 168–77.

21. Emmons, *Garden in the Grasslands,* pp. 99–127.

22. Terry G. Jordan, *Trails to Texas: Southern Roots of Western Cattle Ranching* (Lincoln: University of Nebraska Press, 1981).

23. John Rydjord, *Kansas Place-Names* (Norman: University of Oklahoma Press, 1972), pp. 377–408.

24. Russel L. Gerlach, *Settlement Patterns in Missouri: A Study of Population Origins, with a Wall Map* (Columbia: University of Missouri Press, 1986), p. 23.

25. Rooks County Historical Society, *Lest We Forget,* 2 vols. (Osborne, Kans.: Osborne County Farmer, 1980).

26. Osborne County Historical Society, *The People Came* (Osborne, Kans.: Osborne County Farmer, 1977), esp. p. 220.

27. James R. Shortridge, "The Expansion of the Settlement Frontier in Missouri," *Missouri Historical Review* 75 (1980): 84–85.

28. The citations in C. Robert Haywood's "Comanche County Cowboy: A Case Study of a Kansas Rancher," *Kansas History* 4 (1981): 166–90, provide a good guide to this literature.

29. Jordan, *Trails to Texas,* esp. pp. 41, 51–58, and Michael F. Doran, "Antebellum Cattle Herding in the Indian Territory," *Geographical Review* 66 (1976): 48–58.

30. William G. Cutler, ed., *History of the State of Kansas* (Chicago: A. T. Andreas, 1883), p. 1522.

31. Robert R. Dykstra, *The Cattle Towns* (New York: Alfred A. Knopf, 1968); Homer E. Socolofsky and Huber Self, *Historical Atlas of Kansas* (Norman: University of Oklahoma Press, 1972), plate 32; Vol P. Mooney, *History of*

Butler County, Kansas (Lawrence, Kans.: Standard Publishing Company, 1916), p. 273; J. W. Berryman, "Early Settlement of Southwest Kansas," *Kansas Historical Collections, 1926–1928* 17 (1928): 565.

32. Jordan, *Trails to Texas,* and Jimmy M. Skaggs, *The Cattle-Trailing Industry: Between Supply and Demand, 1866–1890* (Lawrence: University Press of Kansas, 1973).

33. James C. Malin, "An Introduction to the History of the Bluestem-Pasture Region of Kansas," *Kansas Historical Quarterly* 11 (1942): 1–22.

34. Mooney, *History of Butler County,* pp. 273, 794, and Cutler, ed., *History of Kansas,* pp. 1522–23.

35. Edward E. Dale, *The Range Cattle Industry* (Norman: University of Oklahoma Press, 1930), pp. 146–55; Dykstra, *Cattle Towns,* pp. 342–54; Mary Einsel, "Some Notes on the Comanche Cattle Pool," *Kansas Historical Quarterly* 26 (1960): 59–66; Sheridan, *Economic Development,* pp. 57–60.

36. Leola H. Blanchard, *Conquest of Southwest Kansas* (Wichita: Wichita Eagle Press, 1931), p. 58. County maps in the *Fourth Annual Report, 1875,* show the settlement picture in detail.

37. *Third Biennial Report of the State Board of Agriculture, 1881–82* (Topeka: Kansas Publishing House, 1883), p. 186.

38. The literature on Nicodemus is extensive. Good recent studies include Kenneth M. Hamilton, "The Origins and Early Promotion of Nicodemus: A Pre-Exodus, All-Black Town," *Kansas History* 5 (1982): 220–42, and the National Park Service publication edited by J. Keith Everett, *Promised Land on the Solomon: Black Settlement at Nicodemus, Kansas* (Washington, D.C.: Government Printing Office, 1986). For context, see Robert G. Athearn, *In Search of Canaan: Black Migration to Kansas, 1879–80* (Lawrence: Regents Press of Kansas, 1978); Kenneth M. Hamilton, *Black Towns and Profit: Promotion and Development in the Trans-Appalachian West, 1877–1915* (Urbana: University of Illinois Press, 1991); and Nell Irvin Painter, *Exodusters: Black Migration to Kansas after Reconstruction* (New York: Alfred A. Knopf, 1977).

39. Hamilton, "Origins and Early Promotion," pp. 228–33.

40. C. Robert Haywood, "The Hodgeman County Colony," *Kansas History* 12 (1989): 210–21.

41. Athearn, *In Search of Canaan,* p. 183.

42. Painter, *Exodusters,* p. 153.

43. Randall B. Woods, "Integration, Exclusion, or Segregation?: The 'Color Line' in Kansas, 1878–1900," *Western Historical Quarterly* 14 (1983): 194.

44. Athearn, *In Search of Canaan,* pp. 65, 180–81, and H. Craig Miner, *Wichita: The Early Years, 1865–80* (Lincoln: University of Nebraska Press, 1982), p. 164.

45. Athearn, *In Search of Canaan,* p. 181.

46. Woods, "Integration," pp. 181–98; Haywood, "Hodgeman County," p. 214; Hamilton, "Origins and Early Promotion," p. 240.

47. *Mitchell County Historical Essays: 1962–1976* (Beloit, Kans.: Mitchell County Historical Society, 1976), p. 172.

48. Eleanor L. Turk, "Selling the Heartland: Agents, Agencies, Press, and Policies Promoting German Emigration to Kansas in the Nineteenth Century," *Kansas History* 12 (1989): 150–54, and Philip Taylor, *The Distant Magnet: European Emigration to the U.S.A.* (London: Eyre and Spottiswoode, 1971), pp. 7–8, 116–19, 145–66.

49. Taylor, *Distant Magnet,* pp. 1–26; Merle Curti and Kendall Birr, "The Immigrant and the American Image in Europe, 1860–1914," *Mississippi Valley Historical Review* 37 (1950): 203–30; Brian P. Birch, "Popularizing the Plains: News of Kansas in England, 1860–1880," *Kansas History* 10 (1987): 262–74.

50. Emmons, *Garden in the Grasslands,* p. 116.

51. Ibid., pp. 111–12.

52. Curl, "Promotional Efforts," p. 44.

53. Ibid., p. 61.

54. J. Neale Carman, "Germans in Kansas," *American-German Review* 27 (April–May 1961): 4–8.

55. Jacob C. Ruppenthal, "The German Element in Central Kansas," *Kansas Historical Collections, 1913–1914* 13 (1915): 516.

56. J. Neale Carman and Associates, *Foreign-Language Units of Kansas,* vol. 2, *Account of Settlement and Settlements in Kansas* (Lawrence: University Press of Kansas, 1974), p. 133.

57. Clara M. F. Shields, "The Lyon Creek Settlement," *Kansas Historical Collections, 1914–1918* 14 (1918): 143–70.

58. Edward G. Nelson, *The Company and the Community* (Lawrence: University of Kansas School of Business, 1956), pp. 109, 145–57.

59. Carman and Associates, *Account of Settlement,* pp. 453–59.

60. Ibid., pp. 460–69, and Peter Beckman, *The Catholic Church on the Kansas Frontier, 1850–1877* (Washington, D.C.: Catholic University of America Press, 1943), p. 134.

61. Carman and Associates, *Account of Settlement,* pp. 749–54.

62. Ibid., pp. 1301–02.

63. Cutler, ed., *History of Kansas,* p. 1030.

64. Carman and Associates, *Account of Settlement,* p. 1378, and J. Neale Carman, *Foreign-Language Units of Kansas,* vol. 1, *Historical Atlas and Statistics* (Lawrence: University of Kansas Press, 1962), p. 233.

65. Ruth K. Hayden, *The Time That Was* (Colby, Kans.: H. F. Davis Memorial Library, Colby Community College, 1973), pp. 15, 41–49, 71; Carman and Associates, *Account of Settlement,* pp. 492–501; Richard C. Overton, *Burlington West: A Colonization History of the Burlington Railroad* (Cambridge: Harvard University Press, 1941). pp. 283, 400–402, 463.

66. Carman and Associates, *Account of Settlement,* pp. 39–40.

67. Ibid., pp. 1119, 1240, and Ruppenthal, "The German Element," p. 527.

68. Carman and Associates, *Account of Settlement,* pp. 1123–25.

69. Emmons, *Garden in the Grasslands,* p. 108, and C. B. Schmidt, "Reminiscences of Foreign Immigration Work for Kansas," *Kansas Historical Collections, 1905–1906* 9 (1906): 485–97.

70. Harley J. Stucky, "The German Element in Kansas," in *Kansas: The First Century,* ed. John D. Bright, 4 vols. (New York: Lewis Historical Publishing Company, 1956), 1:331.

71. C. B. Schmidt, "Kansas Mennonite Settlements, 1877," trans. Cornelius Krahn, *Mennonite Life* 25 (April 1970): 55.

72. Carman and Associates, *Account of Settlement,* p. 658.

73. Ibid., pp. 1007, 1170, and C. B. Schmidt, "German Settlements along the Atchison, Topeka and Santa Fe Railway," trans. J. Neale Carman, *Kansas Historical Quarterly* 28 (1962): 314–15.

74. Carman and Associates, *Account of Settlement,* pp. 241–44; Carman, *Historical Atlas,* p. 269; Schmidt, "German Settlements," p. 315.

75. Cutler, ed., *History of Kansas,* p. 1405, and Beckman, *Catholic Church,* p. 134.

76. Schmidt, "German Settlements," p. 315.

77. Carman and Associates, *Account of Settlement,* pp. 990–1000, 1538; A. L. Meyers, "Golden Jubilee, 1889–1939," mimeographed booklet prepared by St. Ann's Church, Olmitz, Kansas, 1939 (copy in the Kansas Collection at the University of Kansas); Carman, *Historical Atlas,* pp. 89, 283.

78. Carman and Associates, *Account of Settlement,* pp. 1180, 1375–76, and Schmidt, "German Settlements," p. 316.

79. Carman and Associates, *Account of Settlement,* pp. 1109–10, 1132–35, and "Kansas Farmers and Illinois Dairymen," *Atlantic Monthly* 44 (December 1879): 720.

80. The 33,000 figure includes 18,000 Volga Germans and 15,000 Mennonites from the Crimea, Bessarabia, Volhynia, and other Russian provinces. Albert J. Petersen, "The German-Russian Settlement Pattern in Ellis County, Kansas," *Rocky Mountain Social Science Journal* 5 (April 1968): 52, and Schmidt, "Reminiscences," p. 488.

81. King, "Picturesque Features," p. 135; Emmons, *Garden in the Grasslands,* pp. 113–17; Norman E. Saul, "The Migration of the Russian-Germans to Kansas," *Kansas Historical Quarterly* 40 (1974): 47–48. Noble L. Prentis, a Topeka journalist, was a major publicist for the Mennonites; two samples of this prose are included in his collection, *Kansas Miscellanies* (Topeka: Kansas Publishing House, 1889), pp. 147–67.

82. Saul, "Migration," pp. 38–45. For extended treatment, see Karl Stumpp, *The German-Russians: Two Centuries of Pioneering,* trans. Joseph Height (Bonn: Atlantic-Forum, 1967), and C. Henry Smith, *The Coming of the Russian Mennonites: An Episode in the Settling of the Last Frontier, 1874–1884* (Berne, Ind.: Mennonite Book Concern, 1927).

83. Saul, "Migration," pp. 41–50; Schmidt, "Reminiscences," pp. 490–95; Carman and Associates, *Account of Settlement,* p. 658.

84. Carman and Associates, *Account of Settlement,* p. 266.

85. The four standard sources on the Volga Germans in Kansas are Francis S. Laing, "German-Russian Settlements in Ellis County, Kansas," *Kansas Historical Collections, 1909–1910* 11 (1910): 489–528; Sister Mary Eloise Johannes, *A Study of the Russian-German Settlements in Ellis County, Kansas,* Catholic University of America Studies in Sociology, vol. 14 (Washington, D.C.: Catholic University of America Press, 1946); Albert J. Petersen, "German-Russian Colonization in Western Kansas: A Settlement Geography" (Ph.D. dissertation, Department of Geography and Anthropology, Louisiana State University, 1970); and Norbert R. Dreiling, *Official Centennial History of the Volga-German Settlements in Ellis and Rush Counties in Kansas: 1876–1976* (Hays, Kans.: Volga-German Centennial Association, 1976).

86. Saul, "Migration," pp. 39, 52–58; Carman and Associates, *Account of Settlement,* pp. 133, 276.

87. Carman and Associates, *Account of Settlement,* pp. 264, 269.

88. Ibid., pp. 690–95, 1478–82.

89. Ibid., pp. 656–85, 1174–76, 1425, and Schmidt, "Kansas Mennonite Settlements," pp. 51–58, and "German Settlements," p. 313.

90. Carman and Associates, *Account of Settlement,* pp. 154–55, 660–63, 667–72, 998–99; a list of individual congregations for each of the major Mennonite groups is contained in Carman, *Historical Atlas,* p. 319.

91. A. James Rudin, "Beersheba, Kan.: 'God's Pure Air on Government Land,'" *Kansas Historical Quarterly* 34 (1968): 282–98, and Lipman G. Feld, "New Light on the Lost Jewish Colony of Beersheba, Kansas, 1882–1886," *American Jewish Historical Quarterly* 60 (1970): 159–68.

92. John S. Lindberg, *The Background of Swedish Emigration to the United States* (Minneapolis: University of Minnesota Press, 1930).

93. Emory Lindquist, "The Swedish Immigrant and Life in Kansas," *Kansas Historical Quarterly* 29 (1963): 1–24.

94. Ellen W. Peterson, *A Kansan's Enterprise: The Story of Enterprise, Kansas* (Enterprise, Kans.: Enterprise Baptist Church, 1957), pp. 173–82.

95. The principal sources for the cooperative settlements are Alfred Bergin, "The Swedish Settlements in Cen-

tral Kansas," *Kansas Historical Collections, 1909–1910* 11 (1910): 19–46, and Emory Lindquist, *Smoky Valley People: A History of Lindsborg, Kansas* (Lindsborg, Kans.: Bethany College, 1953).

96. Lindquist, *Smoky Valley People,* and Carman, *Historical Atlas,* p. 189.

97. Carman and Associates, *Account of Settlement,* pp. 781–86; Andrew A. Granstedt, "The Scandinavian People and the Americanization of a Scandinavian Community" (Master's thesis, Department of Sociology, University of Kansas, 1916); Anora Blackburn and Myrtle S. Cardwell, comps., *History of Republic County, 1868–1964* (Belleville, Kans.: Republic County Historical Society, 1964), pp. 248–71; Lonnie J. White, "The Cheyenne Barrier on the Kansas Frontier, 1868–1869," *Arizona and the West* 4 (1962): 51–64.

98. Carman, *Historical Atlas,* p. 295, and Carman and Associates, *Account of Settlement,* pp. 1015, 1569–71.

99. Carman and Associates, *Account of Settlement,* pp. 48, 1121–22, 1418, and Carman, *Historical Atlas,* pp. 189, 193, 231, 247.

100. Carman and Associates, *Account of Settlement,* pp. 1044, 1410–12.

101. Thomas P. Christensen, "The Danish Settlements in Kansas," *Kansas Historical Collections, 1926–1928* 17 (1928): 300–305; Katie M. Peterson, "History of the Scandinavian Settlement in Lincoln County, Kansas" (Master's thesis, Department of History, Kansas State College of Pittsburg, 1939); Carman, *Historical Atlas,* p. 183; Carman and Associates, *Account of Settlement,* pp. 394–400; Kristian Hvidt, *Flight to America: The Social Background of 300,000 Danish Emigrants* (New York: Academic Press, 1975), pp. 169–70.

102. Carman, *Historical Atlas,* pp. 105, 295; Carman and Associates, *Account of Settlement,* pp. 1018, 1587; Hvidt, *Flight to America,* p. 147.

103. Brinley Thomas, *Migration and Economic Growth: A Study in Great Britain and the Atlantic Economy* (Cambridge: Cambridge University Press, 1954).

104. Oscar O. Winther, "The English and Kansas, 1865–1890," in *The Frontier Challenge: Responses to the Trans-Mississippi West,* ed. John G. Clark (Lawrence: University Press of Kansas, 1971), pp. 237, 243–47, and Birch, "Popularizing the Plains."

105. This was George Grant's Victoria Colony; a second highly publicized colony, Runnymede, in Harper County, was not founded until 1889.

106. Winther, "The English," p. 246.

107. The main sources for Wakefield are Winther, "The English," pp. 254–57, and William J. Chapman, "The Wakefield Colony," *Kansas Historical Collections, 1907–1908* 10 (1908): 485–533.

108. James L. Forsythe, "George Grant of Victoria: Man and Myth," *Kansas History* 9 (1986): 102–14; Brian P. Birch, "Victoria Vanquished: The Scottish Press and the Failure of George Grant's Colony," *Kansas History* 9 (1986): 115–24; James L. Forsythe, "The English Colony at Victoria, Another View," *Kansas History* 12 (1989): 175–84.

109. *At Home in Ellis County, Kansas: 1867–1992* (Hays, Kans.: Ellis County Historical Society, 1991), 1:54, 190–91.

110. *Burrton's 75th Anniversary: 1873–1948* (Burrton, Kans.: Burrton Graphic, 1948), pp. 15, 39, and Phillips G. Davies, "The Welsh in Kansas: Settlement, Contributions, and Assimilation," *Welsh History Review* 14 (1989): 380–98.

111. Beckman, *Catholic Church,* p. 101.

112. Stephen Byrne, *Irish Emigration to the United States: What It Has Been and What It Is* (New York: Catholic Publication Society, 1873), p. 125 (this book was reprinted in 1969 by Arno Press as part of their "American Immigration Collection").

113. Everett Dick, *The Sod-House Frontier: 1854–1890* (Lincoln, Nebr.: Johnsen Publishing Company, 1954), p. 334.

114. Vincent LeMoine, *The Chapman Irish* (n.p., 1963).

115. Beckman, *Catholic Church*, pp. 85, 102, 105.

116. Dorothe T. Homan, *Lincoln: That County in Kansas* (Lindsborg, Kans.: Barbos' Printing, 1979), pp. 82–83, 92.

117. Marcus L. Hansen (completed by John B. Brebner), *The Mingling of the Canadian and American Peoples,* vol. 1, *Historical* (New Haven, Conn.: Yale University Press, 1940), pp. 135, 188.

118. Stucky, "German Element," p. 332.

119. Carman and Associates, *Account of Settlement*, pp. 1226–27.

120. Hansen, *Mingling*, pp. 123–30, and Charles B. Campbell, "Bourbonnais; or the Early French Settlements in Kankakee County, Illinois," *Transactions of the Illinois State Historical Society* 11 (1906): 65–72.

121. D. Aidan McQuillan, "The Creation and Survival of French-Canadian Communities in the Upper Midwest during the Nineteenth Century," *Cahiers de Geographie de Quebec* 23 (1979): 53–72; Carman and Associates, *Account of Settlement*, p. 248; Carman, *Historical Atlas*, p. 105.

122. Carman and Associates, *Account of Settlement*, pp. 248–60, and Beckman, *Catholic Church*, pp. 105, 133, 156.

123. Carman and Associates, *Account of Settlement*, p. 253, and Mrs. E. F. Hollibaugh, *Biographical History of Cloud County, Kansas* (n.p., 1903), pp. 200–215.

124. Carman and Associates, *Account of Settlement*, pp. 252–53, 1591–94.

125. Ibid., pp. 212–14, 1469–71; Rooks County, *Lest We Forget;* Sondra Van Meter McCoy and Jan Hults, *1001 Kansas Place Names* (Lawrence: University Press of Kansas, 1989), p. 46.

126. The classic account is Thomas Capek, *The Cechs (Bohemians) in America* (Boston: Houghton Mifflin Company, 1920). See also Karel D. Bicha, *The Czechs in Oklahoma* (Norman: University of Oklahoma Press, 1980), pp. 6–11.

127. Capek, *Cechs (Bohemians)*, pp. 25–68, and Bicha, *Czechs*, pp. 4, 12.

128. Carman and Associates, *Account of Settlement*, pp. 376–88; Bozena Nemcova, "People of Czech (Bohemian) Descent in Republic County, Kansas" (Master's thesis, Department of Sociology, University of Kansas, 1950), pp. 28–32; Mrs. Edward Stepanek and LaVern Kopsa, eds., "Cuba, Kansas Centennial: 1868–1968," mimeographed pamphlet (copy in the Kansas Collection at the University of Kansas); Carman, *Historical Atlas*, p. 251.

129. Carman and Associates, *Account of Settlement*, pp. 380, 1567–68, and Carman, *Historical Atlas*, p. 295.

130. Francis J. Swehla, "Bohemians in Central Kansas," *Kansas Historical Collections, 1913–1914* 13 (1915): 469–512.

131. Carman and Associates, *Account of Settlement*, pp. 1234, 1484–85; Carman, *Historical Atlas*, p. 261; Sondra Van Meter, *Marion County: Past and Present* (Hillsboro, Kans.: Marion County Historical Society, 1972), pp. 44, 295–300; Rush County Book Committee, *Rush County: A Century in Story and Pictures* (La Crosse, Kans.: Rush County Historical Society, 1976), pp. 258–63.

132. Carman and Associates, *Account of Settlement*, pp. 1043, 1165–67, 1401–2, 1471; Carman, *Historical Atlas*, p. 241; Gwendoline Sanders and Paul Sanders, *The Sumner County Story* (North Newton, Kans.: Mennonite Press, 1966), pp. 42–43.

133. Frank R. Kramer, *Voices in the Valley: Mythmaking and Folk Belief in the Shaping of the Middle West* (Madison: University of Wisconsin Press, 1964), pp. 63–104.

134. Curl, "Promotional Efforts," pp. 48, 150.

135. McCoy and Hults, *1001 Kansas Name Places*, pp. 181, 191; Myron C. Burr and Elizabeth Burr, eds., *The Kinsley-Edwards County Centennial, 1873–1973* (Kinsley, Kans.: Nolan Publishers, 1973), pp. 5–6; Cutler, ed., *History of Kansas*, p. 1367.

136. Emmons, *Garden in the Grasslands*, pp. 78–99.

137. John Ise, *Sod and Stubble: The Story of a Kansas Homestead* (1936; rept., Lincoln: University of Nebraska Press, 1967), p. 12, and *At Home in Ellis County*, p. 53.

138. Burr and Burr, *Kinsley-Edwards County*, p. 13.

139. Van Meter, *Marion County*, p. 271, and Cutler, ed., *History of Kansas*, p. 1260.

140. Dick Schamp, *Post Rock to Moon Rock: A Brief History of Russell* (Russell, Kans.: Russell County Historical Society, 1971), pp. 5–8, 23, quotation on p. 8, and Cutler, ed., *History of Kansas*, pp. 1284–86.

141. Miner, *West of Wichita*, p. 74.

142. Burr and Burr, *Kinsley-Edwards County*, p. 7. On the variable roles played by colony organizations, see C. Robert Haywood, "Pearlette: A Mutual Aid Colony," *Kansas Historical Quarterly* 42 (1976): 263–76.

143. Root, "Notes on Kansas Colonies."

144. Cutler, ed., *History of Kansas*, p. 1027.

145. For general background on the Germans in Pennsylvania, see James T. Lemon, *The Best Poor Man's Country: A Geographical Study of Early Southeastern Pennsylvania* (Baltimore: Johns Hopkins University Press, 1972).

146. Curl, "Promotional Efforts," p. 83.

147. Jacob C. Ruppenthal, "Pennsylvania Germans in Central Kansas," *Penn Germania*, n.s. 3 (September 1914): 33–34, and George R. Beyer, "Pennsylvania Germans Move to Kansas," *Pennsylvania History* 32 (1965): 30–32.

148. The quotation is from a letter written by one of the migrants, Jacob Ruppenthal, to J. Neale Carman in 1956, and is cited in Carman and Associates, *Account of Settlement*, p. 1493; Ruppenthal, "Pennsylvania Germans," p. 33.

149. Ruppenthal, "Pennsylvania Germans," p. 34.

150. W. P. Harrington, *History of Gove County, Kansas* (Gove City, Kans.: Republican-Gazette, 1930); Albert B. Tuttle and Mary T. Tuttle, eds. and comps., *History and Heritage of Gove County, Kansas* (n.p.: Gove County Historical Association, 1976), pp. 24–25; Miner, *West of Wichita*, p. 75; *At Home in Ellis County*, p. 53.

151. Minnie D. Millbrook, *Ness: Western County, Kansas* (Detroit: Millbrook Printing Company, 1955), p. 82, and H. Norman, "History of Hodgeman County, Kansas," 1941, mimeographed (copy in the Kansas Collection at the University of Kansas).

152. Cutler, ed., *History of Kansas*, p. 686, and Beyer, "Pennsylvania Germans," pp. 40–43.

153. Carlton O. Wittlinger, *Quest for Piety and Obedience: The Story of the Brethren in Christ* (Nappanee, Ind.: Evangel Press, 1978), pp. 132, 146–48.

154. Emma K. Risser, *History of the Pennsylvania Mennonite Church in Kansas* (Hesston, Kans.: Pennsylvania Mennonite Church, 1958), pp. 1–3.

155. Cutler, ed., *History of Kansas*, pp. 972–1027.

156. Darrel Miller, ed., *Pioneer Plows and Steel Rails: Outriders of Civilization in the Valley of the Solomon* (Downs, Kans.: Downs News and Times, 1961), p. 44; Beyer, "Pennsylvania Germans," pp. 28–30; Miner, *West of Wichita*, pp. 69–72; Howard Ruede, *Sod-House Days: Letters from a Kansas Homesteader, 1877–78*, ed. John Ise (New York: Columbia University Press, 1937), pp. 206, 226.

157. Charles W. Thornthwaite and Helen I. Slentz, *Internal Migration in the United States* (Philadelphia: University of Pennsylvania Press, 1934), p. 10, and Shannon, *Farmer's Last Frontier*, pp. 35–38.

158. Gates, *Fifty Million*, pp. 244–48, and Shannon, *Farmer's Last Frontier*, pp. 295, 303–5.

159. Root, "Notes on Kansas Colonies"; Waldron, "Colonization in Kansas"; Margaret A. Nelson, *Home on the Range* (Boston: Chipman and Grimes, 1947), p. 18.

160. Dollie McCalla, ed., *Memoirs of Old Hawkeye,* from the manuscripts of Amy B. Claar-Rezner (Englewood, Colo: Claar-Rezner Family, n.d.), pp. 7–18.

161. Cutler, ed., *History of Kansas*, pp. 366, 1268–69 (quotation on p. 1269); John R. Gray, *Pioneer Saints and Sinners: Pratt County from Its Beginnings to 1900* (Pratt, Kans.: Pratt Rotary Club, 1961), pp. 44–47, 70; *A Historical Collection of Harper County Churches* (Anthony, Kans.: Harper County Religious Heritage Committee, 1961), p. 1.

162. Douglas K. Meyer, "Illinois Culture Regions at Mid-Nineteenth Century," *Bulletin of the Illinois Geographical Society* 18 (December 1976): 3–13.

163. Carman and Associates, *Account of Settlement*, pp. 675, 1416.

164. Centennial Committee, "History of Ottawa County, Kansas: 1864–1984," mimeographed book (n.p., n.d.; copy in the Kansas Collection at the University of Kansas), pp. 205–7, and M. Winsor and James Scarbrough, *History of Jewell County, Kansas* (Jewell City, Kans.: Diamond Printing Office, 1878), unpaged.

165. Cutler, ed., *History of Kansas*, pp. 686, 699, 1296–97; Root, "Notes on Kansas Colonies"; Waldron, "Colonization in Kansas," p. 146; Miner, *West of Wichita*, pp. 76–78.

166. Waters, *Steel Trails*, pp. 242–43; Glenn D. Bradley, *The Story of the Santa Fe* (Boston: Richard G. Badger, 1920), pp. 124, 127–28; Curl, "Promotional Efforts," pp. 148–50.

167. See the county-level maps of land ownership in the *Fourth Annual Report, 1875,* and Bradley, *Story of Santa Fe,* p. 128.

168. Jesse H. Lowe, *Pioneer History of Kingman County, Kansas* (n.p., n.d.), p.1; *Seventieth Anniversary Edition* (Anthony, Kans.: Anthony Republican and Anthony Bulletin, 1948); Waldron, "Colonization in Kansas," pp. 147–48.

169. Gregory S. Rose, "Hoosier Origins: The Nativity of Indiana's United States–Born Population in 1850," *Indiana Magazine of History* 81 (1985): 201–32.

170. Winsor and Scarbrough, *History of Jewell,* and *The United Methodist Church's 100th Anniversary, 1883–1983* (Smith Center, Kans.: Thornburg United Methodist Church, 1983).

171. Waldron, "Colonization in Kansas," p. 101, and Henry C. Fellow and Melissa S. Fellow, *Semi-Centennial Historical Sketch of Kansas Yearly Meeting of Friends* (Wichita: Friends Book Supply, 1922), pp. 17–22.

172. Cutler, ed., *History of Kansas*, pp. 686, 1288, and *At Home in Ellis County,* p. 53.

173. Cutler, ed., *History of Kansas,* p. 699.

174. Hazel B. Baker, "Some Early Facts on the History of Pawnee County, Kansas, and Stafford County, Kansas" (a collection of newspaper columns held by the Kansas Collection at the University of Kansas, n.d.), p. 33, and *Progress in Pawnee County: 80th Anniversary Edition* (Larned, Kans.: Larned Tiller and Toiler, 1952), p. 43.

175. Cutler, ed., *History of Kansas*, p. 811, and Edna E. Nyquist, *Pioneer Life and Lore in McPherson County, Kansas* (McPherson, Kans.: Democrat-Opinion Press, 1932), pp. 51–52, 96–99.

176. Horace Jones, *The Story of Early Rice County* (Wichita: Wichita Eagle Press, 1932), p. 101; Cutler, ed., *History of Kansas*, pp. 754–57; Nyquist, *Pioneer Life,* p. 97; Emily I. Combes, "Letters from an Eighteen-year-old Kansas Pioneer Girl Written from Manhattan and Rice County to her Fiance in Ohio between April 21, 1871, and December 17, 1871" (manuscript held by the Kansas Collection at the University of Kansas).

177. Alfred B. Bradshaw, *When the Prairies Were New* (Turon, Kans.: Arthur J. Allen, 1957), p. 2.

178. Miner, *Wichita.*

1. Craig Miner, *West of Wichita: Settling the High Plains of Kansas, 1865–1890* (Lawrence: University Press of Kansas, 1986), pp. 190, 204.

2. Frank S. Sullivan, *A History of Meade County, Kansas* (Topeka: Crane and Company, 1916), p. 8.

3. Miner, *West of Wichita,* pp. 212–16.

4. *Fiftieth Anniversary Jubilee* (Ulysses, Kans.: Ulysses News, 1941), p. 23, and Book Committee, *Stanton County, Kansas: 1887–1987* (n.p.: 1987), pp. 73–77 (quotation on page 73).

5. William Allen White, *Forty Years on Main Street,* comp. Russell H. Fitzgibbon (New York: Farrar and Rinehart, 1937), p. 74.

6. Book Committee, *They Came to Stay: Sherman County and Family History,* vol. 1 (Goodland, Kans.: Sherman County Historical Society, 1980), p. 151, and James E. Sherow, *Watering the Valley: Development along the High Plains Arkansas River, 1870–1950* (Lawrence: University Press of Kansas, 1990), pp. 88–94.

7. Miner, *West of Wichita,* p. 218.

8. Ibid., p. 197. See O. P. Byers, "Early History of the El Paso Line of the Chicago, Rock Island, and Pacific Railway," *Kansas Historical Collections, 1919–1922* 15 (1923): 573–78, and A. Bower Sagaser, "Building the Main Line of the Missouri Pacific through Kansas," *Kansas Historical Quarterly* 21 (1955): 326–30.

9. George Root, "Notes on Kansas Colonies," MSS Division, Kansas State Historical Society, Topeka, n.d., and Nell B. Waldron, "Colonization in Kansas from 1861 to 1890" (Ph.D. dissertation, Department of History, Northwestern University, 1923). My information on the officers of townsite companies comes from inspection of the various county histories.

10. Richard C. Overton, *Burlington West: A Colonization History of the Burlington Railroad* (Cambridge: Harvard University Press, 1941), pp. 400–402, 461–63. Detailed maps of railroads for 1887 and 1888 can be found in *The Official State Atlas of Kansas* (Philadelphia: L. H. Everts and Co., 1887) and in the *Sixth Biennial Report of the State Board of Agriculture for the Years 1887–88* (Topeka: Kansas Publishing House, 1889).

11. Book Committee, *The History of Stevens County and Its People* (Hugoton, Kans.: Stevens County Historical Association, 1979), pp. 128–30, and Book Committee, *Stanton County,* p. 48.

12. J. W. Berryman, "Early Settlement of Southwest Kansas," *Kansas Historical Collections, 1926–1928* 17 (1928): 565–67; Elizabeth Hines, "Farming and Ranching in Morton County through 1915: The Historical Geography of a High Plains Frontier" (Master's thesis, Department of Geography, University of Kansas, 1985), p. 52; Pauline Toland, ed., *Seward County, Kansas* (Liberal, Kans.: Seward County Historical Society, 1979), p. 13; Charles L. Wood, "C. D. Perry: Clark County Farmer and Rancher, 1884–1908," *Kansas Historical Quarterly* 39 (1973): 454–56.

13. Terry G. Jordan, *Trails to Texas: Southern Roots of Western Cattle Ranching* (Lincoln: University of Nebraska Press, 1981), pp. 40, 55.

14. Chester M. Destler, "Agricultural Readjustment and Agrarian Unrest in Illinois, 1880–1896," *Agricultural History* 21 (1947): 113.

15. Miner, *West of Wichita,* p. 199.

16. J. Neale Carman and Associates, *Foreign-Language Units of Kansas,* vol. 2, *Account of Settlement and Settlements in Kansas* (Lawrence: University Press of Kansas, 1974), p. 114.

17. Paul Bonnifield, *The Dust Bowl: Men, Dirt, and Depression* (Albuquerque: University of New Mexico Press, 1979), pp. 20–42; Donald Worster, *Dust Bowl: The Southern Plains in the 1930s* (New York: Oxford University

Press, 1979), pp. 80–97; Walter M. Kollmorgen, "The Woodsman's Assaults on the Domain of the Cattleman," *Annals of the Association of American Geographers* 59 (1969): 234–36. The best study of dry farming remains Mary W. M. Hargreaves, *Dry Farming in the Northern Great Plains, 1900–1925* (Cambridge: Harvard University Press, 1957).

18. Book Committee, *History of Stevens County*, pp. 128–30, and Book Committee, *Stanton County*, pp. 48–50.

19. C. Robert Haywood, "Comanche County Cowboy: A Case Study of a Kansas Rancher," *Kansas History* 4 (1981): 167.

20. C. Robert Haywood, *Trails South: The Wagon-Road Economy in the Dodge City–Panhandle Region* (Norman: University of Oklahoma Press, 1986).

21. Charles L. Wood, *The Kansas Beef Industry* (Lawrence: Regents Press of Kansas, 1980), pp. 5–6, 46, and Federal Writers' Project, *The WPA Guide to 1930s Kansas* (Lawrence: University Press of Kansas, 1984), pp. 405, 422.

22. Haywood, "Comanche County Cowboy," pp. 174–75, and John Rydjord, *Kansas Place-Names* (Norman: University of Oklahoma Press, 1972), pp. 300–307, 451–52.

23. Russel L. Gerlach, *Settlement Patterns in Missouri: A Study of Population Origins, with a Wall Map* (Columbia: University of Missouri Press, 1986), pp. 22–23.

24. Bill James and Marge Brown, *A History of Gem, Kansas* (Colby, Kans.: Prairie Printers, 1970), p. 122, and Carman and Associates, *Account of Settlement*, p. 1286.

25. Book Committee, *History of Kearny County, Kansas,* vol. 1 (Dodge City, Kans.: Kearny County Historical Society, 1964), p. 68; Book Committee, *History of Stevens County*, p. 95; Kiowa County Libraries History Book Committee, *A History of Kiowa County: 1880–1980* (Lubbock, Tex.: Taylor Publishing Company, 1979), pp. 78, 242–45, 271, 286, 293, 339, 356, 407, 414, 457, 536; Weston F. Cox, *The Community of Haviland, Kansas* (Haviland, Kans.: Friends Bible College Press, 1966), p. 52.

26. Book Committee, *History of Logan County, Kansas* (Oakley, Kans.: Logan County Historical Society, 1986), pp. 13, 33, 408–10.

27. Useful summaries of immigration for this time and area can be found in Merle Curti and Kendall Birr, "The Immigrant and the American Image in Europe, 1860–1914," *Mississippi Valley Historical Review* 37 (1950): 203–30; Douglas Hale, "European Immigrants in Oklahoma: A Survey," *Chronicles of Oklahoma* 53 (1975–1976): 179–203; and Frederick C. Luebke, "Ethnic Group Settlement on the Great Plains," *Western Historical Quarterly* 8 (1977): 405–30.

28. Glenn D. Bradley, *The Story of the Santa Fe* (Boston: Richard G. Badger, 1920), p. 136, and Miner, *West of Wichita*, pp. 199–201.

29. Carman and Associates, *Account of Settlement*, pp. 1013, 1127–28, 1286; J. Neale Carman, *Foreign-Language Units of Kansas,* vol. 1, *Historical Atlas and Statistics* (Lawrence: University of Kansas Press, 1962), p. 310; Book Committee, *History of Kearny County*, p. 205.

30. Carman and Associates, *Account of Settlement*, p. 807.

31. Ibid., p. 1126a, and Ellen R. Krenzel, ed., *History of Wichita County, Kansas,* vol. 1 (Leoti, Kans.: Wichita County History Association, 1980), pp. 386–90, 397.

32. Albert B. Tuttle and Mary T. Tuttle, eds. and comps., *History and Heritage of Gove County, Kansas* (n.p.: Gove County Historical Association, 1976), pp. 46–47, and Carman and Associates, *Account of Settlement*, pp. 1148–52, 1209.

33. Krenzel, ed., *History of Wichita County*, p. 406; Carman, *Historical Atlas*, pp. 154–55, 309–10; Carman and Associates, *Account of Settlement*, pp. 426–31, 1157–58, 1210, 1283.

34. Curti and Birr, "Immigrant," p. 224.

35. Carman and Associates, *Account of Settlement,* pp. 1013, 1153, 1520, 1541, and Tuttle and Tuttle, eds. and comps., *History and Heritage,* pp. 96–97.

36. Carman and Associates, *Account of Settlement,* pp. 1208–9, and Book Committee, *History of Logan County,* pp. 19, 374–75.

37. Carman and Associates, *Account of Settlement,* pp. 1561–62; Wallace County Historians, *Wallace County History: A Story of Grass, Grit and Chips* (Sharon Springs, Kans.: Wallace County Historians, 1979), pp. 36, 42–43, 243 (quotation on p. 43); Greeley County Historical Book Committee, *History of Early Greeley County,* vol. 1 (Tribune, Kans.: Greeley County Historical Book Committee, 1981), p. 154.

38. Wallace County Historians, *Wallace County History,* pp. 36, 43, 243.

39. Carman and Associates, *Account of Settlement,* pp. 426–47; Larry G. Rutter, "Mexican Americans in Kansas: A Survey and Social Mobility Study, 1900–1970" (Master's thesis, Department of History, Kansas State University, 1972), pp. 20–54; Robert Oppenheimer, "Acculturation or Assimilation: Mexican Immigrants in Kansas, 1900 to World War II," *Western Historical Quarterly* 16 (1985): 429–48.

40. Ernest S. Osgood, *The Day of the Cattleman* (Minneapolis: University of Minnesota Press, 1929), p. 222. The local situation is described well in David L. Wheeler, "Winter on the Cattle Range: Western Kansas, 1884–1886," *Kansas History* 15 (1992): 2–17.

41. Floyd Edwards, *Hamilton County, Kansas, History* (Syracuse, Kans.: Hamilton County Historical Society, 1979), pp. 16–20.

42. Tuttle and Tuttle, eds. and comps., *History and Heritage,* pp. 24–25, and W. P. Harrington, *History of Gove County, Kansas* (Gove City, Kans.: Republican-Gazette, 1930).

43. Edwards, *Hamilton County,* p. 20.

44. Sherow, *Watering the Valley,* p. 87.

45. Book Committee, *History of Logan County,* pp. 16, 30.

46. Destler, "Agricultural Readjustment," p. 108, and Overton, *Burlington West,* pp. 400–402; 461–63.

47. Ellen M. Stanley, *Early Lane County History: 12,000 B.C.–A.D. 1884* (Dighton, Kans.: Ellen M. Stanley, 1993), p. 172; Book Committee, *History of Logan County,* p. 374; Wallace County Historians, *Wallace County History,* p. 43; Krenzel, ed., *History of Wichita County,* p. 385; Tuttle and Tuttle, eds. and comps., *History and Heritage,* p. 71; Book Committee, *They Came to Stay,* p. 212.

48. Book Committee, *History of Early Scott County* (Scott City, Kans.: Scott County Historical Society, 1977), p. 15; Book Committee, *They Came to Stay,* p. 134; Tuttle and Tuttle, eds. and comps., *History and Heritage,* pp. 32–33.

49. Greeley County Historical Book Committee, *History of Early Greeley County,* p. 15.

50. Destler, "Agricultural Readjustment," pp. 108–12, and *Chicago Vanguard,* June 4, 1892 (cited in Destler, p. 112).

51. Greeley County Historical Book Committee, *History of Early Greeley County,* p. 154; Rydjord, *Kansas Place-Names,* pp. 284–85; Kiowa County Libraries History Book Committee, *History of Kiowa County,* p. 68.

52. Kiowa County Libraries History Book Committee, *History of Kiowa County,* p. 34; Michael E. Crowe, ed., *Comanche County History* (Coldwater, Kans.: Comanche County Historical Society, 1981), pp. 74, 104; Haywood, *Trails South,* p. 42; Book Committee, *Stanton County,* pp. 38, 64; Rydjord, *Kansas Place-Names,* p. 279.

53. Cox, *Community of Haviland,* pp. 6–8, 26–28, 34–36.

54. Henry C. Fellow and Melissa S. Fellow, *Semi-Centennial Historical Sketch of Kansas Yearly Meeting of Friends*

(Wichita: Friends Book Supply, 1922), p. 26; Crowe, ed., *Comanche County*, p. 171; Book Committee, *History of Stevens County*, pp. 189–90.

55. For background on recent changes in southwestern Kansas, see "When the Packers Came to Town: Changing Ethnic Relations in Garden City," a special issue of *Urban Anthropology*, ed. Donald D. Stull, 19 (Winter 1990), and David E. Kromm and Stephen E. White, eds., *Groundwater Exploitation in the High Plains* (Lawrence: University Press of Kansas, 1992).

CHAPTER 6. POPULATION ORIGINS IN PERSPECTIVE

1. Robert D. Mitchell, "The Formation of Early American Cultural Regions: An Interpretation," in *European Settlement and Development in North America: Essays on Geographical Change in Honour and Memory of Andrew Hill Clark*, ed. James R. Gibson (Toronto: University of Toronto Press, 1978), pp. 66–90; Douglas K. Meyer, "Illinois Culture Regions at Mid-Nineteenth Century," *Bulletin of the Illinois Geographical Society* 18 (December 1976): 3–13; Gregory S. Rose, "Hoosier Origins: The Nativity of Indiana's United States–Born Population in 1850," *Indiana Magazine of History* 81 (1985): 201–32; Hubert G. H. Wilhelm, "The Origin and Distribution of Settlement Groups: Ohio: 1850," Department of Geography, Ohio University, 1982, mimeographed.

2. Norval D. Glenn and J. L. Simmons, "Are Regional Cultural Differences Diminishing?" *Public Opinion Quarterly* 31 (1967): 176–93; John S. Reed, *The Enduring South: Subcultural Persistence in Mass Society* (Chapel Hill: University of North Carolina Press, 1974); Roger W. Stump, "Regional Divergence in Religious Affiliation in the United States," *Sociological Analysis* 45 (1984): 283–99.

3. J. Neale Carman, *Foreign-Language Units of Kansas*, vol. 1, *Historical Atlas and Statistics* (Lawrence: University of Kansas Press, 1962).

4. The most complete source for name origins is John Rydjord, *Kansas Place-Names* (Norman: University of Oklahoma Press, 1972). I supplemented this information with material from Sondra Van Meter McCoy and Jan Hults, *1001 Kansas Place Names* (Lawrence: University Press of Kansas, 1989), and from recently published county histories.

5. Norman E. Saul, "Myth and History: Turkey Red Wheat and the 'Kansas Miracle,'" *Heritage of the Great Plains* 22 (Summer 1989): 1–13.

6. Lewis C. Gray, *History of Agriculture in the Southern United States to 1860*, 2 vols. (1933; rept., New York: Peter Smith, 1958), 2:876; Terry G. Jordan, "The Imprint of the Upper and Lower South on Mid-Nineteenth-Century Texas," *Annals of the Association of American Geographers* 57 (1967): 683–84; Robert B. Lamb, *The Mule in Southern Agriculture*, University of California Publications in Geography, vol. 15 (Berkeley: University of California Press, 1963).

7. Emory K. Lindquist, *Smoky Valley People: A History of Lindsborg, Kansas* (Lindsborg, Kans.: Bethany College, 1953), pp. 68–69, and D. Aidan McQuillan, *Prevailing Over Time: Ethnic Adjustment on the Kansas Prairies, 1875–1925* (Lincoln: University of Nebraska Press, 1990), p. 53.

8. Norman E. Saul, "The Migration of the Russian-Germans to Kansas," *Kansas Historical Quarterly* 40 (1974): 61; McQuillan, *Prevailing Over Time*, p. 65; Sister Mary Eloise Johannes, *A Study of the Russian-German Settlements in Ellis County, Kansas*, Catholic University of America Studies in Sociology, vol. 14 (Washington, D.C.: Catholic University of America Press, 1946), p. 33; Albert J. Petersen, "German-Russian Colonization in Western Kansas:

A Settlement Geography" (Ph.D. dissertation, Department of Geography and Anthropology, Louisiana State University, 1970), pp. 104–6. The thirty-eight acres of tobacco shown in Cloud County on Map 6.6 is apparently an anomaly; no tobacco was planted there the following year.

9. Church and denominational school data from the state census are available in the *Fifth Biennial Report of the Kansas State Board of Agriculture, 1885–1886* (Topeka: Kansas Publishing House, 1887). The Congregational, Unitarian, and Universalist churches are descendants of New England Puritan groups. Seventh-Day Adventists and the Wesleyan Methodists both have roots in New York. In contrast, the Christian church grew out of frontier mission work in the heart of South-Midland culture: Kentucky, Missouri, and Tennessee. Baptists, although present in both the North and the South, increasingly became known as a Southern denomination after 1820. See Edwin S. Gaustad, *Historical Atlas of Religion in America* (New York: Harper and Row, 1962).

10. Useful sketchs of this election can be found in William F. Zornow, *Kansas: A History of the Jayhawk State* (Norman: University of Oklahoma Press, 1957), pp. 190–96, and in Homer E. Socolofsky, *Kansas Governors* (Lawrence: University Press of Kansas, 1990), pp. 109–118. County-by-county results are in *Fifth Biennial Report of the Secretary of State of the State of Kansas, 1885–1886* (Topeka: Kansas Publishing House, 1886), pp. 66–67.

11. J. Neale Carman and Associates, *Foreign-Language Units of Kansas*, vol.2, *Account of Settlement and Settlements in Kansas* (Lawrence: University Press of Kansas, 1974), pp. 56–57.

12. Ethnic political orientations are summarized in Walter T. K. Nugent, *The Tolerant Populists: Kansas Populism and Nativism* (Chicago: University of Chicago Press, 1963), pp. 35–53, and in Robert S. Bader, *Prohibition in Kansas: A History* (Lawrence: University Press of Kansas, 1986), pp. 66–71. On Bohemians, see Bozena Nemcova, "People of Czech (Bohemian) Descent in Republic County, Kansas" (Master's thesis, Department of Sociology, University of Kansas, 1950), p. 50, and Francis J. Swehla, "Bohemians in Central Kansas," *Kansas Historical Collections, 1913–1914* 13 (1915): 495. The most comprehensive group study is David A. Haury's "German-Russian Immigrants to Kansas and American Politics," *Kansas History* 3 (1980): 226–37.

13. County-by-county data for the Prohibition referenda of 1880, 1934, and 1948 and for the liquor-by-the-drink referendum of 1970 are in Bader, *Prohibition in Kansas*, pp. 269–70.

14. Ibid., p. 60.

15. *Statistics of the Population of the United States at the Tenth Census*, vol. 1 (Washington, D.C.: Government Printing Office, 1883), Table 14: "Native and Foreign-Born Population, by Counties."

16. Robert M. Crisler, "Missouri's 'Little Dixie,'" *Missouri Historical Review* 42 (1948): 130–39.

17. Joel Garreau, *The Nine Nations of North America* (Boston: Houghton Mifflin Company, 1981), pp. 328–61; Raymond D. Gastil, *Cultural Regions of the United States* (Seattle: University of Washington Press, 1975), pp. 216–24; Wilbur Zelinsky, *The Cultural Geography of the United States*, rev. ed. (Englewood Cliffs, N.J.: Prentice-Hall, 1992), pp. 117–34.

18. Larry Rutter, "Mexican Americans in Kansas: A Survey and Social Mobility Study, 1900–1970" (Master's thesis, Department of History, Kansas State University, 1972), p. 51; Carman, *Historical Atlas*, pp. 112, 187, 223, 236, 304; Michael J. Broadway, "The Characteristics of Southeast Asian Refugees Residing in Garden City, Kansas," *Kansas Geographer* 19 (1985): 5–18; Joseph B. Herring, *The Enduring Indians of Kansas: A Century and a Half of Acculturation* (Lawrence: University Press of Kansas, 1990).

19. The foremost student of rural demography in the United States is Calvin Beale; see Peter A. Morrison, ed., *A Taste of the Country: A Collection of Calvin Beale's Writings* (University Park: Pennsylvania State University Press, 1990).

20. Suzi Jones, "Regionalization: A Rhetorical Strategy," *Journal of the Folklore Institute* 13 (1976): 105–20. A recent elaboration of Jones's ideas is Barbara Allen and Thomas J. Schlereth, eds., *Sense of Place: American Regional Cultures* (Lexington: University Press of Kentucky, 1990).

21. Peter J. McCormick, "The 1992 Secession Movement in Southwest Kansas," senior honors thesis, Department of Geography, University of Kansas, 1993, and James R. Shortridge, "The Heart of the Prairie: Culture Areas in the Central and Northern Great Plains," *Great Plains Quarterly* 8 (1988): 206–21.

22. Paul E. Phillips, "An Assessment of the Validity of an East-West Cultural Dichotomy for Kansas" (Ph.D. dissertation, Department of Geography, University of Kansas, 1977). The character of western Kansas is described well in Cary W. de Wit, "Sense of Place on the Kansas High Plains" (Master's thesis, Department of Geography, University of Kansas, 1992).

23. Huber Self, *Environment and Man in Kansas: A Geographical Analysis* (Lawrence: Regents Press of Kansas, 1978), p. 89.

24. Religious data are available in Bernard Quinn et al., *Churches and Church Membership in the United States, 1980* (Atlanta: Glenmary Research Center, 1982), pp. 111–20, and Martin H. Bradley et al., *Churches and Church Membership in the United States, 1990* (Atlanta: Glenmary Research Center, 1992), pp. 155–66; Albert B. Cook, "Kansas Word Geography: A Summary of Findings," *Kansas Quarterly* 22 (Fall 1990): 77–107. Political data are available in *Election Statistics, State of Kansas: 1990 Primary and General Elections* (Topeka: Secretary of State Bill Graves, n.d.).

25. Lindquist, *Smoky Valley People,* pp. 199–204; Haury, "German-Russian Immigrants"; William E. Powell, "European Settlement in the Cherokee-Crawford Coal Field of Southeastern Kansas," *Kansas Historical Quarterly* 41 (1975): 150–65; Daniel C. Fitzgerald, "'We Are All in This Together': Immigrants in the Oil and Mining Towns of Southern Kansas, 1890–1920," *Kansas History* 10 (1987): 17–28; James R. Shortridge, *Kaw Valley Landscapes: A Traveler's Guide to Northeastern Kansas,* rev. ed. (Lawrence: University Press of Kansas, 1988), pp. 3–20.

26. United States Department of Commerce, Bureau of the Census, *1980 Census of Population and Housing,* vol. 1, *General Social and Economic Characteristics of the Population,* Table 60: "Selected Ancestry Groups." Complete data for all groups are on summary tape file 4, also published by the Bureau of the Census. Russian affiliation was chosen by very few of the descendants of Russian-German immigrants; the highest percentage, for Gray County, was two.

27. On the concept of ethnicity in modern American society, see Werner Sollors, *Beyond Ethnicity: Consent and Descent in American Culture* (New York: Oxford University Press, 1986), and Richard D. Alba, *Ethnic Identity: The Transformation of White America* (New Haven, Conn.: Yale University Press, 1990).

28. The most articulate spokesman for the reestablishment of human connections to particular places has been Wendell Berry; see especially his *The Unsettling of America: Culture and Agriculture* (San Francisco: Sierra Club Books, 1977). A good recent study is Scott R. Sanders, *Staying Put: Making a Home in a Restless World* (Boston: Beacon Press, 1993).

29. Wilbur Zelinsky, "Selfward Bound? Personal Preference Patterns and the Changing Map of American Society," *Economic Geography* 50 (1974): 144–79, and idem, *Cultural Geography of the United States,* pp. 134–39, 177–85.

30. McQuillan, *Prevailing Over Time,* quotation on p. 201.

Bibliography

THE KANSAS CENSUS

The decennial censuses of Kansas, which form the principal data source for this book, were initiated in 1865. They were seen as important supplements to the federal censuses during the period of rapid growth in the state, demonstrations to potential immigrants and others of the progress being made on the central plains. The first effort, coordinated by the secretary of state, was never published. Responsibility for subsequent surveys passed to officials at the Kansas State Board of Agriculture, who issued them as part of their regular bulletins through 1925. The plan for each state survey followed closely that of the preceding federal census, but Kansans, because of their special concern with immigrants, added a question asking where each resident had lived just prior to his or her immigration to the state. I did not use these data on previous residence for my study, but, in combination with nativity figures, they offer opportunities to gain additional insights into the migration process.

At the county level, nativity statistics on individual states and countries of birth are available in the *Fourth Annual Report of the Kansas State Board of Agriculture* and in the *Fifth, Tenth, Fifteenth, Twentieth,* and *Twenty-fifth Biennial Reports* of the same organization, all published in Topeka by the state printer. These reports also contain finer, township-level resolutions for race and for native- versus foreign-born populations, but such detail for individual states and countries of birth can be obtained only by making counts directly from the census rolls. Microfilm copies of the original manuscripts are available from the Kansas State Historical Society in Topeka and also can be found in major libraries throughout the state. The microfilm collection includes the unpublished 1865 census.

OTHER SOURCES

Alba, Richard D. *Ethnic Identity: The Transformation of White America.* New Haven, Conn.: Yale University Press, 1990.

Allen, Barbara, and Thomas J. Schlereth, eds. *Sense of Place: American Regional Cultures.* Lexington: University Press of Kentucky, 1990.

At Home in Ellis County, Kansas: 1867–1992. Vol. 1. Hays, Kans.: Ellis County Historical Society, 1991.

Athearn, Robert G. *In Search of Canaan: Black Migration to Kansas, 1879–80.* Lawrence: Regents Press of Kansas, 1978.

Bader, Robert S. *Prohibition in Kansas: A History.* Lawrence: University Press of Kansas, 1986.

———. *Hayseeds, Moralizers, and Methodists: The Twentieth-Century Image of Kansas.* Lawrence: University Press of Kansas, 1988.

Baker, Hazel B. "Some Early Facts on the History of Pawnee County, Kansas, and Stafford County, Kansas." A collection of newspaper columns held by the Kansas Collection at the University of Kansas, no date.

Barry, Louise. "The Emigrant Aid Company Parties of 1854." *Kansas Historical Quarterly* 12 (1943): 115–55.

———. "The New England Emigrant Aid Company Parties of 1855." *Kansas Historical Quarterly* 12 (1943): 227–68.

Beckman, Peter. *The Catholic Church on the Kansas Frontier, 1850–1877.* Washington, D.C.: Catholic University of America Press, 1943.

———. "The Overland Trade and Atchison's Beginnings." In *Territorial Kansas: Studies Commemorating the Centennial,* pp. 148–63. Lawrence: University of Kansas Publications, 1954.

Bergin, Alfred. "The Swedish Settlements in Central

Kansas." *Kansas Historical Collections, 1909–1910* 11 (1910): 19–46.

Berry, Wendell. *The Unsettling of America: Culture and Agriculture.* San Francisco: Sierra Club Books, 1977.

Berryman, J. W. "Early Settlement of Southwest Kansas." *Kansas Historical Collections, 1926–1928* 17 (1928): 561–70.

Beyer, George R. "Pennsylvania Germans Move to Kansas." *Pennsylvania History* 32 (1965): 27–48.

Bicha, Karel D. *The Czechs in Oklahoma.* Norman: University of Oklahoma Press, 1980.

Birch, Brian P. "Victoria Vanquished: The Scottish Press and the Failure of George Grant's Colony." *Kansas History* 9 (1986): 115–24.

———. "Popularizing the Plains: News of Kansas in England, 1860–1880." *Kansas History* 10 (1987): 262–74.

Blackburn, Anora, and Myrtle S. Cardwell, comps. *History of Republic County, 1868–1964.* Belleville, Kans.: Republic County Historical Society, 1964.

Blanchard, Leola H. *Conquest of Southwest Kansas.* Wichita: Wichita Eagle Press, 1931.

Bogue, Allan G. *From Prairie to Corn Belt: Farming on the Illinois and Iowa Prairies in the Nineteenth Century.* Chicago: University of Chicago Press, 1963.

Bonnifield, Paul. *The Dust Bowl: Men, Dirt, and Depression.* Albuquerque: University of New Mexico Press, 1979.

Book Committee. *History of Early Scott County.* Scott City, Kans.: Scott County Historical Society, 1977.

Book Committee. *History of Kearny County, Kansas.* Vol. 1. Dodge City, Kans.: Kearny County Historical Society, 1964.

Book Committee. *History of Logan County, Kansas.* Oakley, Kans.: Logan County Historical Society, 1986.

Book Committee. *The History of Stevens County and Its People.* Hugoton, Kans.: Stevens County Historical Association, 1979.

Book Committee. *Stanton County, Kansas: 1887–1987.* N.p., 1987.

Book Committee. *They Came to Stay: Sherman County and Family History.* Vol. 1. Goodland, Kans.: Sherman County Historical Society, 1980.

Bowen, William A. *The Willamette Valley: Migration and Settlement on the Oregon Frontier.* Seattle: University of Washington Press, 1978.

Bradley, Glenn D. *The Story of the Santa Fe.* Boston: Richard G. Badger, 1920.

Bradley, Martin H., et al. *Churches and Church Membership in the United States, 1990.* Atlanta: Glenmary Research Center, 1992.

Bradshaw, Alfred B. *When the Prairies Were New.* Turon, Kans.: Arthur J. Allen, 1957.

Bright, John D., ed. *Kansas: The First Century.* Vol. 1. New York: Lewis Historical Publishing Company, 1956.

Broadway, Michael J. "The Characteristics of Southeast Asian Refugees Residing in Garden City, Kansas." *Kansas Geographer* 19 (1985): 5–18.

Brown, Lula L. *The Cherokee Neutral Lands Controversy.* Girard, Kans.: Girard Press, 1931.

Burgess, Charles W. "Mining Costs in the Missouri-Kansas District." *Mining and Engineering World* 38 (April 1913): 801–5.

Burr, Myron C., and Elizabeth Burr, eds. *The Kinsley-Edwards County Centennial, 1873–1973.* Kinsley, Kans.: Nolan Publishers, 1973.

Burrton's 75th Anniversary: 1873–1948. Burrton, Kans.: Burrton Graphic, 1948.

Byers, O. P. "Early History of the El Paso Line of the Chicago, Rock Island, and Pacific Railroad." *Kansas Historical Collections, 1919–1922* 15 (1923): 573–78.

Byrne, Stephen. *Irish Emigration to the United States: What It Has Been and What It Is.* New York: Catholic Publication Society, 1873.

Campbell, Charles B. "Bourbonnais; or the Early French Settlements in Kankakee County, Illinois." *Transactions of the Illinois State Historical Society* 11 (1906): 65–72.

Capek, Thomas. *The Cechs (Bohemians) in America.* Boston: Houghton Mifflin Company, 1920.

Carman, J. Neale. "Continental Europeans in Rural

Kansas, 1854–1861." In *Territorial Kansas: Studies Commemorating the Centennial*, pp. 164–96. Lawrence: University of Kansas Publications, 1954.

———. "Germans in Kansas." *American-German Review* 27 (April–May 1961): 4–8.

———. *Foreign-Language Units of Kansas*. Vol. 1. *Historical Atlas and Statistics*. Lawrence: University of Kansas Press, 1962.

Carman, J. Neale, and Associates. *Foreign Language Units of Kansas*. Vol. 2. *Account of Settlement and Settlements in Kansas*. Lawrence: University Press of Kansas, 1974.

Case, Nelson. *History of Labette County, Kansas*. Topeka: Crane and Company, 1893.

Castel, Albert. *A Frontier State at War: Kansas 1861–1865*. 1958. Reprint. Lawrence: Kansas Heritage Press, 1992.

Centennial Committee. "History of Ottawa County, Kansas: 1864–1984." Mimeographed, n.d. Copy in the Kansas Collection, University of Kansas.

Chapman, William J. "The Wakefield Colony." *Kansas Historical Collections, 1907–1908* 10 (1908): 485–533.

Cheatham, Gary L. "Divided Loyalties in Civil War Kansas." *Kansas History* 11 (1988): 93–107.

———. "Desperate Characters: The Development and Impact of the Confederate Guerrillas in Kansas." *Kansas History* 14 (1991): 144–61.

Christensen, Thomas P. "The Danish Settlements in Kansas." *Kansas Historical Collections, 1926–1928* 17 (1928): 300–305.

Clark, John G. *Towns and Minerals in Southeastern Kansas: A Study in Regional Industrialization, 1890–1930*. Special Distribution Publication 52. Lawrence: State Geological Survey of Kansas, 1970.

———, ed. *The Frontier Challenge: Responses to the Trans-Mississippi West*. Lawrence: University Press of Kansas, 1971.

Clark, W. A. V. *Human Migration*. Scientific Geography Series. Vol. 7. Beverly Hills, Calif.: Sage Publications, 1986.

Combes, Emily I. "Letters from an Eighteen-year-old Kansas Pioneer Girl Written from Manhattan and Rice County to her Fiance in Ohio between April 21, 1871, and December 17, 1871." Manuscript, the Kansas Collection, University of Kansas.

Connelley, William E. *An Appeal to the Record*. Topeka: William E. Connelley, 1903.

———. "The Lane Trail." *Kansas Historical Collections, 1913–1914* 13 (1915): 268–79.

Cook, Albert B. "Perspectives for a Linguistic Atlas of Kansas." *American Speech* 53 (Fall 1978): 199–209.

———. "Kansas Word Geography: A Summary of Findings." *Kansas Quarterly* 22 (Fall 1990): 77–107.

Cooper, Arnold. "'Protection to All, Discrimination to None': The Parsons Weekly Blade, 1892–1900." *Kansas History* 9 (1986): 58–71.

Cox, Weston F. *The Community of Haviland, Kansas*. Haviland, Kans.: Friends Bible College Press, 1966.

Craik, Elmer L. "Southern Interest in Territorial Kansas, 1854–1858." *Kansas Historical Collections, 1919–1922* 15 (1923): 334–450.

Crisler, Robert M. "Missouri's 'Little Dixie.'" *Missouri Historical Review* 42 (1948): 130–39.

Crowe, Michael E., ed. *Comanche County History*. Coldwater, Kans.: Comanche County Historical Society, 1981.

Curl, Thelma J. "Promotional Efforts of the Kansas Pacific and Santa Fe to Settle Kansas." Master's thesis, Department of History, University of Kansas, 1961.

Curti, Merle, and Kendall Birr. "The Immigrant and the American Image in Europe, 1860–1914." *Mississippi Valley Historical Review* 37 (1950): 203–30.

Cutler, William G., ed. *History of the State of Kansas*. Chicago: A. T. Andreas, 1883.

Dale, Edward E. *The Range Cattle Industry*. Norman: University of Oklahoma Press, 1930.

Dary, David. *More True Tales of Old-Time Kansas*. Lawrence: University Press of Kansas, 1987.

Davies, Phillips G. "The Welsh in Kansas: Settlement, Contributions, and Assimilation." *Welsh History Review* 14 (1989): 380–98.

Destler, Chester M. "Agricultural Readjustment and Agrarian Unrest in Illinois, 1880–1896." *Agricultural History* 21 (1947): 104–16.

de Wit, Cary W. "Sense of Place on the Kansas High Plains." Master's thesis, Department of Geography, University of Kansas, 1992.

Dick, Everett. *The Sod-House Frontier: 1854–1890.* Lincoln, Nebr.: Johnsen Publishing Company, 1954.

Doran, Michael F. "Population Statistics of Nineteenth Century Indian Territory." *Chronicles of Oklahoma* 53 (1975–1976): 492–515.

———. "Antebellum Cattle Herding in the Indian Territory." *Geographical Review* 66 (1976): 48–58.

Drake, Charles C. *Who's Who: A History of Kansas and Montgomery County, Including the Cities of Coffeyville, Independence, Cherryvale, and Caney.* Coffeyville, Kans.: Coffeyville Journal Press, 1943.

Dreiling, Norbert R. *Official Centennial History of the Volga-German Settlements in Ellis and Rush Counties in Kansas: 1876–1976.* Hays, Kans.: Volga-German Centennial Association, 1976.

Duncan, L. Wallace, and Charles F. Scott, eds. *History of Allen and Woodson Counties, Kansas.* Iola, Kans.: Iola Register, 1901.

Dykstra, Robert R. *The Cattle Towns.* New York: Alfred A. Knopf, 1968.

Edwards, Floyd. *Hamilton County, Kansas, History.* Syracuse, Kans.: Hamilton County Historical Society, 1979.

Einsel, Mary. "Some Notes on the Comanche Cattle Pool." *Kansas Historical Quarterly* 26 (1960): 59–66.

Emmons, David M. *Garden in the Grasslands: Boomer Literature of the Central Great Plains.* Lincoln: University of Nebraska Press, 1971.

Everett, J. Keith, ed. *Promised Land on the Solomon: Black Settlement at Nicodemus, Kansas.* Washington, D.C.: Government Printing Office, 1986.

Faragher, John M. *Sugar Creek: Life on the Illinois Prairie.* New Haven, Conn.: Yale University Press, 1986.

Federal Writers' Project. *The WPA Guide to 1930s Kansas.* Lawrence: University Press of Kansas, 1984.

Feld, Lipman G. "New Light on the Lost Jewish Colony of Beersheba, Kansas, 1882–1886." *American Jewish Historical Quarterly* 60 (1970): 159–68.

Fellman, Michael. *Inside War: The Guerrilla Conflict in Missouri during the American Civil War.* New York: Oxford University Press, 1989.

Fellow, Henry C., and Melissa S. Fellow. *Semi-Centennial Historical Sketch of Kansas Yearly Meeting of Friends.* Wichita: Friends Book Supply, 1922.

Fiftieth Anniversary Jubilee. Ulysses, Kans.: Ulysses News, 1941.

Fitzgerald, Daniel C. "'We Are All in This Together': Immigrants in the Oil and Mining Towns of Southern Kansas, 1890–1920." *Kansas History* 10 (1987): 17–28.

Fleming, Walter L. "The Buford Expedition to Kansas." *American Historical Review* 6 (October 1900): 38–48.

Forsythe, James L. "George Grant of Victoria: Man and Myth." *Kansas History* 9 (1986): 102–14.

———. "The English Colony at Victoria, Another View." *Kansas History* 12 (1989): 175–84.

Foucault, Michel. *Power/Knowledge: Selected Interviews and Other Writings, 1972–1977.* Edited by Colin Gordon. New York: Pantheon Books, 1980.

Gaeddert, G. Raymond. *The Birth of Kansas.* Lawrence: University of Kansas Publications, 1940.

Garreau, Joel. *The Nine Nations of North America.* Boston: Houghton Mifflin Company, 1981.

Gastil, Raymond D. *Cultural Regions of the United States.* Seattle: University of Washington Press, 1975.

Gates, Paul W. "The Homestead Act in an Incongruous Land System." *American Historical Review* 41 (1936): 652–81.

———. *Fifty Million Acres: Conflicts over Kansas Land Policy, 1854–1890.* Ithaca, N.Y.: Cornell University Press, 1954.

———. *History of Public Land Law Development.* Washington, D.C.: Government Printing Office, 1968.

Gaustad, Edwin S. *Historical Atlas of Religion in America*. New York: Harper and Row, 1962.

Gerlach, Russel L. *Settlement Patterns in Missouri: A Study of Population Origins, with a Wall Map*. Columbia: University of Missouri Press, 1986.

Gibson, Arrell M. *Wilderness Bonanza: The Tri-State District of Missouri, Kansas, and Oklahoma*. Norman: University of Oklahoma Press, 1972.

Gibson, James R., ed. *European Settlement and Development in North America: Essays on Geographical Change in Honour and Memory of Andrew Hill Clark*. Toronto: University of Toronto Press, 1978.

Giddens, Anthony. *The Constitution of Society*. Berkeley: University of California Press, 1984.

Glenn, Norval D., and J. L. Simmons. "Are Regional Cultural Differences Diminishing?" *Public Opinion Quarterly* 31 (1967): 176–93.

Granstedt, Andrew A. "The Scandinavian People and the Americanization of a Scandinavian Community." Master's thesis, Department of Sociology, University of Kansas, 1916.

Graves, W. W. *History of Neosho County*. Vol. 1. St. Paul, Kans.: Journal Press, 1949.

Gray, John R. *Pioneer Saints and Sinners: Pratt County from Its Beginnings to 1900*. Pratt, Kans.: Pratt Rotary Club, 1961.

Gray, Lewis C. *History of Agriculture in the Southern United States to 1860*. Vol. 2. 1933. Reprint. New York: Peter Smith, 1958.

Greeley County Historical Book Committee. *History of Early Greeley County*. Vol. 1. Tribune, Kans.: Greeley County Historical Book Committee, 1981.

Gruening, Ernest, ed. *These United States: A Symposium*. Vol. 1. New York: Boni and Liveright, 1923.

Hale, Douglas. "European Immigrants in Oklahoma: A Survey." *Chronicles of Oklahoma* 53 (1975–76): 179–203.

Hamilton, Kenneth M. "The Origins and Early Promotion of Nicodemus: A Pre-Exodus, All-Black Town." *Kansas History* 5 (1982): 220–42.

———. *Black Towns and Profit: Promotion and Development in the Trans-Appalachian West, 1877–1915*. Urbana: University of Illinois Press, 1991.

Hansen, Marcus L., completed by John B. Brebner. *The Mingling of the Canadian and American Peoples*. Vol. 1. *Historical*. New Haven, Conn.: Yale University Press, 1940.

Hargreaves, Mary W. M. *Dry Farming in the Northern Great Plains, 1900–1925*. Cambridge: Harvard University Press, 1957.

Harper, Paul F. *Surely It Floweth with Milk and Honey: A History of Montgomery County, Kansas, to 1930*. Independence, Kans.: Independence Community College Press, 1988.

Harrington, W. P. *History of Gove County, Kansas*. Gove City, Kans.: Republican-Gazette, 1930.

Harris, Cole. "Power, Modernity, and Historical Geography." *Annals of the Association of American Geographers* 81 (1991): 671–83.

Hart, Charles D. "The Natural Limits of Slavery Expansion: Kansas-Nebraska, 1854." *Kansas Historical Quarterly* 34 (1968): 32–50.

Haury, David A. "German-Russian Immigrants to Kansas and American Politics." *Kansas History* 3 (1980): 226–37.

Haworth, Erasmus. *Annual Bulletin on Mineral Resources of Kansas for 1897*. Lawrence: University Geological Survey of Kansas, 1898.

Hayden, Ruth K. *The Time That Was*. Colby, Kans.: H. F. Davis Memorial Library, Colby Community College, 1973.

Haywood, C. Robert. "Pearlette: A Mutual Aid Colony." *Kansas Historical Quarterly* 42 (1976): 263–76.

———. "Comanche County Cowboy: A Case Study of a Kansas Rancher." *Kansas History* 4 (1981): 166–90.

———. *Trails South: The Wagon-Road Economy in the Dodge City–Panhandle Region*. Norman: University of Oklahoma Press, 1986.

———. "The Hodgeman County Colony." *Kansas History* 12 (1989): 210–21.

Herring, Joseph B. *The Enduring Indians of Kansas: A Century and a Half of Acculturation.* Lawrence: University Press of Kansas, 1990.

Hines, Elizabeth. "Farming and Ranching in Morton County through 1915: The Historical Geography of a High Plains Frontier." Master's thesis, Department of Geography, University of Kansas, 1985.

Historical Collection of Harper County Churches. Anthony, Kans.: Harper County Religious Heritage Committee, 1961.

Hollibaugh, Mrs. E. F. *Biographical History of Cloud County, Kansas.* N.p., 1903.

Holloway, John N. *History of Kansas.* Lafayette, Ind.: James, Emmons and Company, 1868.

Homan, Dorothe T. *Lincoln: That County in Kansas.* Lindsborg, Kans.: Barbos' Printing, 1979.

Howell, Frederick N. "Pittsburg, Kansas, and Its Industries." Master's thesis, Department of History, University of Kansas, 1930.

Hudson, John C. "Two Dakota Homestead Frontiers." *Annals of the Association of American Geographers* 63 (1973): 442–62.

———. "Migration to an American Frontier." *Annals of the Association of American Geographers* 66 (1976): 242–65.

———. "Theory and Methodology in Comparative Frontier Studies." In *The Frontier: Comparative Studies,* edited by David H. Miller and Jerome O. Steffen, pp. 11–31. Norman: University of Oklahoma Press, 1977.

———. "The Study of Western Frontier Populations." In *The American West: New Perspectives, New Dimensions,* edited by Jerome O. Steffen, pp. 35–60. Norman: University of Oklahoma Press, 1979.

———. "The Middle West as a Cultural Hybrid." *Pioneer America Society Transactions* 7 (1984): 35–45.

———. "North American Origins of Middlewestern Frontier Populations." *Annals of the Association of American Geographers* 78 (1988): 395–413.

Hvidt, Kristian. *Flight to America: The Social Background of 300,000 Danish Emigrants.* New York: Academic Press, 1975.

Ise, John. *Sod and Stubble: The Story of a Kansas Homestead.* 1936. Reprint. Lincoln: University of Nebraska Press, 1967.

James, Bill, and Marge Brown. *A History of Gem, Kansas.* Colby, Kans.: Prairie Printers, 1970.

Johannes, Sister Mary Eloise. *A Study of the Russian-German Settlements in Ellis County, Kansas.* Catholic University of America Studies in Sociology, Vol. 14. Washington, D.C.: Catholic University of America Press, 1946.

Johnson, Samuel A. *The Battle Cry of Freedom: The New England Emigrant Aid Company in the Kansas Crusade.* Lawrence: University of Kansas Press, 1954.

Jones, Carolyn. *The First One Hundred Years: A History of the City of Manhattan, Kansas, 1855–1955.* Manhattan, Kans.: Manhattan Centennial, 1955.

Jones, Horace. *The Story of Early Rice County.* Wichita: Wichita Eagle Press, 1932.

Jones, Suzi. "Regionalization: A Rhetorical Strategy." *Journal of the Folklore Institute* 13 (1976): 105–20.

Jordan, Terry G. "The Imprint of the Upper and Lower South on Mid-Nineteenth-Century Texas." *Annals of the Association of American Geographers* 57 (1967): 667–90.

———. "Population Origins in Texas, 1850." *Geographical Review* 59 (1969): 83–103.

———. "Population Origin Groups in Rural Texas." *Annals of the Association of American Geographers* 60 (1970): 404–5, with a color map.

———. *Trails to Texas: Southern Roots of Western Cattle Ranching.* Lincoln: University of Nebraska Press, 1981.

Jordan, Terry G., and Matti Kaups. *The American Backwoods Frontier: An Ethnic and Ecological Interpretation.* Baltimore: Johns Hopkins University Press, 1989.

"Kansas Farmers and Illinois Dairymen." *Atlantic Monthly* 44 (December 1879): 717–25.

Kansas in 1875: Strong and Impartial Testimony to the

Wonderful Productiveness of the Cottonwood and Arkansas Valleys. Topeka: Atchison, Topeka and Santa Fe Railroad Company, 1875.

King, Edward. "The Great South: The New Route to the Gulf." *Scribner's Monthly* 6 (July 1873): 257–88.

King, Henry. "Picturesque Features of Kansas Farming." *Scribner's Monthly* 19 (November 1879): 132–40.

Kiowa County Libraries History Book Committee. *A History of Kiowa County: 1880–1980.* Lubbock, Tex.: Taylor Publishing Company, 1979.

Kniffen, Fred B. "Folk Housing: Key to Diffusion." *Annals of the Association of American Geographers* 55 (1965): 549–77.

Kollmorgen, Walter M. "The Woodsman's Assaults on the Domain of the Cattleman." *Annals of the Association of American Geographers* 59 (1969): 215–39.

Kramer, Frank R. *Voices in the Valley: Mythmaking and Folk Belief in the Shaping of the Middle West.* Madison: University of Wisconsin Press, 1964.

Krenzel, Ellen R., ed. *History of Wichita County, Kansas.* Vol. 1. Leoti, Kans.: Wichita County History Association, 1980.

Kromm, David E., and Stephen E. White, eds. *Groundwater Exploitation in the High Plains.* Lawrence: University Press of Kansas, 1992.

Laing, Francis S. "German-Russian Settlements in Ellis County, Kansas." *Kansas Historical Collections, 1909–1910* 11 (1910): 489–528.

Lamb, Robert B. *The Mule in Southern Agriculture.* University of California Publications in Geography. Vol. 15. Berkeley: University of California Press, 1963.

Lee, Everett S. "A Theory of Migration." *Demography* 3 (1966): 47–57.

LeMoine, Vincent. *The Chapman Irish.* N.p., 1963.

Lemon, James T. *The Best Poor Man's Country: A Geographical Study of Early Southeastern Pennsylvania.* Baltimore: Johns Hopkins University Press, 1972.

Lewis, Lloyd. "Propaganda and the Kansas-Missouri War." *Missouri Historical Review* 34 (1939): 3–17.

Lindberg, John S. *The Background of Swedish Emigration to the United States.* Minneapolis: University of Minnesota Press, 1930.

Lindquist, Emory. *Smoky Valley People: A History of Lindsborg, Kansas.* Lindsborg, Kans.: Bethany College, 1953.

———. "The Swedish Immigrant and Life in Kansas." *Kansas Historical Quarterly* 29 (1963): 1–24.

Lowe, Jesse H. *Pioneer History of Kingman County, Kansas.* N.p., n.d.

Luebke, Frederick C. "Ethnic Group Settlement on the Great Plains." *Western Historical Quarterly* 8 (1977): 405–30.

Malin, James C. "The Proslavery Background of the Kansas Struggle." *Mississippi Valley Historical Review* 10 (1923): 285–305.

———. "The Kinsley Boom of the Late Eighties." *Kansas Historical Quarterly* 4 (1935): 23–49, 164–87.

———. "The Turnover of Farm Population in Kansas." *Kansas Historical Quarterly* 4 (1935): 339–72.

———. "An Introduction to the History of the Bluestem-Pasture Region of Kansas." *Kansas Historical Quarterly* 11 (1942): 1–22.

———. *John Brown and the Legend of Fifty Six.* Philadelphia: American Philosophical Society, 1942.

———. *The Nebraska Question, 1852–1854.* Lawrence, Kans.: privately printed, 1953.

———. "Kansas: Some Reflections on Culture Inheritance and Originality." *Journal of the Central Mississippi Valley American Studies Association* 2 (Fall 1961): 3–19.

Martin, John A. "The Progress of Kansas." *North American Review* 142 (1886): 348–55.

Masterson, V. V. *The Katy Railroad and the Last Frontier.* Norman: University of Oklahoma Press, 1952.

McCalla, Dollie, ed. *Memoirs of Old Hawkeye.* Englewood, Colo.: Claar-Rezner Family, n.d.

McCormick, Peter J. "The 1992 Secession Movement

in Southwest Kansas." Senior honors thesis, Department of Geography, University of Kansas, 1993.

McCoy, Sondra Van Meter, and Jan Hults. *1001 Kansas Place Names.* Lawrence: University Press of Kansas, 1989.

McQuillan, D. Aidan. "The Creation and Survival of French-Canadian Communities in the Upper Midwest during the Nineteenth Century." *Cahiers de Géographie de Quebec* 23 (1979): 53–72.

———. *Prevailing Over Time: Ethnic Adjustment on the Kansas Prairies, 1875–1925.* Lincoln: University of Nebraska Press, 1990.

McVicar, Peter. *A Historical Sketch of Washburn College.* Burlington, Kans.: Republican-Patriot Printers, 1886.

Meyer, Douglas K. "Illinois Culture Regions at Mid-Nineteenth Century." *Bulletin of the Illinois Geographical Society* 18 (December 1976): 3–13.

———. "Native-Born Immigrant Clusters on the Illinois Frontier." *Proceedings of the Association of American Geographers* 8 (1976): 41–44.

Meyers, A. L. "Golden-Jubilee, 1889–1939." St. Ann's Church, Olmitz, Kans. Mimeographed, 1939. Copy in the Kansas Collection, University of Kansas.

Millbrook, Minnie D. *Ness: Western County, Kansas.* Detroit: Millbrook Printing Company, 1955.

Miller, Darrel, ed. *Pioneer Plows and Steel Rails: Outriders of Civilization in the Valley of the Solomon.* Downs, Kans.: Downs News and Times, 1961.

Miller, David H., and Jerome O. Steffen, eds. *The Frontier: Comparative Studies.* Norman: University of Oklahoma Press, 1977.

Miner, H. Craig. *Wichita: The Early Years, 1865–80.* Lincoln: University of Nebraska Press, 1982.

———. *West of Wichita: Settling the High Plains of Kansas, 1865–1890.* Lawrence: University Press of Kansas, 1986.

Miner, H. Craig, and William E. Unrau. *The End of Indian Kansas: A Study of Cultural Revolution, 1854–1871.* Lawrence: Regents Press of Kansas, 1978.

Mitchell County Historical Essays: 1962–1976. Beloit: Mitchell County Historical Society, 1976.

Mitchell, Robert D. "The Formation of Early American Cultural Regions: An Interpretation." In *European Settlement and Development in North America: Essays on Geographical Change in Honour and Memory of Andrew Hill Clark,* edited by James R. Gibson, pp. 66–90. Toronto: University of Toronto Press, 1978.

Mooney, Vol P. *History of Butler County, Kansas.* Lawrence: Standard Publishing Company, 1916.

Morrison, Peter A., ed. *A Taste of the Country: A Collection of Calvin Beale's Writings.* University Park: Pennsylvania State University Press, 1990.

Nelson, Edward G. *The Company and the Community.* Lawrence: University of Kansas School of Business, 1956.

Nelson, Margaret A. *Home on the Range.* Boston: Chipman and Grimes, 1947.

Nemcova, Bozena. "People of Czech (Bohemian) Descent in Republic County, Kansas." Master's thesis, Department of Sociology, University of Kansas, 1950.

Newton, Milton B., Jr. "Cultural Preadaptation and the Upland South." *Geoscience and Man* 5 (1974): 143–54.

Nichols, Alice. *Bleeding Kansas.* New York: Oxford University Press, 1954.

Norman, H. "History of Hodgeman County, Kansas." Mimeographed, 1941. Copy in the Kansas Collection, University of Kansas.

North, F. A. *The History of Jasper County, Missouri.* Des Moines, Iowa: Mills and Company, 1883.

Nugent, Walter T. K. *The Tolerant Populists: Kansas Populism and Nativism.* Chicago: University of Chicago Press, 1963.

Nyquist, Edna E. *Pioneer Life and Lore in McPherson County, Kansas.* McPherson, Kans.: Democrat-Opinion Press, 1932.

O'Brien, Michael J. *Grassland, Forest, and Historical Settlement: An Analysis of Dynamics in Northeast*

Missouri. Lincoln: University of Nebraska Press, 1984.

Official State Atlas of Kansas. Philadelphia: L. H. Everts and Company, 1887.

Oppenheimer, Robert. "Acculturation or Assimilation: Mexican Immigrants in Kansas, 1900 to World War II." *Western Historical Quarterly* 16 (1985): 429–48.

Osborne County Historical Society. *The People Came.* Osborne, Kans.: Osborne County Farmer, 1977.

Osgood, Ernest S. *The Day of the Cattleman.* Minneapolis: University of Minnesota Press, 1929.

Ostergren, Robert. *A Community Transplanted: The Formative Experience of a Swedish Immigrant Community in the Upper Middle West, 1835–1915.* Madison: University of Wisconsin Press, 1988.

Overton, Richard C. *Burlington West: A Colonization History of the Burlington Railroad.* Cambridge: Harvard University Press, 1941.

Painter, Nell Irvin. *Exodusters: Black Migration to Kansas after Reconstruction.* New York: Alfred A. Knopf, 1977.

Parrish, William E. *David Rice Atchison of Missouri: Border Politician.* Columbia: University of Missouri Press, 1961.

Petersen, Albert J. "The German-Russian Settlement Pattern in Ellis County, Kansas." *Rocky Mountain Social Science Journal* 5 (April 1968): 52–62.

———. "German-Russian Colonization in Western Kansas: A Settlement Geography." Ph.D. dissertation, Department of Geography and Anthropology, Louisiana State University, 1970.

Petersen, Katie M. "History of the Scandinavian Settlement in Lincoln County, Kansas." Master's thesis, Department of History, Kansas State College of Pittsburg, 1939.

Peterson, Ellen W. *A Kansan's Enterprise: The Story of Enterprise, Kansas.* Enterprise, Kans.: Enterprise Baptist Church, 1957.

Phillips, Paul E. "An Assessment of the Validity of an East-West Cultural Dichotomy for Kansas." Ph.D. dissertation, Department of Geography, University of Kansas, 1977.

Powell, William E. "European Settlement in the Cherokee-Crawford Coal Field of Southeastern Kansas." *Kansas Historical Quarterly* 41 (1975): 150–65.

Power, Richard L. "Wet Lands and the Hoosier Stereotype." *Mississippi Valley Historical Review* 22 (1935): 33–48.

Prentis, Noble L. *Kansas Miscellanies.* Topeka: Kansas Publishing House, 1889.

Progress in Pawnee County: 80th Anniversary Edition. Larned, Kans.: Larned Tiller and Toiler, 1952.

Quinn, Bernard, et al. *Churches and Church Membership in the United States, 1980.* Atlanta: Glenmary Research Center, 1982.

Rager, T. F., and John S. Gilmore. *History of Neosho and Wilson Counties, Kansas.* Fort Scott, Kans.: L. Wallace Duncan, 1902.

Ramsdell, Charles W. "The Natural Limits of Slavery Expansion." *Mississippi Valley Historical Review* 16 (1929): 151–71.

Ravenstein, E. G. "The Laws of Migration." *Journal of the Royal Statistical Society* 48, part 2 (1885): 167–227.

Reed, John S. *The Enduring South: Subcultural Persistence in Mass Society.* Chapel Hill: University of North Carolina Press, 1974.

Revard, Frances. "Osage Mission." *St. Paul Journal,* May 7, 1942. Included in a scrapbook of clippings about Coffey and Neosho counties held by the Kansas Collection at the University of Kansas.

Rich, Everett, ed. *The Heritage of Kansas: Selected Commentaries on Past Times.* Lawrence: University of Kansas Press, 1960.

Risser, Emma K. *History of the Pennsylvania Mennonite Church in Kansas.* Hesston, Kans.: Pennsylvania Mennonite Church, 1958.

Roark, Michael O. "Oklahoma Territory: Frontier Development, Migration, and Culture Areas." Ph.D. dissertation, Department of Geography, Syracuse University, 1979.

Robbins, Roy M. *Our Landed Heritage: The Public*

Domain, 1776–1970. 2d ed. Lincoln: University of Nebraska Press, 1976.

Rooks County Historical Society. *Lest We Forget.* 2 vols. Osborne, Kans.: Osborne County Farmer, 1980.

Root, George. "Notes on Kansas Colonies." Manuscripts Division. Kansas State Historical Society, Topeka, n.d.

Rose, Gregory S. "Hoosier Origins: The Nativity of Indiana's United States–Born Population in 1850." *Indiana Magazine of History* 81 (1985): 201–32.

———. "Information Sources for Nineteenth Century Midwestern Migration." *Professional Geographer* 37 (1985): 66–72.

Roseman, Curtis C. "Migration as a Spatial and Temporal Process." *Annals of the Association of American Geographers* 61 (1971): 589–98.

Rudin, A. James. "Beersheba, Kan.: 'God's Pure Air on Government Land.'" *Kansas Historical Quarterly* 34 (1968): 282–98.

Ruede, Howard. *Sod-House Days: Letters from a Kansas Homesteader, 1877–78.* Edited by John Ise. New York: Columbia University Press, 1937.

Ruppenthal, Jacob C. "Pennsylvania Germans in Central Kansas." *Penn Germania,* N.s. 3 (September 1914): 33–38.

———. "The German Element in Central Kansas." *Kansas Historical Collections, 1913–1914* 13 (1915): 513–34.

Rush County Book Committee. *Rush County: A Century in Story and Pictures.* La Crosse, Kans.: Rush County Historical Society, 1976.

Rutter, Larry G. "Mexican Americans in Kansas: A Survey and Social Mobility Study, 1900–1970." Master's thesis, Department of History, Kansas State University, 1972.

Rydjord, John. *Kansas Place-Names.* Norman: University of Oklahoma Press, 1972.

Sagaser, A. Bower. "Building the Main Line of the Missouri Pacific through Kansas." *Kansas Historical Quarterly* 21 (1955): 326–30.

Sanders, Gwendoline, and Paul Sanders. *The Sumner County Story.* North Newton, Kans.: Mennonite Press, 1966.

Sanders, Scott R. *Staying Put: Making a Home in a Restless World.* Boston: Beacon Press, 1993.

Saul, Norman E. "The Migration of the Russian-Germans to Kansas." *Kansas Historical Quarterly* 40 (1974): 38–62.

———. "Myth and History: Turkey Red Wheat and the 'Kansas Miracle.'" *Heritage of the Great Plains* 22 (Summer 1989): 1–13.

Schamp, Dick. *Post Rock to Moon Rock: A Brief History of Russell.* Russell, Kans.: Russell County Historical Society, 1971.

Schmidt, C. B. "Reminiscences of Foreign Immigration Work for Kansas." *Kansas Historical Collections, 1905–1906* 9 (1906): 485–97.

———. "German Settlements along the Atchison, Topeka and Santa Fe Railway," J. Neale Carman, translator. *Kansas Historical Quarterly* 28 (1962): 310–16.

———. "Kansas Mennonite Settlements, 1877," Cornelius Krahn, translator. *Mennonite Life* 25 (April 1970): 51–58.

Scott, Angelo. "How Natural Gas Came to Kansas." *Kansas Historical Quarterly* 21 (1954): 233–46.

Self, Huber. *Environment and Man in Kansas: A Geographical Analysis.* Lawrence: Regents Press of Kansas, 1978.

Seventieth Anniversary Edition. Anthony, Kans.: Anthony Republic and Anthony Bulletin, 1948.

Shannon, Fred A. *The Farmer's Last Frontier: Agriculture, 1860–1897.* New York: Holt, Rinehart, and Winston, 1945.

Sheridan, Richard. *Economic Development in Southcentral Kansas, Part 1A: An Economic History, 1500–1900.* Lawrence: University of Kansas School of Business, 1956.

———. "From Slavery in Missouri to Freedom in Kansas: The Influx of Black Fugitives and Contrabands into Kansas, 1854–1865." *Kansas History* 12 (1989): 28–47.

Sherman, William C. *Prairie Mosaic: An Ethnic Atlas*

of Rural North Dakota. Fargo: North Dakota Institute for Regional Studies, 1983.

Sherman, William C., and Playford V. Thorson, eds. *Plains Folk: North Dakota's Ethnic History*. Fargo: North Dakota Institute for Regional Studies, 1988.

Sherow, James E. *Watering the Valley: Development along the High Plains Arkansas River, 1870–1950*. Lawrence: University Press of Kansas, 1990.

Shields, Clara M. F. "The Lyon Creek Settlement." *Kansas Historical Collections, 1914–1918* 14 (1918): 143–70.

Shortridge, James R. "The Post Office Frontier in Kansas." *Journal of the West* 13 (July 1974): 83–97.

———. "The Expansion of the Settlement Frontier in Missouri." *Missouri Historical Review* 75 (1980): 64–90.

———. "The Heart of the Prairie: Culture Areas in the Central and Northern Great Plains." *Great Plains Quarterly* 8 (1988): 206–21.

———. *Kaw Valley Landscapes: A Traveler's Guide to Northeastern Kansas,* rev. ed. Lawrence: University Press of Kansas, 1988.

Skaggs, Jimmy M. *The Cattle-Trailing Industry: Between Supply and Demand, 1866–1890*. Lawrence: University Press of Kansas, 1973.

Smith, C. Henry. *The Coming of the Russian Mennonites: An Episode in the Settling of the Last Frontier, 1874–1884*. Berne, Ind.: Mennonite Book Concern, 1927.

Socolofsky, Homer E. *Kansas Governors*. Lawrence: University Press of Kansas, 1990.

Socolofsky, Homer E., and Huber Self. *Historical Atlas of Kansas*. Norman: University of Oklahoma Press, 1972.

Sollors, Werner. *Beyond Ethnicity: Consent and Descent in American Culture*. New York: Oxford University Press, 1986.

Standard Highway Mileage Guide. Chicago: Rand McNally and Company, 1982.

Stanley, Ellen M. *Early Lane County History: 12,000 B.C.– A.D. 1884*. Dighton, Kans.: Ellen M. Stanley, 1993.

Steffen, Jerome O., ed. *The American West: New Perspectives, New Dimensions*. Norman: University of Oklahoma Press, 1979.

Steiner, Michael, and Clarence Mondale. *Region and Regionalism in the United States: A Source Book for the Humanities and Social Sciences*. New York: Garland Publishing Company, 1988.

Stepanek, Mrs. Edward, and LaVern Kopsa, eds. "Cuba, Kansas Centennial: 1868–1968." Mimeographed, 1968. Copy in the Kansas Collection, University of Kansas.

Stephenson, Wendell H. *The Political Career of General James H. Lane*. Publications of the Kansas State Historical Society. Vol. 3. Topeka: Kansas State Printing Plant, 1930.

Stone, Irene G. "The Lead and Zinc Field of Kansas." *Kansas Historical Collections, 1901–1902* 7 (1902): 243–60.

Stucky, Harley J. "The German Element in Kansas." In *Kansas: The First Century*. Vol. 1. Edited by John D. Bright, pp. 329–54. New York: Lewis Historical Publishing Company, 1956.

Stull, Donald D., ed. "When the Packers Came to Town: Changing Ethnic Relations in Garden City." Special issue. *Urban Anthropology* 19 (Winter 1990).

Stump, Roger W. "Regional Divergence in Religious Affiliation in the United States." *Sociological Analysis* 45 (1984): 283–99.

Stumpp, Karl. *The German-Russians: Two Centuries of Pioneering,* Joseph Height, translator. Bonn: Atlantic-Forum, 1967.

Sullivan, Frank S. *A History of Meade County, Kansas*. Topeka: Crane and Company, 1916.

Swehla, Francis J. "Bohemians in Central Kansas." *Kansas Historical Collections, 1913–1914* 13 (1915): 469–512.

Taylor, Philip. *The Distant Magnet: European Emigration to the U.S.A.* London: Eyre and Spottiswoode, 1971.

Thomas, Brinley. *Migration and Economic Growth: A Study in Great Britain and the Atlantic Economy*. Cambridge: Cambridge University Press, 1954.

Thornthwaite, Charles W., and Helen I. Slentz. *Internal Migration in the United States.* Philadelphia: University of Pennsylvania Press, 1934.

Toland, Pauline, ed. *Seward County, Kansas.* Liberal, Kans.: Seward County Historical Society, 1979.

Turk, Eleanor L. "Selling the Heartland: Agents, Agencies, Press, and Policies Promoting German Emigration to Kansas in the Nineteenth Century." *Kansas History* 12 (1989): 150–59.

Tuttle, Albert B., and Mary T. Tuttle, eds. and comps. *History and Heritage of Gove County, Kansas.* N.p.: Gove County Historical Association, 1976.

United Methodist Church's 100th Anniversary, 1883–1983. Smith Center, Kans.: Thornburg United Methodist Church, 1983.

Van Meter, Sondra. *Marion County: Past and Present.* Hillsboro, Kans.: Marion County Historical Society, 1972.

Waldron, Nell B. "Colonization in Kansas from 1861 to 1890." Ph.D. dissertation, Department of History, Northwestern University, 1923.

Wallace County Historians. *Wallace County History: A Story of Grass, Grit and Chips.* Sharon Springs, Kans.: Wallace County Historians, 1979.

Walther, Thomas R., and Robert K. Ratzlaff. "Industrialization on the Frontier: A Case Study, Crawford County, Kansas, 1870–1914." *Red River Valley Historical Review* 6 (Fall 1981): 15–23.

Ware, Eugene F. "The Neutral Lands." *Kansas Historical Collections, 1897–1900* 6 (1900): 147–69.

———. "History of Sun-Gold Section." In *The Heritage of Kansas: Selected Commentaries on Past Times,* edited by Everett Rich, pp. 82–95. Lawrence: University of Kansas Press, 1960.

Waters, L. L. *Steel Trails to Santa Fe.* Lawrence: University of Kansas Press, 1950.

Weisberger, Bernard A. "The Newspaper Reporter and the Kansas Imbroglio." *Mississippi Valley Historical Review* 36 (1950): 633–56.

Wheeler, David L. "Winter on the Cattle Range: Western Kansas, 1884–1886." *Kansas History* 15 (1992): 2–17.

White, Lonnie J. "The Cheyenne Barrier on the Kansas Frontier, 1868–1869." *Arizona and the West* 4 (1962): 51–64.

White, William A. "Kansas: A Puritan Survival." In *These United States: A Symposium.* 2 vols. Edited by Ernest Gruening, 1:1–12. New York: Boni and Liveright, 1924.

———. *Forty Years on Main Street,* Russell H. Fitzgibbon, compiler. New York: Farrar and Rinehart, 1937.

Wilhelm, Hubert G. H. "The Origin and Distribution of Settlement Groups: Ohio: 1850." Department of Geography, Ohio University, 1982. Mimeographed.

Williams, Walter. *The State of Missouri.* Columbia, Mo.: K. W. Stephens Press, 1904.

Winsor, M., and James Scarbrough. *History of Jewell County, Kansas.* Jewell City, Kans.: Diamond Printing Office, 1878.

Winther, Oscar O. "The English and Kansas, 1865–1890." In *The Frontier Challenge: Responses to the Trans-Mississippi West,* edited by John G. Clark, pp. 235–73. Lawrence: University Press of Kansas, 1971.

Wittlinger, Carlton O. *Quest for Piety and Obedience: The Story of the Brethren in Christ.* Nappanee, Ind.: Evangel Press, 1978.

Wood, Charles L. "C. D. Perry: Clark County Farmer and Rancher, 1884–1908." *Kansas Historical Quarterly* 39 (1973): 449–77.

———. *The Kansas Beef Industry.* Lawrence: Regents Press of Kansas, 1980.

Woods, Randall B. "Integration, Exclusion, or Segregation?: The 'Color Line' in Kansas, 1878–1900." *Western Historical Quarterly* 14 (1983): 181–98.

Worster, Donald. *Dust Bowl: The Southern Plains in the 1930s.* New York: Oxford University Press, 1979.

Zelinsky, Wilbur. "Selfward Bound? Personal Preference Patterns and the Changing Map of American Society." *Economic Geography* 50 (1974): 144–79.

———. *The Cultural Geography of the United States.* Rev. ed. Englewood Cliffs, N.J.: Prentice-Hall, 1992.

Zornow, William F. *Kansas: A History of the Jayhawk State.* Norman: University of Oklahoma Press, 1957.

Index